FASHION AND JAZZ

Dress, Body, Culture

Series Editor: Joanne B. Eicher, *Regents' Professor*, *University of Minnesota*

Advisory Board:
Djurdja Bartlett, *London College of Fashion, University of the Arts*
Pamela Church-Gibson, *London College of Fashion, University of the Arts*
James Hall, *University of Illinois at Chicago*
Vicki Karaminas, *University of Technology, Sydney*
Gwen O'Neal, *University of North Carolina at Greensboro*
Ted Polhemus, *Curator, "Street Style" Exhibition, Victoria and Albert Museum*
Valerie Steele, *The Museum at the Fashion Institute of Technology*
Lou Taylor, *University of Brighton*
Karen Tranberg Hansen, *Northwestern University*
Ruth Barnes, *Ashmolean Museum, University of Oxford*

Books in this provocative series seek to articulate the connections between culture and dress which is defined here in its broadest possible sense as any modification or supplement to the body. Interdisciplinary in approach, the series highlights the dialogue between identity and dress, cosmetics, coiffure and body alternations as manifested in practices as varied as plastic surgery, tattooing, and ritual scarification. The series aims, in particular, to analyse the meaning of dress in relation to popular culture and gender issues and will include works grounded in anthropology, sociology, history, art history, literature, and folklore.

ISSN: 1360-466X

Previously published in the Series

Helen Bradley Foster, *"New Raiments of Self": African American Clothing in the Antebellum South*
Claudine Griggs, *S/he: Changing Sex and Changing Clothes*
Michaele Thurgood Haynes, *Dressing Up Debutantes: Pageantry and Glitz in Texas*
Anne Brydon and Sandra Niessen, *Consuming Fashion: Adorning the Transnational Body*
Dani Cavallaro and Alexandra Warwick, *Fashioning the Frame: Boundaries, Dress and the Body*
Judith Perani and Norma H. Wolff, *Cloth, Dress and Art Patronage in Africa*
Linda B. Arthur, *Religion, Dress and the Body*
Paul Jobling, *Fashion Spreads: Word and Image in Fashion Photography*
Fadwa El Guindi, *Veil: Modesty, Privacy and Resistance*
Thomas S. Abler, *Hinterland Warriors and Military Dress: European Empires and Exotic Uniforms*
Linda Welters, *Folk Dress in Europe and Anatolia: Beliefs about Protection and Fertility*
Kim K.P. Johnson and Sharron J. Lennon, *Appearance and Power*
Barbara Burman, *The Culture of Sewing*
Annette Lynch, *Dress, Gender and Cultural Change*
Antonia Young, *Women Who Become Men*
David Muggleton, *Inside Subculture: The Postmodern Meaning of Style*
Nicola White, *Reconstructing Italian Fashion: America and the Development of the Italian Fashion Industry*
Brian J. McVeigh, *Wearing Ideology: The Uniformity of Self-Presentation in Japan*
Shaun Cole, *Don We Now Our Gay Apparel: Gay Men's Dress in the Twentieth Century*
Kate Ince, *Orlan: Millennial Female*
Ali Guy, Eileen Green and Maura Banim, *Through the Wardrobe: Women's Relationships with their Clothes*
Linda B. Arthur, *Undressing Religion: Commitment and Conversion from a Cross-Cultural Perspective*
William J.F. Keenan, *Dressed to Impress: Looking the Part*
Joanne Entwistle and Elizabeth Wilson, *Body Dressing*
Leigh Summers, *Bound to Please: A History of the Victorian Corset*
Paul Hodkinson, *Goth: Identity, Style and Subculture*
Leslie W. Rabine, *The Global Circulation of African Fashion*
Michael Carter, *Fashion Classics from Carlyle to Barthes*
Sandra Niessen, Ann Marie Leshkowich and Carla Jones, *Re-Orienting Fashion: The Globalization of Asian Dress*
Kim K. P. Johnson, Susan J. Torntore and Joanne B. Eicher, *Fashion Foundations: Early Writings on Fashion and Dress*
Helen Bradley Foster and Donald Clay Johnson, *Wedding Dress Across Cultures*
Eugenia Paulicelli, *Fashion under Fascism: Beyond the Black Shirt*
Charlotte Suthrell, *Unzipping Gender: Sex, Cross-Dressing and Culture*
Irene Guenther, *Nazi Chic? Fashioning Women in the Third Reich*
Yuniya Kawamura, *The Japanese Revolution in Paris Fashion*
Patricia Calefato, *The Clothed Body*
Ruth Barcan, *Nudity: A Cultural Anatomy*
Samantha Holland, *Alternative Femininities: Body, Age and Identity*
Alexandra Palmer and Hazel Clark, *Old Clothes, New Looks: Second Hand Fashion*

FASHION AND JAZZ

Dress, identity and subcultural improvisation

ALPHONSO D. McCLENDON

Bloomsbury Academic
An imprint of Bloomsbury Publishing Plc

B L O O M S B U R Y
LONDON · NEW DELHI · NEW YORK · SYDNEY

Bloomsbury Academic

An imprint of Bloomsbury Publishing Plc

50 Bedford Square
London
WC1B 3DP
UK

1385 Broadway
New York
NY 10018
USA

www.bloomsbury.com

**BLOOMSBURY and the Diana logo are registered trademarks of
Bloomsbury Publishing Plc**

First published 2015

British Library Cataloguing-in-Publication Data

A catalogue record for this book is available from the British Library.

ISBN HB: 978-0-8578-5126-0
PB: 978-0-8578-5127-7
ePDF: 978-0-8578-5129-1
ePub: 978-0-8578-5128-4

Library of Congress Cataloging-in-Publication Data

McClendon, Alphonso.
Fashion and jazz: dress, identity and subcultural improvisation / Alphonso McClendon.
pages cm. — (Dress, body, culture)
ISBN 978-0-85785-127-7 (paperback) — ISBN 978-0-85785-126-0 (hardback)   1.   Clothing
and dress—History.   2.   Fashion—History.   3.   Jazz—Social aspects.   I.   Title.
GT596.M378 2015
391—dc23
2014022528

Series: Dress, Body, Culture

Typeset by RefineCatch Limited, Bungay, Suffolk
Printed and bound in India

CONTENTS

ILLUSTRATIONS

ACKNOWLEDGMENTS

Many individuals have supported me throughout the execution of this book. First, I would like to thank Bloomsbury Publishing, especially Anna Wright and Joanne B. Eicher, who were extremely supportive from the genesis through the duration of this project. Very special thanks to Joseph Hancock for his unyielding mentorship from the beginning. Thanks also to Hannah Crump for guidance through the production.

Next, I would like to thank the Antoinette Westphal College of Media Arts & Design at Drexel University for financial support, particularly the Westphal Faculty Mini-Grant Program and the Westphal Creativity Fund. With much appreciation, I thank Allen Sabinson, Roberta Gruber, Karin Kunstler, Kathi Martin, Renee Chase, Clare Sauro, and other Westphal colleagues.

The extensive and invaluable history in this book would not be possible without the assistance of the Institute of Jazz Studies at Rutgers University, the Schomburg Center for Research in Black Culture, the Archives Center at the National Museum of American History, the Hogan Jazz Archive at Tulane University, the Free Library of Philadelphia, and the *Philadelphia Tribune*. In addition, thanks to the seniors at the Philadelphia Senior Center who shared their amazing stories of jazz in the city. A special thanks to Tad Hershorn for his direction during my research at Rutgers; and my immeasurable gratitude to Michel Fontanes for sharing his extensive knowledge, passion and experience of jazz in France.

For their endless love, encouragement and knowledge, I thank my parents, Alphonso and Ada McClendon, as well Rita Anderson, Alana Babb-McGowan, and other family members. Also, for providing a listening ear and words of support in various ways: Michael Daniels, Stephen Jackson, Peter Clark, Mel Greenwich, Daniel Golden, Patrick Durkin, Mario Martines, Stefan Moore, George Starks, and John Pfeiffer. My great thanks go to Cynthia Sesso and Don Peterson for their assistance with the photographs that accent this book and its cover. Finally, I acknowledge Billie Holiday's legacy of artistry, style, storytelling, defiance and fortitude that was the impetus of *Fashion and Jazz* as well my direction in this life of jazz.

INTRODUCTION

From infancy to evolution, the trajectory of jazz has comprised an emphatic way of being that drives its genetic dialogue. The merger of conspicuous fashion and multiform cadence organized a mutually beneficial relationship, where aesthetics were put forth that imparted identity and showmanship. Creative output, an aspiration of each discipline, is achieved through exploration of textiles and construction in fashion, and likewise the improvisation of melody and harmony in jazz. With American origins in the nineteenth century, the path of jazz in both dominant and marginal standings has spanned one hundred years of vitality. This history has contained dress, appearance and behavioral representations that provide critical context to cultural development.

Jazz is an impassioned style of music that takes hold of a listener, urging the body toward rhythmic and spirited movement. It's about feeling and expressing that which one has experienced be it great happiness, love, hardship or grief. Sidney Bechet, in characterizing the totality of jazz, declared: "it's the rhythm . . . and that feeling you put around it, always keeping the melody, that's all there is to it . . . 1910, 1923, 1950—there's no difference in that" (Bechet 2002: 213).

The drive of this book is to perform a broad examination and measurement of jazz aesthetics inclusive of the fashion, culture, identities and behaviors of performers and the community. For consideration, the first half of the twentieth century ranging from the musical styles of ragtime to modern jazz proposes a meaningful span of time, contrary to a momentary focus on limited styles and fashion trends. A narrative will be woven demonstrating the pivotal role of African Americans in shaping the art, beauty and taste of this music as insiders and outsiders. The contributions of published sheet music, recordings, film and media that intersect and build this cultural capital will be assessed.

In the present day, the genre continues to boldly resonate, for example in the popularity of Ken Burns' "Jazz", a multi-episode documentary released in 2000. The highly stylized film of nineteen hours utilized recordings, photographs, interviews and video clips to brand jazz to a new audience, equally satisfying a societal longing for past musical brilliance. Instrumental to the appeal was the visually compelling images of performers in uniforms, tuxedos, gowns and sportswear. Louis Armstrong, Bessie Smith, Duke Ellington, Billie Holiday and others embodied culture through performance, dress and style that set the impetus for this book.

Second, this text aims to present topics of race, class and gender through practices that elevated and scorned identities. Through this lens, it is evident that the roots of jazz extend to Africa, and so the human disparities, techniques of tyranny and battles for freedom find expression in twentieth-century observations on this fresh musical culture. Performers defied racial and social classification through pursuits of modernism. Particularly for African Americans, this sensibility was a departure from oppressive segregation defined by the Jim Crow era. Elizabeth Hurlock, in discussion of changes in fashion leadership of the modern period, issued: "fashion arbiters will be recruited from the men and women of the world who have attained prestige and power through their ability to accomplish great things" (Hurlock 1929: 126). Costume history, especially of the European Renaissance, has shown that royalty and aristocrats occupied this position. This book will explore the adoption of exclusivity through appearance and behavior that transformed jazz artists into idols and public figures, despite differences of culture. In contrast to the reverence held by clergy, teachers, business owners and civil rights activists, entertainers, their image and the production of secular music became an enterprise for equality. The music without limits of imagination was produced, finding recognition among those keen to hear it. Referencing this zeitgeist, Bechet described the music as natural, free, happy and simply "a way of speaking" (Bechet 2002: 213, 217).

Also in relation to jazz identities, there were projections of negativity from the development of abstract musical constructions and the appendage of narcotics use. Such attention resulted in alterations to dress and appearance for various outcomes. The style considered by some as subcultural, as being of a separate social group, was equally inter-cultural communication, employing camouflage through popular and fashionable veneers to negate and advance difference. Hence, a continued re-engineering of music and presence occurred beyond systemic control. As to the art's favor, Cornel West informed the audience's reprise: "hummed on the streets, whistled by shoeshine boys and even danced to in the house parties in urban black communities" (West 1999: 475).

Prominence of jazz aesthetics, as the third objective, will be discerned through icons, performance locations and contemporary references. Decisive garments and accessories had resonance, yet with insight into the attitudes and consciousness of musicians, decoding of public images is gained. For instance, Duke Ellington's qualitative moniker, the "Aristocrat of Jazz", has import that traces to his early childhood experiences. Patrizia Calefato, in *The Clothed Body*, argues that fashion and music "are languages that construct spaces and identities" (Calefato 2004: 119). In branding performers, the visual and mental qualities have a primary role. An understated area of study is performance venues that backed the worth of the music. These establishments generated enthusiasm of genres and artists by accessing traits of elegance, popularity and attraction. As a final theme, the aesthetics of jazz reverberate in today's popular culture, validating that genetic traits shaped earlier still find appetite, consumption and value in the twenty-first century.

At the outset, the image of jazz artists had the power to advance the performer and sway audiences. Chapter 1 will provide context to assess the role of fashion and cultural theory in this representation. Work within the field of sociology and psychology informs that the clothing applied to the body contains codes with societal germaneness. The development of a rhythmic art and the habits of its messengers amended traditions in mainstream society. A case in point; male band musicians established formal dress as customary uniform at the dawn of the twentieth century; formal dress operated as an aesthetic conduit from performer to listener. W. C. Handy, of his days with the Mahara Minstrels, recalled an impressive colleague and his demeanor. "The star of our show . . . was 'Clever Billy Young.' Beau Brummell of the first magnitude, Billy also qualified as a gentleman" (Handy 1969: 39–40). Bolstering attributes of European aristocracy, African American male performers assumed fashion leadership through skill and presence.

In Chapter 2, the jazz aesthetic will be qualified through the judgment and expression of beauty that transformed over fifty years. This analysis will identify silhouettes, cuts and fabrics of garments along with social and political trends that contributed to a collective meaning. Barthes, in *Elements of Semiology*, issued that the study of signs can incorporate "images, gestures, musical sounds, objects . . . which form the content of ritual, convention or public entertainment" (Barthes 1973: 9). Accordingly, the clothing of performers constructed value and communicated information about the wearer. The following announcement published in the *Philadelphia Tribune* merges dress and artistry into a single vision. "Ella Fitzgerald, robed in a stunning mink coat, signs autograph for delighted fans who heard her Saturday at Town Hall" (*Philadelphia Tribune* 1939a). In similar manner, the *Pittsburgh Courier* fused the hierarchy of dress by labeling Duke Ellington, "the debonair prince of popular jazz" (*Pittsburgh Courier* 1931).

Chapter 3 will explore the progress towards modernism. Having evolved in a time of racial inequality, the forward manner of jazz offered resistance to stringent morality, bias and stereotypes. This strategy beyond garment styling was evidenced in posture, written text, fine art and language. As argued by J. C. Flügel, "the ultimate and essential cause of fashion lies in competition" (Flügel 1950: 138), principally the social elements. The modernistic agencies in jazz that challenged past traditions will be outlined. Amiri Baraka, in *Blues People: Negro Music in White America*, designated this feat as a "realization by Negroes of a more human hypothesis on which to base their lives" (Baraka 2002: 93), experienced through the escalation of popular jazz orchestras and female blues singers in the 1920s.

Adding weight to the modern premise are analyses of class and gender in Chapters 4 and 5. Strategically, jazz artists set forth elite codes that employed perceptions of fashion, talent and knowledge to counteract inequality. It is notable that changes in economic position buttressed the practice of ornamentation, adoption of affluent dress and fancying-up of social behavior. By the mid-century, the mature images of performers identified prestige and quality in corporate advertising, advising social gains and marking the music as grown-up. Juan Williams, in a foreword to *The Power of Pride*, declared that "in jazz . . . the men and women who can reinvent their identity right before your eyes—compel you to see them differently, in a new and better light—are the geniuses" (Marks and Edkins 1999: 9). These chapters, outlining identity through dress, provide evidence of emancipation from limiting societal classifications.

With its innovativeness and strong cultural identity, jazz culture confronted antagonism in film plots, musical lyrics and fictional text. Chapter 6 will commence with the rejection of jazz by African American elite societies, concluding with piety as redemption to this radical rhythm. Part of this fear was the uncensored communication of black hardship, desire, faith and tradition in blues songs of the 1920s. In *Jazz: A History*, Frank Tirro framed the cathartic platform: "the words are usually direct, sometimes laced with disguised meaning, but always full of real-life experience" (Tirro 1977: 115). The subversive representation of jazz in popular culture is explored in Chapter 7, where narcotic habits that damaged reputations altered the dress motive of performers. The actuality of drug use in the 1940s found exploitation in subsequent decades through vivid performance in film and media. These narratives along with the performers' experiences provide the hypothesis of addiction being fashionable. Signifiers that proposed a relationship between appearance and drug addiction will be examined. In support, fashion scholarship has proven that subgroups within society transform dress to counter negative labels and mitigate forms of oppression (Lynch 1999: 1–5). The employment of high-status fashion to conceal and balance substance dependence will be addressed as a social response.

Finally in consideration of icons and nostalgia, the creation of jazz idols is deconstructed through artistic personas and media partiality. Jazz performers, despite language and travel barriers, were influential around the world. Michel Fontanes, French musician and author, in description of Billie Holiday, asserted: "for me, she is a major contributor to the American culture . . . she was a rebel and you could not impose anything to her" (Fontanes 2010). Chapter 8 goes beyond the ubiquitous gardenia impression to trace the icon's versatile and stylish image. Furthering this method, Chapter 9 traces the pedigrees of jazz dandies that enlighten the complex identities around masculinity and fame. Male musicians transformed the suit by adding their hyper-individuality and cultural style, creating the modern day dandy. In explanation of this transmission, Flügel maintained that "narcissistic self-feelings ultimately fuse clothes and body into a harmonious unity" (Flügel 1950: 100) triggering sartorial exhibition.

Philadelphia, the birthplace of Billie Holiday, the proving ground of Dizzy Gillespie and the eternal home of Bessie Smith, breathes the history of jazz in underrepresented fashion. It will be shown that nightlife within the African American neighborhoods signified the jazz demand and the transition of performers to celebrities. Additionally, Chapter 10 highlights the outward thrust of the genre in contemporary society that fulfills a desire for nostalgia not purely of music, but enthusiastically of dress, appearance, behavior and class. A similar resurgence was evidenced in the mid-century. John Wilson, a writer for the *New York Times*, listed revivals in jazz that denoted "tributes" and lovesick glances of the happier days of ragtime, big band, and bop (Wilson 1958c). "There's a leaning toward remembrance of things past in the current jazz releases . . . great floods of nostalgia are bound to be unleashed" (Wilson 1955). Not even a full decade away from the heyday of 52nd Street when jazz legends filled the nightclubs, these comments demonstrate a generation's yearning for past jazz aesthetics and genuine cultural expression.

Significance of a fashion and jazz history

This book constructs a framework to analyse the visual and behavioral representations of jazz and African American aesthetics that influence fashion and popular culture. Supported by theoretical scholarship, it aims to be a companion to fashion and music disciplines investigating themes, patterns, motives and outcomes of the jazz phenomenon. Also, it goes beyond a narrow approach of the 1920s with examination of antebellum origins, vernacular, cinema, nightlife spaces, masculine and feminine depictions and exploitation over several decades. Anyone with an interest in the evolution of musical artists and their mutable identities will find this compilation essential. Uniting the voices of performers, words of literary witnesses, storytelling of film directors and transcripts of journalists and writers accomplishes a wide-ranging historical survey. Furthermore, the timeline of jazz linked with changes in social and political response is communicated in text, as well a purposeful assembly of photographs from the work of Charles Peterson, Herman Leonard, Burt Goldblatt and Marcel Fleiss. It is hoped that fashion, music, popular culture, gender and African American studies are enlightened by this narrative of cultural diversity that considers performance, dress, visual image, subcultural improvisation and addiction through a unique lens.

1
DRESS THEORY, FASHION AND A JAZZ AESTHETIC

Pattern of influence between fashion and jazz

Fashion and jazz are disciplines that have significantly influenced one another in the first half of the twentieth century. Aesthetics, defined as "the identification of the beautiful" (Weiner 2012: 8), were generated, shared and communicated through a merger of visual, behavioral and acoustic qualities among performers. In *Cultural Passions*, Elizabeth Wilson related the wearing of clothes with the appeal to pleasure and beauty, emphasizing that the practices are "universal human, cultural activities" (Wilson 2013: 52). Strategically, jazz musicians and singers utilized garments and accessories to articulate their individual style and secure an affirmative response. For instance, trumpeter Oran "Hot Lips" Page projects cool style with polished hair, finely tailored suit and formal posture during a 1942 jam session (Figure 1.1).

These individual and group ways of accentuating the beautiful drew upon their cultural and social definitions of attractiveness. In effect, the clothing became coded with "a particular meaning of the body, of the person" (Barthes 2006: 96). It is apparent in the fashion system that designers incorporate meanings into their artifacts through choices of inspiration, color, textiles, silhouette and make that influence society. When performers appropriate clothing for the stage, the initial design codes are merged with their personal style and intellect to bolster the music, demonstrate technical rank and stir the audience. The art and aesthetics of fashion and music occur simultaneously with explorations and expressions of cultural heritage, struggle and transformation allowing performers to break down social borders.

For jazz artists, dress was deliberate, valued and situated inside of performance obligations as demonstrated by pianist Mary Lou Williams, who retained extensive receipts of clothing purchases and garment maintenance from 1930 to 1980. These documents archived at the Institute of Jazz Studies at Rutgers

Figure 1.1 Oran "Hot Lips" Page, trumpeter, personifies the jazz aesthetic at a jam session, New York, 1942. Photo by Charles Peterson. Courtesy of Don Peterson

University revealed invoices for dresses, shoes, blouses, hosiery and furs with classifications such as "work," "concert," "interview," and "job." Williams conducted business with stores across the country including Kline's, O'Connor & Goldberg, Lord & Taylor, I. Miller, Gimbles, I. Magnin, and Saks Fifth Avenue. Such interest in fashion did not exceed the musical technique or her authority as a woman in the male dominated field. "You've got to play, that's all . . . you automatically become strong, though this doesn't mean you're not feminine," stated Williams in an interview (McPartland 1957). Hence, she entered the cycle of fashion as an African American leader, adopting and dispersing cultural meaning through clothing. Fred Davis, in considering the sociological importance of fashion, affirmed that "through clothing people communicate some things about their persons, and at the collective level this results typically in locating them symbolically in some structured universe" (Davis 1994: 4). This happening establishes a pattern of influence when one discipline—jazz—intensifies the art of another—fashion—through the exhibition of expressive articles.

Freedom of expression in fashion and jazz

A measurable display of style was promoted among jazz artists to obtain greater freedom, gain financial success, and achieve creative recognition. Such efforts have the function of a road map, relaying aesthetic features associated with a given point in time. The path of jazz, both in dominant and marginal forms, has spanned over a century in America. This history contained dress, appearance and behavioral representations that gave vital context to fashion and cultural development. American philosopher John Dewey, in *Freedom and Culture*, positioned that the production of culture in society is determined by "the arts of expression and communication" (Dewey 1989: 25). As the pioneer to rhythm and blues and rock-n-roll, the narrative of fashion's role in jazz informs related associations with style in subsequent generations of music.

Especially among African American musicians, the aspiration to express their existence was palpable in song. This is prominently displayed on Louis Armstrong's arrangement of "West End Blues" (1928), where his trumpet playing with stylish charm and raw melancholic emotion gave voice to African American culture. The composition with New Orleans brass band style and a distinct religious moan imparted equally the pride and hardship of southern living. In a 1956 interview, Billie Holiday, legendary jazz singer, described Armstrong's arrangement that inspired her technique. "He doesn't say any words you know . . . and I liked the feeling he got from it so I wanted Louis Armstrong's feeling" (Connover 1956). Holiday co-penned the iconic song "Lady Sings the Blues" in the year of the interview. The title is direct testimony to a performer's ability to convey feeling through spoken word. Armstrong and Holiday's employment of the blues demonstrates the artist's desire to communicate cultural aesthetics, and equally signify the social environment in music. As Paul Gilroy notes, black musical expression amplifies political engagement by "communicating information, organizing consciousness and testing out . . . forms of subjectivity" (Gilroy 2011: 497).

Within fashion, Madeleine Vionnet, proponent of the 1920s bias cut, sought the liberation of the dressed female body through simplicity. "Unrestricting, easy to slip on and off and often free of all fastenings, so clever was the cut, they had everything to commend them" (Ewing 1986: 102). Also, the modernist approach of Gabrielle Chanel to women's clothing design through the incorporation of nautical, equestrian and menswear details showed a process of communication. Richard Martin and Harold Koda suggested that Chanel's spirit of design was not only an exploration of haute couture, but also a "compelling picture of society" (Martin and Koda 1995: 16). Confirming the social meaning, Elizabeth Ewing proclaimed: "the Chanel suit is more a way of life than just a fashion" (Ewing 1986: 100). Therefore, an idiom of style, mood and expression was conceived in fashion that paralleled its exercise in jazz. Calefato argued that "fashion and music are two intimately connected forms of worldliness, two social practices that go hand in hand" (Calefato 2004: 117). These creative forms impacted history through their influence on economic and political development. As a product of human creation, fashion and jazz represent voices of agreement, opposition, rebellion and transformation in society. This authority was enhanced by technological ingenuity that allowed for the proliferation of fashion and music beyond the privileged classes. As the sewing machine and sized paper patterns aided the momentum of fashion production, the phonograph and recording disc revolutionized music distribution. These nineteenth-century innovations were critical for fashion and jazz to gain mass-market persuasion and authority.

Beyond the technological improvements that supported a creative union, fashion and jazz had multicultural influences that spawned a new modernity. Milbank, in support of this fashion amalgamation, defined the "appetite for European imports" and "American taste for simplicity" (Milbank 1989: 19) that was emerging in the late 1800s. France, Germany and England inspired novelty fashion, while African, Creole and European traditions nourished jazz improvisation. Here, Duke Ellington's declaration concerning the liberating aspect of the music:

> Jazz is like the automobile and airplane. It is modern and it is American. I don't like the word jazz but it is the one that is usually used. Jazz is freedom. Jazz is the freedom to play anything, whether it has been done before or not. It gives you freedom.

> (*PM* 1945: 4)

Ellington's quote mirrored fashion shifts including removal of the corset and bustle that initiated a dress revolt among women of the early 1900s. Reformers of dress like the early musicians of jazz navigated tradition seeking liberty from garment constraint. Designers were challenged to increase or decrease mobility with the inclusion of seams, darts, pleats and shirring. These construction techniques engineer textiles to conform, expand, enclose and gather on the body. From earliest times to modern day, the design process has rational perspective, steeped in "theoretical considerations and calculations" for body contour (De Castro 2009: 9). Welters and Cunningham's case of the free expression of 1920s "shapeless dresses" noted: "the styles allowed for freedom of movement that the dress reformers of the past only dreamed of" (Welters and Cunningham 2005: 57). Comparisons can be drawn between challenges to dress standards and pursuits of original forms of music, solidifying a common strategy of unbound expression among fashion and jazz. Dewey reasoned that culture is inclusive of "ideas used by men to justify and to criticize the fundamental conditions under which they live, their social philosophy" (Dewey 1989: 25). The predicament of freedom is a fundamental aspect of American existence questioned by the authors of the United States Constitution and diverse cultural groups having inequity in the country's development.

The role of fashion

The meaning and process of fashion supports the understanding of its role in the field of jazz. Case in point, it would be difficult to overlook the crisp houndstooth blazer worn by Duke Ellington in numerous publicity images of the 1940s. The textile weave of Scottish origin along with Ellington's pose promoted the high quality of structured music to be produced. Once joined, artifact and performer, and expressed in public, the appearance contains added meaning, taking on cultural substance inscribed in the origins of jazz and fashion. Most important is the acknowledgment of influence and understanding of attached meanings. This example reveals a chief motive of dress posited by scholars in the field of dress psychology. Flügel described "decoration" as a purpose of clothing (Flügel 1950: 16). The act of adorning the body with materials that display, attract, entice and define status can be attributed to Ellington's houndstooth blazer. Ellington, a key player of the swing era, was highly shrewd with image, reputation and performance venue, hence the use of specific textiles and formal garments aided in the goal of attraction. Since the late 1800s, an astute practice of dressing is found in numerous performers of jazz. Analysing the artifacts and motives fueled this scholarship that frames identities and societal implications.

Understandably, the narration of jazz is incomplete without scrutiny of the clothing of performers. By the same token, the history of costume that overlooks the contributions of jazz artists and spectators would be inadequate. Duke Ellington, interviewed by *PM*, accentuated the presence of style in music. "Our music grew out of the personalities in the band. We see an old man walking along the street. We play a song that goes with the man" (*PM* 1945). This succinct quote captured the fundamental association between two art forms. It proposes that human style is intrinsic and can be given imitable form by designers and musicians. Fashion provides the visual representation of the enthusiasm, while music signifies it through performance and recorded sound. Regarding the path and genuine meaning of fashion, Edward Sapir indicated the importance of group compulsion rather than individual taste and the power of symbolism in dress and exhibition (Sapir 2007: 45). The creation of music and fashion are similar in their extension of ideas into commodities that frame a social impulse.

To appreciate the dynamic relationship between fashion and jazz, a working definition of fashion is essential. Wilson's contemporary evaluation asserts that fashion is change, reaction, aesthetic representation and the expression of ideas through distinct preferences (Wilson 2003: 3–8). As with Hurlock's psychological approach to dress, Wilson maintains that the exhibition of fashion can ultimately signify "hidden desires and dreams" (Wilson 2013: 52). For example, jazz singer Anita O'Day's adoption of the male band member's jacket in the 1940s challenged tradition, altered the group aesthetic, declared risk taking and contributed to a fashion movement that thrived during the war years. O'Day's practice led to imitation, which Anne Hollander, dress historian, describes as fashion's mode of originating from a capricious act of an individual desiring autonomy followed by admiration (Hollander 1993: 353).

Thus, the discussion of jazz style will connote the influencer (fashion) and the act of producing (dressing). In defining fashion, Hurlock provides support with her quote of Edward Ross. "Fashion is marked by rhythmic imitation and innovation, by alternate uniformity and change, but neither of these phases obeys the principle of utility" (Hurlock 1929: 4). This statement establishes two critical realities that fashion is not stagnant nor is it restricted to practical purpose. The continual movements of trends bear witness to shifts in clothing tastes and needs. Often, economic and political events influence the direction. During the 1960s, the jazz scene adopted a noticeably casual and rugged style that aesthetically represented the music's disjointed status among more youthful sounds, as well as an edgier approach to technique that mirrored struggles for freedom. "I think the music has grown up so much that today it's outgrown the word," stressed Ellington in questioning the label of jazz for modern music development (Greuenberg 1961). As it mushroomed, "the avant-garde refused to be pinned down to any one style or idiom" (Giddins and DeVeaux 2009: 449). Unkempt facial hair, utility shirts with epaulets, turtlenecks, knit caps and short sleeves suggested a fragmented independence among the male performers that was absent during the unified dress of the swing era. The technique and compositional traits of a particular period are often mirrored in the style choices of musicians, and so, with a reading of appearance and historical import, an insight into fashion within the jazz genres is initiated.

A language of dress in jazz

Within this dialogue of fashion, the language of "dress" and "dressing" aids in describing the conduct of individuals. The established work of scholars in the fields of fashion theory, costume history, psychology and sociology has provided a common platform. Barthes, in *The Language of Fashion*, defined "dress" as the object and "dressing" as the method of wearers displaying group-influenced clothing (Barthes 2006: 9). This structure is critical for differentiating between the artifact and the action. Artifacts represent the clothing, accessories and ornamentation, while dressing stipulated the psychological motivation to apply these articles to the body. Hence, the fact that Billie Holiday frequently had a white gardenia affixed to the side of her head not only communicated a striking feature, but questioned the utility and associated stimulus to wear it. Holiday alternated between real and artificial flowers as accessories. In later years without acknowledgment of fashion, she explained in interview that the gardenia practice was a childish habit. Wilson alludes to another likely reason for the dress that being its link to aesthetics, pleasure and beauty (Wilson 2013: 52).

Highly influenced by their celebrity, musicians and singers had great sensitivity to appearance, being in front of audiences and industry critics. In broader terms, the performance costume had a secondary role of return on investment that followed attraction. Managers, agents and recording companies entered this financial equation with anticipated returns on their operations. Artists were under significant pressure to maintain profit margins, relevance and popularity. Ethel Waters, who launched her singing career in the 1920s, verbalized the management of her business, "as my salary increased, so did my personal expenses . . . as a headliner I had to buy plenty of expensive clothes" (Waters and Samuels 1992: 156). As well, Waters juggled the decision of collecting her earnings or paying accompaniment when show revenue was down. Theory has shown that elaborate dress prior to the twentieth century suggested a life of leisure and the absence of productive labor (Hurlock 1929: 152; Flügel 1950: 112). Contrary to this notion, it will be evidenced that the restrictive tuxedos, strapless ball gowns and other posh clothing of jazz artists indicated regular work and conspicuous expenditures; even more so, for women it defied inferiority to male earnings, social status and influence. "It goes without saying that no apparel can be considered elegant, or even decent, if it shows the effect of manual labor on the part of the wearer, in the way of soil or wear" (Veblen 2007: 341). Responding to this aristocratic code, performers although working and at times facing grueling road trips were compelled to fashion their artistry as intellectual effort. Expenses, cash flow, risks and impressions transformed the simple act of dressing into an intricate economic model.

For the reason that clothing occurs in a community for public view, the artifact of dress is social, where it is expressed and perceived by individuals. Barthes interpreted the object with meaning as "a standardized picture of expected collective behavior" (Barthes 2006: 14). The combination of fashion and music, each with desired outcomes, proffers a complex analysis of influential qualities. There are tangible components within jazz that can be aesthetically judged similar to fashion. Evidence is found in timbre, a characteristic sound quality produced by musicians and singers (Tirro 1977: 17). The listener can detect a distinct sound through instrumental and vocal manipulation. A religious, celebratory or gloomy quality is evoked through the speed, texture and volume of a composition. Through the receiver's interpretation, this characteristic has emotional meaning indicative of love, happiness, ecstasy, sadness or anger. Teddy Wilson, jazz pianist, recalled during his days with the Benny Goodman band that a fervor took hold with audiences displaying wild behaviors, and "jumping up and down and tearing up seats," while hearing bluesy versions of "Don't Be That Way" and "St. Louis Blues" (Wilson, Ligthart and Van Loo 2001: 39). Giddins and DeVeaux submitted that the stylistic technique of timbre persuaded musicians "to lend their instruments the same qualities of human speech" (Giddins and Deveaux 2009: 3). Hence, dress and timbre comparably elicit meaning, and "bear witness to the creative power of society" (Barthes 2006: 15).

The influential fashion system

In society, the process of applying sewn fabrics to the body represents additional functions beyond style. Fashion is a fluctuating system, where persuasive dress and dressing equate to economic and cultural capital. Furthermore, clothes represent goods that are exchanged for revenue and promotion. The analysis of supply and demand is critical in manufacturing these products. When goods are favorable to consumers, the demand curve slopes upward. Designers, producers, entertainers and governments have impacted this quotient through the manipulation of demand via silhouette, sumptuary law, exhibition and production. The accumulation of wealth allows individuals to consume greater quantities and higher valued items. Jazz artists have displayed this capital on stage, in public and through printed press, thereby influencing demand. As such, the dress of jazz performers is relevant because the selection and presentation of clothing impacts the fashion cycle. This flow is supported by microeconomics, a study of "the behavior of particular households, firms, and industries" (Collins and Devanna 1992: 79), and likewise consumer trends that vary the economy as a whole. According to Veblen, the "admitted expenditure for display . . . is, perhaps, more universally practiced in the matter of dress than in any other line of consumption" (Veblen 2007: 339).

Second, movements in society transform the fashion system. Some of the most powerful interests were witnessed when civil rights, women's rights and youth rebellion took hold. Groups expressed their desire for social, political and economic change with voice and body. This egalitarian pursuit was intensified through appearance and behavior. Quoted earlier was Duke Ellington's declaration that jazz embodied freedom. From its birth, the genres of jazz have sought equal artistic expression. The growing admiration of performers, particularly African American, became compelling through the stream of fashion. These artists acquired clothing, augmented it with their personal style and displayed it to audiences, who responded with imitation. Fashion passed from supplier to the entertainer, thenceforth to the desire of spectators, touching

diverse economic classes. This transmission in communities was juxtaposed to realities of housing, religion, employment, entertainment and retail. As illustration, S. Rubin & Sons, a tailoring and hatter business, advertised regularly in the 1920s to African American men. Rubin's location neighboring the black vaudeville houses on South Street determined clothing offerings and demand. Marketing printed in the *Philadelphia Tribune* cited attraction, quality and value:

> Be a Good Dresser and have "Rubin" tailor your "SPRING SUITS." "RUBIN CLOTHES" are all quality and give fullest satisfaction and service. English Suitings for the young men who want plenty of snap will surely be pleased with our One Button-Double-Flare Models. Moderate Prices.
>
> (*Philadelphia Tribune* 1920b)

Based on the economic model, the retailer responded to trends by offering specific styles utilizing promotional idioms such as "plenty of snap." Moskin's Credit Clothing Co. and Koshland Clothier and Furnisher promoted multiple brand offerings and value. Of the latter's assurance, "there never was a season when it was so vitally important to choose clothing of well-known standard make and at a reputable, reliable house" (*Philadelphia Tribune* 1921a). Locality, clientele and aesthetics influenced designers and retailers; as much, jazz provoked the fashion system to notice the improvisation of style.

As a third point, social enterprise thrived within the system, sustained by human interaction. Clothing worn by an individual acts as a guide, in some measure, distinguishing ethnicity, geography, religion, social inclination and sexual orientation. Communities assign meanings in dress through values, rituals, affirmations and repudiations. As an immigrant nation, America's history configured a place where multicultural customs, varied belief systems and inequalities both social and financial collided. The proliferation of jazz entertainment in the early part of the twentieth century increased aspirational style among economically diverse populations and international audiences. On November 29, 1934, the *Philadelphia Tribune* related Parisian exhilaration following "eccentric" Louis Armstrong's performance:

> Armstrong immaculately attired in a full dress suit, with his gold "Selmer" trumpet in one hand and a white linen handkerchief in the other ran out on the Salle Rameau's stage . . . their snappy costumes and their magnificent display of instruments in itself was a delight to the eyes of these people who are devotees of beauty and art.
>
> (*Philadelphia Tribune* 1934b)

The manner of jazz, with its various traits, had an intrinsic ability to challenge class difference, spawn interaction and mutate within social environments.

Together with this act, fashion communicated well-understood ideas of attraction, prosperity, influence and respectability.

The representation of dress

Clothing, being the product of a fashion system where various parties have an interest to create, manufacture, advertise and sell items of value, contains a set of messages with meaning in society. An historic evaluation of jazz dress considers visual output spanning print to video; thereby, communication has been delivered at a point of time beyond the event. Also, the original image can be a reproduction in archives and film or viewed in a different medium. Messages have a complex makeup of stimuli, displays and interpretations. Thus, a view of jazz dress through photography, film, literature and marketing will consider biographies and events that swayed a meaning of fashion and music allowing thoughtful conclusion.

A fundamental approach to fashion and jazz starts with knowledge that clothes with assigned meaning were acquired. Desiring a reaction, performers presented this image alongside music to an audience, resulting in the representation having meaning to the receiver. The introduction of behavior of the artist and environment of presentation transformed the definition of the clothes, for example, Ben Webster and Billy Kyle merging fashionable clothing including suspenders, fedora and tweed overcoat in a 1940 studio session (Figure 1.2).

The measurement of image and meaning is informed by the writings of Ferdinand de Saussure, Stuart Hall and Roland Barthes in the areas of semiology, representation and fashion language, respectively. Barthes, in construction of a clothes idiom, affirmed: "dress . . . is a strong form of meaning, it constitutes an intellectual, notifying relation between a wearer and their group" (Barthes 2006: 10).

For jazz artists, clothing and accessories were obtained and manipulated for view. This is the point of representation. Hall, in concise wording, labeled it "the production of meaning through language" (Hall 2012: 16). Within the genre, a conscious attitude towards fashion was evident. The aim of artistic, social and financial liberty stimulated the dress of performers. From the roots of jazz, qualities of free expression, display and persuasiveness were fused together. Sidney Bechet, in discussion of his grandfather's drumming in New Orleans, described the relevance:

> Sundays when the slaves would meet—that was their free day—he beat out rhythms on drums at the Square . . . everyone loved him. They waited for him

Figure 1.2 Ben Webster, saxophonist, and Billy Kyle, pianist, display the harmony of fashion and jazz, 1940. Photo by Charles Peterson. Courtesy of Don Peterson

> to start things: dances, shouts, moods even. Anything he wanted to do, he'd lead them. He had a power. He was a strong man. His name was Omar.
>
> (Bechet 2002: 6)

This quote is a demonstrative example of a black musician, likely of the early 1800s period, conveying an influential spirit. Bechet's grandfather swayed the audience with musical talent; yet, the visual quality seems to have had a similar function in his appeal.

Gwendolyn O'Neal ascertained that African American men exhibited aesthetic elements of dress that could be traced to 1800s West Africa (O'Neal 2010), where color affinity, improvisation and fine dress were documented. Even earlier, African art of the fifteenth and sixteenth centuries gave emphasis to the head, considered the location of "knowledge, perception, and skill" (Arnoldi and Kreamer 1995: 12). Elaborate headdresses, intricate border motifs and highly decorative kilts were found in sculptures, reliefs and masks from the Mali, Songhai, Ashanti and Benin Kingdoms. In the seventeenth century, writings from Dutch travelers including Dierick Ruyters and Olfert Dapper, detailed trade-driven cities, where inhabitants were "magnificently dressed, wearing necklaces of jasper or fine coral" (Davidson 1966: 104); in like manner, British traders of the 1800s noted an abundance of impressive cloths and silks, robes that shimmered and multi-colored leather sandals (Davidson 1966: 107–8). Thus, early African history exhibited skilled technique in jewelry design, weaving, dyeing, printing and animal skin production that contributed to a strong visual aesthetic that was preserved in cultural artifacts and documented by observers. From these traditions and expressions, jazz of the twentieth century embodied the performance of drumming, singing and dancing as well the representation of cultural beauty.

It will be evident that dress and style was pronounced among performers following their entry into the entertainment industry. However at an early age, these aspiring artists were cognizant of fashion, dress motives and the outcome of influence. Count Basie, in a chronicle of his adolescence circa 1920, specified navigation around generational norms:

> In those day you wore short pants, knee breeches, or sailor-boy pants until you were in your teens . . . My first pair of long pants were sailor pants with the narrow hips and the square-flap button placket and bell bottoms . . . I couldn't put them on at home because when I was growing up you were not supposed to wear long pants until you came of age.
>
> (Basie and Murray 2002: 36)

Farid Chenoune, dress historian, described the same custom in the eighteenth century when the upper class dressed little boys as "sailors," prior to emancipation (Chenoune 1993: 23). The permanent transition to pantaloons and trousers took place in the next century owing to circulatory comfort, aesthetic conformity and social transformation. Regarding the breeches worn during Basie's childhood, he described a trend among the youth who modified conventional dress:

> Some guys used to wear them like baseball pants, and if you could get away with letting them hang down, that was kind of raunchy, and if you wore one leg up and one down, that was very sporty, especially if you wore your cap cocked at a special angle or with the visor flipped up or turned around to the back.
>
> (Basie and Murray 2002: 36)

These similar alterations, when applied to contemporary dress of disaffected black teenagers, have been identified as subversive style. Considering the provocative depiction and anxiety generated by hipsters, beats and teddy boys decades earlier, Hebdige asserted that the output expresses the "tension between those in power and those condemned to subordinate positions and second-class lives" (Hebdige 2009: 132). Hence, the drooping pants, curved and flat brim caps, oversized white t-shirts and untied sneakers of black urban teenagers and white suburban youth popularized in the late twentieth century have added weight in view of past practices. Contrary to the negative traits applied to modern adolescent adaptations, the inventive stylings of the knee breeches, as Basie detailed, were interpreted as the wearer being "mannish" or "in too much of a hurry to be grown up" (Basie and Murray 2002: 36). The dress and representation of performers is multifaceted, happening and evolving over several decades amid both genders with cultural genetics.

Defining a jazz aesthetic

Emission of melodic sounds and words serves the primary tool of communication in music. As previously outlined, the output is the expression of performers, who have strategic goals to share and influence. The attractive, pleasing or aesthetic element of jazz is registered in both audible and visual form. Improvisation has been intimately tied with music, indeed, linked with technical explorations like abstract constructions in modern jazz. The category of free jazz "seemed to epitomize an aesthetic of anarchy and nihilism" (Tirro 1977: 341) Translating the coded music, the sharp, strident and bluesy sound became a representation of the essence of young black Americans demanding civil rights. For instance in the late 1950s, Ornette Coleman, a pioneer of free jazz, released the expressively titled albums, *The Shape of Jazz to Come*, *Change of the Century* and *This Is Our Music*. *Ebony* paying tribute to Coleman and other black musicians asserted that their efforts in creativity sought "to change the operating modality . . . in the art forms they choose to engage" (Riley 1972).

Inherent in the term "code" is secrecy; performers that improvised invented an idiom of meaning that was "specific to a particular group of people" (Rose 2001: 89). Early on, the creation of music occurred on the spot, wherever the playing was happening, also influenced by surroundings. As such, to gain understanding, it was advantageous to be aware of the origins, alterations and challenges taking place within a composition and its environment. This guardianship of style lessened as the music became admired beyond select factions, and technology spread its exposure and technique. Bechet summarized the conduit, "the music makes a voice, and, no matter what happens, the man that cares to hear that voice, he can hear it" (Bechet 2002: 217). Free will, risk taking, emotional expression and spirituality formulate jazz aesthetics. From Louis Armstrong's husky lyrical delivery to Dinah Washington's crystalline blues, a certain way of being steeped in cultural fortitude permeates the performer's core. Simply stated, the listener, consumed by a spiritual feeling that radiates from the chest cavity, is "amused, amazed, shaken, and moved" (Giddins and DeVeaux 2009: 2).

Conclusion

The contributions of the visual and performing arts are noted by their participation in the cultural development of nations. A history of America would be incomplete without a narrative of women's hemlines rising above the ankles, the performance of popular songs in cork-applied blackface or the mixing of segregated audiences in the 1950s. Thus, fashion and jazz have played a factor in social, economic and political change. Tradition, culture and activism are conveyed in both art forms. Often, these images have the power to persuade, particularly the youth in society.

In jazz, the "persistent existence of social tension between the adolescent and parental generations" was evidenced (MacDonald 1989: 159). The latter cohort embraced sentiments from religious groups, political leaders and music traditionalists. In the late 1800s, a similar generational conflict resided in fashion, where Victorian and Edwardian sensibilities of taste and gentility were a stronghold among the older and wealthier populations. Here, Joseph Willson's observations of African American higher classes in 1800s Philadelphia:

> Unlike fashionable people of other communities . . . they manage well to maintain even appearances, and support such comforts, conveniences and luxuries . . . in this way they avoid many of the embarrassments that are common to those whose sole claim to "fashion" consist in the success they may meet with in making a commanding "show" on particular occasions.
>
> (Winch 2000: 98)

Willson linked the binary premise of modesty and ostentation in his declaration, establishing that the unrestrained display of wealth by certain youthful societies was judged crude among the older populace. Conflicts are often generational and suggest reluctance to cultural change.

Production technology, new channels of distribution and diverse consumers in fashion and music ignited an increasingly youthful demand in the twentieth century. Musicians, painters, photographers, writers and editors provided witness to these events; thus, a comprehensive narrative is obtained through various forms of representation. The exhibitions of dress and behavior within jazz are relevant and critical as scholarship owing to the music's pivotal role in the transformation of American popular culture and history, and likewise the genre's influence on worldwide aesthetics.

2

A STYLISH HISTORY OF JAZZ: 1900–1960

Origins of jazz expression

Decades before the Civil War, a gathering of inspired people seeking self-determination initiated the birth of a musical genre that flourished throughout America. Congo Square in New Orleans, Louisiana is the highly renowned ground where slaves gathered for spiritual communion on free Sunday. By 1800, these assemblies swelled to six hundred individuals, who engaged in a visceral response of drumming, dancing and singing that had direct African roots (Gioia 1998: 4). The expression and celebration of the "moral and religious convictions that underlay their daily life" (Davidson 1966: 143) had been the art of African civilizations for centuries. From the Bini to the Ashanti, the recognition of harvest, hunt, birth, death, puberty and marriage was conveyed through rituals and traditional art (Davidson 1966: 148). Extensive slave narratives from Solomon Northup and accounts compiled by the Works Progress Administration in the late 1930s corroborate that these assemblies occurred in various locales, especially during Christmas celebrations. Following his twelve years of bondage, the writings of Northup detail the great quantity of slaves that gathered for the holiday supper: "usually from three to five hundred are assembled, coming together on foot, in carts, on horseback, on mules, riding double and triple" (Northup 2010: 118). A common objective of slavery was to destroy familial bonds by separating families, often mother and child. Consequently, the emotional rituals were a way to empathize and carry forward legacy that could not be physically taken. Recounting his grandfather's musical experience in Congo Square, Bechet described:

> First one drum, then another one answering it. Then a lot of drums. Then a voice, one voice. And then a refrain, a lot of voices joining and coming into each other. And all of it having to be heard. The music being born right inside itself, not knowing how it was getting to be music, one thing being responsible for another. Improvisation . . . that's what it was.
>
> (Bechet 2002: 8)

These African-related performances combined arm motions, vocal elements, dance and cultural rituals that created an art with distinct union to African Americans. For instance, Northup's narrative recounted a lively aspect practiced during dances. "The patting is performed by striking the hands on the knees then striking the hands together, then striking the right shoulder with one hand, the left with the other—all the while keeping time with the feet and singing" (Northup 2010: 121). In the late twentieth century, director Spike Lee accentuated the performance of stepping in his film, *School Daze* (1988), which flaunted the dance routines and dress of African American fraternities and sororities. This form of expression derived from the West African ring shout. It is carried forward and practiced in modern times by the McIntosh County Shouters of the Gullah-Geechee region in Georgia, who aim to preserve the cultural heritage. "The call-and-response singing, the polyrhythms of the stick and hands and feet, the swaying and hitching of the shouters, all derive from African forms," noted Rosenbaum in *Shout Because You're Free* that chronicles the tradition that was performed in South Carolina, Georgia and Florida "by slaves and their descendants" (Rosenbaum, Rosenbaum and Buis 1998: 1–4).

As noted by Bechet's descriptions and various slave narratives, music was instrumental to the spirit of the assemblies with solos, accompaniment, praise and response produced on drums, quills, fiddles, banjos and violins. This improvisational element is significant to the creation of jazz. Giddins and DeVeaux described this quality as rhythmic contrast, based on "two distinct layers," a fixed chorus and a variable accent on top (Giddins and DeVeaux 2009: 26). The latter part, played by a soloist, embellishes the continuous melody generated by the rhythm section: piano, bass, guitar and drums. A precursor to the modern jazz ensemble was exhibited in Bini art, especially bronze plaques and ivory carvings that commemorated the culture of the Benin Kingdom located in southern Nigeria. Originating from the fifteenth century, these reliefs show citizens in action with drumming and acrobatic performance. Bini musicians produced additional sound through "bells, gourd rattles and elephant-tusk trumpets" (Davidson 1966: 112). Citing the continent's influence, W. C. Handy, an African American musician and composer, recalled his creation of "Jogo Blues" published in 1913. "The inspiration for the new composition was a humorous Negro custom that could be traced to the Gullahs and from them all the way back to Africa" (Handy 1969: 116).

Early forms of cultural expression including ring shouts, spirituals, work songs and folk pieces integrated African traditions and ripened in the late 1800s into a syncopated form called ragtime. By the mid-1900s, an abstract method of jazz was launched from blues and swing rhythms furthering the freedom seeking and exploration inherent in the genre. Dizzy Gillespie, in summarizing the evolution, asserted: "it shares the rhythmic content of the African music, music of the Western Hemisphere and various lands of the East, and has merged this rhythm with European harmonies, the soul of the slaves, the blues, and the spirituals to create jazz" (Gillespie and Fraser 2009: 485). The distinct formulation was essential to the development of ragtime, blues, swing, bebop, and modern jazz.

Ragtime music

A zeitgeist of unapologetic rhythm was initiated by ragtime style of the early twentieth century. Initially a piano style, the name was generally acknowledged as an extraction from "ragged time," meaning the simultaneous utilization of contrasting rhythms (Giddins and DeVeaux 2009: 67; Gioia 1998: 21). The proliferation of the piano made it the choice instrument that yielded ragtime music. "Piano professors" was the name of African American men who trained on the popular mechanism, finding novel ways of rhythmic expression and melody dissemination (Peress 2004: 29). Accounts of the 1893 World's Columbian Exposition in Chicago suggested the music being in circulation at the fair (Peress 2004: 37). Ragtime arrived on the tailcoats of the cakewalk that snowballed in popularity among Americans. By the late 1800s, the humorous dance highlighted the behaviors of antebellum plantation owners at social gatherings, where aristocratic displays of excessive gentility were observed. Slave narratives indicate that "cuttin' de pigeons wings," "dancin' on de spot," and "set de flo" were similar to the cakewalk dance that required participants to be agile and remain in a defined space with the winner receiving a cake (Berlin, Favreau and Miller 1998: 179–80). Traditional dances of European heritage including the waltz and quadrille cultivated group sequence and aesthetics as opposed to self-showmanship. The cakewalk with comedic traits and acrobatic movements challenged this structure.

Ridicule of African Americans came through the dance's appropriation by white performers in black face. This process of darkening the skin with burnt cork was popularized around 1820 with Thomas Dartmouth Rice, the father of Negro minstrelsy. The *Washington Post* reported that Rice, following the study of an older slave named Jim Crow, "made up precisely as the original . . . singing a score of humorous verses to the air-slightly changed and quickened-of the poor, wretched cripple" (Quinn 1895). Minstrel performance and the grotesque Jim Crow masquerade crossed the Atlantic during the mid-century. Rice, in addition to Johnny Raynor (Christy's Minstrels) and George Washington "Pony" Moore, performed in England, finding great popularity and financial success (*Washington Post* 1897). Fifty years later, the influence of minstrel entertainment in the country was indicated when a ban followed by a reinstatement of playing Negro melodies and ragtime occurred in London. On May 9, 1909, the *New York Times* reported that the four-year prohibition was due to the excessively popular music being played in park concerts. The London County Council yielding to demands for ragtime songs, including "Suwanee River," "Watermelon Patch," and "Darkies'

Cake Walk," offered an apologetic comment "that tastes in music differ as in other things." Confirming the notoriety, J. Ashby-Sterry, in the *Washington Post* via the *London Graphic*, declared that Negro minstrelsy had captivated London for at least a half century (Ashby-Sterry 1909).

The Jim Crow label as frequently mentioned in this book represents not only the original distortion of an African American slave but the oppressive laws that instituted racial segregation, thereby restricting the liberties of blacks following the Civil War. Minstrel entertainment with its link to Jim Crow has direct association to denigration and inequality. Into the 1920s, minstrelsy and the cakewalk found expression with upbeat tempos that complemented the acrobatics of the dance infused with snobbish bearing, high steps and twirling canes.

To mark its status, the art of ragtime became published compositions by the last decade of the 1800s. The piano style is notable for its energetic speed, lightness, modulations and thumping accents. For conventional analysis by jazz scholars, the technique was a spectacle matching the disciplined conduct of the left hand and the madcap explorations in cadence of the right hand (Gioia 1998: 21, Giddins and DeVeaux 2009: 67). Scott Joplin, one of the most well-known ragtime musicians, composed "Maple Leaf Rag" (1899), a work that articulated a modernity that was hungering among African Americans pursuing human rights juxtaposed to white Americans desiring economic prosperity. W. E. B. Du Bois personified this pursuit with his publication, *The Souls of Black Folks*, and his leadership in the burgeoning National Association for the Advancement of Colored People. Likewise, Henry Ford's founding of Ford Motor Company in 1903 represented American ingenuity that proceeded from agriculture to urban industrialization. Joplin, Du Bois and Ford were members of the post-Civil War generation that contributed to a modernity swelling in America. Of the three, Joplin would be the only one that would not see the full impact his talent had on this new course. Showing a limited period of popularity, ragtime had begun to wane by Joplin's death in 1917, stepping aside for fresher takes on improvisation and melody. A younger generation born around the 1900s created the label "jazz" that would entice mainstream American interests.

Ragtime era fashion

Early twentieth century fashion, comparable to ragtime, had a liberating quality that allowed for increased movement, expression and optimism. By far the most profound change was volume reduction in women's dresses, as negotiated by couturier Charles Fredrick Worth. Hoop skirts and the bustle of the post-antebellum period gave way to streamlined skirts that were paired with jackets to form practical street suits. Furthermore, options for comfort were found in the shirtwaist, often worn with just a skirt for day. Milbank, in describing this trend, alluded to the consumer's voice in fashion: "American women . . . resisted attempts by couturiers to introduce blouses, of silk or other materials" (Milbank 1989: 51), preferring the ease of laundry care with cotton shirts. Additional functionality was gained through bell-flared and paneled seamed skirts; to this effect, a slight elevation from the ground augmented mobility and hem cleanliness (Milbank 1989: 50). By the end of the first decade, the fashion silhouette for women had hastily shifted to a narrow cylindrical drape with a high waistline or Empire silhouette. Thus, the modern sentiment and rhythm exploration in ragtime had an equivalent intonation in women's fashion design.

Pertaining to men's fashion, simplicity was obtained through departures from long-tailed coats, ornate vests and multi-fabric ensembles. The ditto suit, originating around 1860, had reached widespread influence by the turn of the century. Consisting of coat, pant and vest matched to the same fabric and color, this less elaborate look was attainable by diverse economic groups (Bigelow 1970: 194). The contour of the ditto suit complemented the wearer's body, equally advancing mobility with a coat cut to the low hip, sloped shoulders and single breasted-closure. A Hackett Carhart & Co. advertisement in the *New York Times* on April 19, 1912 hinted at comfort options for men's suits: "All of the American adaptations of the English initiative in unpadded shoulders, soft roll lapel and narrow trousers . . . no matter how skeptical you are, here are all the prevailing modes" (*New York Times* 1912). Also in the same year, L. Wollenberger, a Philadelphia tailor and clothier, promoted "good-fitting suits, made of the very best material" (*Philadelphia Tribune* 1912).

Headwear was the second most important aspect of a man's wardrobe during this time. Evolving from the rigid structure of the top hat, these styles were shorter in height, fabricated of softer materials and sanctioned a crease along the crown. The bowler, homburg, panama and pork pie, each with international origin, epitomized the hats that would dominate this era. In the mid-century, Lester Young's distinctive adornment of the pork pie hat aroused popularity of the headwear among a younger generation (Figure 2.1).

A prominent photograph of Kid Ory's Woodland Band in 1905 featured six band members with individualized hats either perched on their leg or an instrument (Godbolt 1990: 10). The rounded crown of the derby was represented, as was the indented top of the homburg. Each hat embodied the silhouette of the musician's instrument from the bell-like end of the trumpet and trombone to the slightly curved surface of the bass, violin and guitar. Chenoune noted that the bowler originated as "sporting or country wear" transitioning to an accessory for formal attire (Chenoune 1993: 130). As evidenced in early jazz images, these head coverings revealed an approach that individualized musicians. A uniquely styled hat, along with posture, countenance, and dress, accentuated band members in photographs. During the 1920s, Willie "The Lion" Smith, a prominent stride-form pianist, styled his performance with cigars, horn-rimmed glasses and

Figure 2.1 Lester Young accentuates "cool" style in pork pie hat, Newport Jazz Festival, 1958. © Ted Williams/Cynthia Sesso, CTSIMAGES

sharp clothes. "He always sported a derby that he kind of cocked at a special angle and also wore while he played" (Basie and Murray 2002: 79). In the same way, pianists, James P. Johnson and Fats Waller, employed aspects of the guise.

Prominence of male musicians was achieved through bands and orchestras in white and black communities. Brass bands were vital to American life, having recurring roles in parades, funerals, circuses, baseball games and political assemblies, where patriotism flourished. These groups ranged from large to small ensembles were unity through sound and dress was dominant. A review in the *Washington Post* on May 7, 1901 connected the irresistible force of the

United States Marine Band's music and stylish dress. The writer conveyed that "no better spectacular effect could have been devised for the stage than the view of the musicians in their brilliant red uniforms with gilt decorations" (*Washington Post* 1901).

Integration of dress was essential to brass bands that maintained traits of military dress and precision. Mandarin collars, fully buttoned coats, regimental stripes, spiral embroideries and caps with insignias signified structure, cohesiveness and authority within the group. Equally for soldiers, these accoutrements designated rank, pride of service and gravity of war, fostering an effective fighter. "The psychological effect of banners, bands, the flash and glitter of steel and gold, blaze of colors, the rhythmic tramp of feet, the thunder of hoofs, was incalculable in the wars of the past . . . the soldier who is proud of his uniform is proud of the service" (Curtis 1902). Reasonably for the Colored Waif's Home Brass Band featuring a young Louis Armstrong, the Superior Orchestra, the Reliance Brass Band and the Holmes Band of Lutcher uniforms solidified common ambition, measurable talent, boldness and the desire to look good. Extraordinary photographs of these bands and orchestras from 1900 to 1915 document gracefully aligned men in sharp dress possessing sophistication and determination.

The Superior and Reliance musicians wore a hip-length, buttoned coat with mandarin collar. By the mid-twentieth century, a version of this garment would be labeled the Nehru jacket, inspired by the dress of Jawaharlal Nehru, Indian Prime Minister (Ghurye 1995: 208; Bigelow 1970: 271). The coat's collar and drape has references to fifteenth-century Imperial China, while braids, ribbons, lace and rosettes pull from decorative details of the justaucorps, an outer coat of the seventeenth-century Baroque period (Bigelow 1970: 123). Comparable dress was displayed among college musicians. Ensembles such as the Hampton Institute Indian Orchestra and the Claflin University Brass Band modernized this uniform with military style hats featuring insignias (Figure 2.2).

Hurlock's assertion of standardized masculine fashion supports the act of conformity in early brass bands. "The well-dressed man . . . his aim is to conform to the standards held by the other men of his social class" (Hurlock 1929: 154). Band members gained acceptance, prestige and access to musical expertise by adhering to the standards of dress. "Fashion can serve the purpose of satisfying our desire to be one with the group" (Hurlock 1929: 38). Hence, the application of the uniform signified that the individual identified with the band in thought, technique and acknowledgment of a hierarchy. Sidney Bechet corroborated the majesty of the Grand Marshals who led the strutting bands adorned in full dress suits, long sashes, shoulder emblems and gold bangles. Bechet stressed the visual quality of the leader's showmanship. "It's what you want from a parade: you want to see it as well as hear it . . . they got a whole lot of pleasure out of just watching him" (Bechet 2002: 66).

Figure 2.2 The Claflin University Brass Band exhibits dress conformity with fully buttoned coats, swirling embroideries and crested caps, c.1900. © CORBIS

Blues music

Piano thumpers tickled the ivories in the saloons to attract customers, furnishing a theme for the prayers at Beale Street Baptist Church and Avery Chapel (Methodist). Scores of powerfully built roustabouts from river boats sauntered along the pavement, elbowing fashionable browns in beautiful gowns. Pimps in boxback coats and undented Stetsons came out to get a breath of early evening air and to welcome the young night. The poolhall crowd grew livelier than they had been during the day. All that contributed to the color and spell of Beale Street mingled outside.

(Handy 1969: 118)

The "Father of the Blues," W. C. Handy, illustrates the Memphis setting in 1914 when he composed many of his blues including the infinitely recorded "St. Louis Blues." Handy's account divulges the rhythm of life, love and spirituality, which shaped the authenticity of the blues. With a keen reference to the aesthetics, the individuals on Beale Street that he paints are appealing, stylish and self-assured.

A form of poetic expression with roots in call-and-response techniques took hold in the second decade of the twentieth century. The improvisation had been exhibited in religious and work songs of slaves, thus approximating its birth decades before its peak. Given the title "blues," it illustrated an individual who was sad, despondent, indeed, a target of life's hardships but not surrendering. The inclusion of loss of life and its related adversities placed the blues alongside gospel hymns that expressed sorrow and a need for salvation. Within the African American community, a new generation was experiencing lack of opportunity, hostility and violence that had been faced by their parents. The melody and lyrics of the blues expressed their feelings and desires. Cornel West described the visceral response of African American culture as "creative ways of fashioning power and strength through the body and language which yield black joy and ecstasy" (West 1999: 102). Two distinct varieties, classic and country, defined the blues genre. Lyrics concerning the difficulties of love, lack of money and natural disasters, especially floods, consumed the blues divas. Ma Rainey, Mamie Smith, Bessie Smith and Alberta Hunter propelled this art into popular culture through their famous recordings and performances of the 1920s, while the men gained their fame, posthumously, via a 1960s resurgence of the vocal guitar style. Around 1903 in Tutwiler, Mississippi, Handy witnessed the rural or folk version of the blues that would in later years be linked to Robert Johnson and Blind Lemon Jefferson:

A lean, loose-jointed Negro had commenced plunking a guitar beside me while I slept. His clothes were rags; his feet peeped out of his shoes. His face had on it some of the sadness of the ages . . . the singer repeated the line three times, accompanying himself on the guitar with the weirdest music I had ever heard.

(Handy 1969: 74)

The arrangement of the blues song is identified as two repeated lines followed by a rhyming line (Gioia 1998: 13). Thirty years after its climax, Billie Holiday honored this twelve-bar arrangement with her composition of "Stormy Blues" (1954). Holiday expressed two of the blues themes inserting problematic love and inclement weather. In contrast to ragtime with its upbeat tempo, the blues symbolized a realization that social freedom and equality would be a protracted struggle. This reflection on the past, the south and darker times led to its falling out of favor in the urban cities of the north.

Blues era fashion

Contrary to the sad lyrics they espoused, the blues ladies dressed in extravagant designs that articulated their growing wealth, as well as "the changing attitudes of women" (Ewing 1986: 91). The most striking alterations were the introduction of fur trimmings, the pear-shape silhouette with considerable volume below the bust, aspects of Orientalism and the chemise dress. On January 4, 1914 the *New York Times* heralded the fur rage with the following declaration: "whether or not the fur of the day is genuine or mostly imitation is not to be considered . . . it is everywhere" (*New York Times* 1914). This frenzy, as with other trends, originated in Europe, where the preferences of couturiers and high society maintained a strong hold on American interests. "Paris fashions had been shown at the Chicago Fair of 1893 and American *Vogue* followed this course . . . angling its fashions strongly to Paris" (Ewing 1986: 72). While the blues technique utilized past elements of African vocal delivery, the fashions of Paris explored the history of great empires, particularly of North Africa and Western Asia. "The Egyptian influence was more pronounced than ever . . . bright colors which seemed to be subdued by age were said to be exact reproductions of those found in the museum," declared the *New York Times* in review of a fashion show in 1923 (*New York Times* 1923).

In a publicity photo for Columbia Records of the same year, Bessie Smith, Empress of the Blues, captured the Oriental aesthetic, elegantly draped in a sleeveless net tunic embroidered with beads and floral appliqués that scalloped at the hem (Marks and Edkins 1999: 120). Smith was known for her opulent headdresses that exploited beads, fringe and feathers, conceivably a strategy to emphasize the head as practiced by early African societies. Instrumental to this exotic escapism was the 1922 discovery of Pharaoh Tutankhamun's tomb, followed by the 1923 opening of the chamber by Howard Carter, British archaeologist. The *New York Times* cautioned women on the Egyptian trend in clothes: "do not exaggerate it, modify it, and choose the beautiful parts only" (*New York Times* 1923). Due to the delicate and revealing dresses, the *Washington Post* questioned societal virtue through a church official's decree that "short skirts and bobbed hair . . . take us back in ancient fashions to those who have lost their character" (*Washington Post* 1927a).

"Skirts were minimal, they began at the hip-line and only just covered the knees but in the evening the hem line varied, and handkerchief-points, flared godets and fringes in uncertain lengths fluttered and swayed as the wearer walked or danced" (Black and Garland 1975: 322). With this fashion shift, the straight silhouette of the chemise dress was ideal for performers on the vaudeville and TOBA (Theater Owner's Booking Association) circuits. These theatrical shows combined singing, dancing and comedy routines; accordingly, the looseness of the drape and the above ankle skirt length supported movement and generated attraction. In the *Philadelphia Tribune*, Gibson's New Standard Theater highlighted in advertisements that upcoming shows featured "mostly girls" and "nearly all girls" as well the paper listed international themes of tango dancing and exploits in Africa (*Philadelphia Tribune* 1914; 1919). Women, inclusive of classic blues singers, were agents in transmitting global style that contained elements of African and Asian origins.

Men's fashion of the blues period resisted the deliberate extravagance of Eastern destinations. However in 1919, exoticism made a strong appearance with Benny Peyton's Jazz Kings in London. The black American band was photographed in elaborate feathered turbans accompanied with Nehru jackets enveloped in contrasting horizontal stripes. The ostentatious outfit was likely restricted to publicity shots or lower tier performances. Band member Sidney Bechet referred to high-quality dress at the Embassy Club in London: "a smart place where we had to wear white tie and tails" (Bechet 2002: 129). However, turbans and Oriental flare continued to thrive among women. A *New York Times* advertisement for Lord & Taylor proclaimed "The Turban Dominates the Mode" (*New York Times* 1919a). The ad listed prices up to four hundred dollars, necessitated by intricate pearls, beads, plumes and metallic embroideries. Similar to the cultural references of blues singing, the era's fashion demonstrated storytelling through textiles, silhouettes and accessories of ancient cultures.

Swing music

In the late teens, a faction of musicians with honed skills on a variety of instruments departed New Orleans for Chicago, Kansas City, Los Angeles and New York. This black and white movement facilitated the influence of the Dixie style to new populations. Performers circulated the technique in urban centers, where it mimicked the hectic rhythms of crowded tenements, factory work and nightlife. The music was given the designations "jass" and "jazz." The latter name, being the adopted title, embodied the vibrant energy and harmonic blend of the ensemble. In analysis of the genre's ubiquity, Gioia asserted: "it seems almost anything in fashion would, sooner or later, be classified as jazz" (Gioia 1998: 77).

The pursuit of freedom continued to be a theme that found voice in the generation born after 1900. Many were part of the great migration, a time when African Americans left the south for opportunity in large cities of the north. Although faced with continued segregation and economic barriers, these groups found solace in religion, as well visual, literary and performance art. This out-flowing initiated the Harlem Renaissance, a period between 1919 and 1929 that demonstrated interest, patronage and elevation of black arts. Although the experience was beneficial for a select group, a broader view places the renaissance as an essential marker on the path to civil rights for African Americans. The artists of the renaissance disseminated black aesthetics through fine art, photography, literature, stage performance and music. In a similar capacity, a youthful white population, coveting an escape from the

First World War and the National Prohibition Act of 1919 that regulated the commerce of "intoxicating liquors," indulged in socially liberating behavior. The music and dance exchanged between blacks and whites during the jazz age spawned challenges to racial constructs that would be triumphant in decades to come.

Following the period of marching bands, vaudeville, tent shows and minstrel performances, the swing aesthetic exemplified the most polished of these fares. It fused visual and artistic qualities of each entertainment style into a single package. Considering this richness, Louis Armstrong recalled the musical assortment of the Joe Oliver Band in 1920s Chicago, when the ensemble traded between theatrical playing, dance tunes and blues renditions (Armstrong 1999: 53). Swing bands prospered into the 1930s with a unique blend of symphonic composition, polyrhythms, famed soloists and uncompromising appearance. Duke Ellington, Paul Whiteman, Count Basie and Benny Goodman developed considerable fame during this period, when elements of African American art were absorbed into the white mainstream. As recorded by the *Pittsburgh Courier* in 1929, an article featuring Harlem's Cotton Club as a mecca of beauty and grace noted: "the crowd of New York's white elite pounding the tables with tiny hammers for more" (*Pittsburgh Courier* 1929).

The art of Aaron Douglas that explored "African aesthetics and use of Black subject matter" contributed to the visual of the swing period (Campbell et al. 1994: 110). Douglas' paintings incorporated a softened approach to the technique of Cubism, accelerated by Pablo Picasso and George Braque in the early 1900s. African vegetation, tribal warriors and spiritual rituals are synthesized with geometric patterns, collage and silhouette in Douglas' art. Equally, swing musicians augmented their performances with African embellishment as stage backdrops, promotional materials, show themes and song references. The representations of African heritage in swing performance utilized primitiveness and tribal qualities. Warner Brothers Pictures released an all-black film short in 1933, starring the Mills Blue Rhythm Band. During a party scene, the director transformed smartly dressed couples engaged in contemporary dance into natives with nude torsos, grass skirts and untamed hair. The visual transition suggested the regression of urbane dancers to primitive natives, therefore reinforcing stereotypes of cultural origins that minimized African societies and ceremonial practices. Langston Hughes, in his autobiography, articulated the nightly migrations of downtown white patrons to Harlem: "the strangers were given the best ringside tables to sit and stare at the Negro customers—like amusing animals in a zoo" (Hughes 1997: 225). Despite their hand in the music, African American audiences were barred from the Cotton Club and other venues that adopted Jim Crow policies. Nevertheless, swing jazz was deemed hot, wild and jumping that resulted in popular imitation, widespread growth and ultimately in a rebellion for a divergent sound.

Swing era fashion

Transpiring at the middle of the swing era in 1929, the stock market crash brought an abrupt end to the Harlem Renaissance and the carefree spending of the Jazz Age. Women's clothing saw conservative shifts that echoed the austerity required for the 1930s economy. For daywear, the simplicity of the printed dress in synthetic rayon or silk dominated. Milbank noted the garment's details: "its waistline was placed at the natural waist . . . and the prints were smaller and more delicate than the patterns of the previous decade" (Milbank 1989: 102). For evening, the hemlines of dresses lengthened from below the knee to dragging the floor. Ostentatious displays of wealth and sexuality were discarded for glamour that emphasized refinement and maturity. Although the nation was stricken with high unemployment and a loss of retirement savings, Hollywood studios produced an abundance of films that portrayed high-society affairs, where old-money wealth and nouveau riche segments clashed. *Dinner at Eight*, *Gold Diggers of 1933* and *Baby Face*, all released in 1933, signified films that illuminated devious ways to obtain wealth. The bias cut gown was prominent in these productions outlining the figures of Jean Harlow and Barbara Stanwyck. Cutting on a diagonal grain enabled the fabric, particularly satin and silk chiffon, to cascade. This drape technique was a reference to Greek and Roman antiquity.

In opposition to mainstream cinema, all-black productions concentrated on moral themes, wherein characters struggled between vice linked to jazz clubs and devotion to God. *Hallelujah!* (1929), *Moon Over Harlem* (1939), and *Swing!* (1938), comparable to mainstream films, contained women's day-time printed dresses and bias cut evening gowns. Thus, the universality of the fashion cycle was evident. During this period, the careers of Billie Holiday and Ella Fitzgerald, renowned jazz vocalists, gained ground through positions in the Count Basie and Chick Webb bands, respectively. Their early dress, austere in nature, would signify the economic depression of the early 1930s, advancing to well-defined allure by the end of the decade (Figure 2.3).

Jazz orchestras exacted formal modes of dress for men that simulated the exclusivity of jockey clubs of the nineteenth century. In Paris, these elite male societies were a "bastion of aristocratic pleasures and lifestyle," where hegemonic manner was the mission (Chenoune 1993: 61). "Lack of title or fortune was an almost insurmountable handicap" for membership (Chenoune 1993: 61). While jazz bands did not stringently calculate legacy or wealth, the player's talent and appearance replaced status criteria for admission. Miles Davis referred to his growing popularity circa 1945, when as a teenager he started to play with local bands. "I was starting to have a little reputation . . . as an up-and-coming trumpet player . . . some of the best musicians around East St. Louis wanted me to play with them" (Davis and Troupe 2011: 36). As with the previous decades of jazz, the chief dress among the male musicians was the tuxedo and suit. Davis

Figure 2.3 Ella Fitzgerald poses in a beaded, full-length evening dress with fingerless gloves, c.1940. © Bettmann/CORBIS

recalled his early captivation with this attire when it merged with the performer's personality. "All the cats in the band had their hair slicked back, was wearing hip shit—tuxedos and white shirts—and acting and talking like they was the baddest motherfuckers in the world" (Davis and Troupe 2011: 45). Complementing this narrative of formal dress, Basie recounted the necessity of wearing the garment while touring on the 1924 Columbia Circuit. "The management let us draw some money in advance . . . one thing the newcomers had to get for the act was tuxedos" (Basie and Murray 2002: 56). Thus, inclusion was achieved through conformity of attire with highbrow qualities, validating the weight of fashion alongside musical proficiency.

Originating in the late 1880s, the tuxedo, aka the dinner jacket, shortened the life of the long tailcoat for formal occasions. The title came from the Tuxedo Park Club in New York, where Griswold Lorillard, son of an American tobacco manufacturer, challenged established approaches to men's dress (Chenoune 1993: 111). Although the exact details are contested, Lorillard's coat was without tails, thus considered relaxed for high society. The identifying look of the tuxedo, often with satin lapels, was widespread among jazz bands; consequently attention to specific instrumentalists demanded solo exploits and distinctions in behavior (Figure 2.4).

According to Basie, Duke Ellington, whose orchestra adhered to the tuxedo dress, practiced this "colorful" habit. "Duke was always so interesting to look at along with that music he played . . . to watch him you could understand where the music was coming from and how he was walking around the stage bringing it out" (Basie and Murray 2002: 176). Hence, the standardization of fashion was a catalyst to increased experimentation and showmanship among musicians.

In 1910, Oscar "Papa" Celestin along with William "Baba" Ridgley intertwined the tuxedo garment and jazz through the formation of the Original Tuxedo

Figure 2.4 The Paul Banks Orchestra conveys uniformity of dress with tuxedos, c.1927.
© Bettmann/CORBIS

Orchestra. The impetus for the title came from the Tuxedo Dance Hall in Storyville (the Red Light District of New Orleans), where Celestin's band played until the Hall's closure in 1913 (Tirro 1977: 159). Initially tuxedos were not worn; however they were soon adopted by the group following the suggestion of a supporter (Ridgley 1978: 3). The transition to formal dress established three socioeconomic outcomes including syncopated music as popular dance music, elevated performance venues with better pay and African American musicians as influential. According to Ridgley in a transcribed interview at Tulane University, pay scales ranged from a low of $1.50 to a high of $25 per band member for premiere bookings at the New Orleans Country Club, Southern Yacht Club, Roosevelt Hotel and Carnival Balls (Ridgley 1978: 22–3). A correspondence from J. Calvin Drake of the Southern Yacht Club demonstrated the high opinion garnered. "Your orchestra has unquestionably contributed very largely to the success and increased attendance of our weekly dances" (Ridgley 1928a). In addition, a recommendation from the manager of the Conn New Orleans Company posited that Ridgley's Tuxedo Orchestra had "played with entire satisfaction a large number of very good engagements" (Ridgley 1928b). Such favorable endorsements necessitated good appearance and behavior, reliability and pleasing performances. Band members were under written agreement to adhere to formal dress standards of tuxedos or suits. In the late 1920s, Ridgley contracted members "to wear a dark suit, i.e., blue or black, with a white shirt and black bow tie" (Ridgley 1928c). Distinguished dress along with rhythmic jazz produced encounters, albeit socially restrictive between black musicians and white audiences, that would propel integration in future decades.

For less formal events, the suit was most acceptable. It had evolved from the sack version to a tailored form shadowing the lines of the upper torso. Toward the end of the decade, the waistband was high, trouser legs grew in width and cuffs were added at the hem. Photographer Charles Peterson, in 1937, captured the John Kirby Orchestra in light-colored suits that typified the trending features (Figure 2.5).

In addition, a jacket style with roots in the crossed redingote worn by the French Incroyables of the 1800s gained prominent exposure in Hollywood films and jazz orchestras. Known as the mess jacket, the military style garment "was waist length, tailless, and cut with a deep V across the back hem" (Bigelow 1970: 250). The tuxedo, suit and mess jacket were accessorized with oxford shoes featuring straight-toe caps; thereafter variation was achieved with two-toned versions and wing tips. Men's jazz dress of the swing period began as a singular, dark and formal presentation, yielding to challenges of standardization with the glen plaid, houndstooth and pinstripe woven patterns—equally wider lapels and double-breasted closures.

Figure 2.5 John Kirby Orchestra in dapper dress (note the pocket squares, white oxfords and wide-cuffed hems) at Onyx Club, New York, 1937. Photo by Charles Peterson. Courtesy of Don Peterson

Bebop music

On the precipice of the Second World War, a modern structure of music was born that emulated the radicalness of Cubist art conceived decades earlier. Bebop deconstructed the lucid music formula of the swing era with small ensembles that employed sharp punches, fast tempos, unpredictable solo placements and high-pitch, vocal-like instrumentation. In analysis, Gioia described bop qualities as "slightly off-balance," "crystalline," and "doubling of the stated time" (Gioia 1998: 202). Charlie Parker, Dizzy Gillespie, Kenny Clarke and Thelonious Monk are regularly cited as architects of this work having experimented with the arrangement at Minton's Playhouse, a defunct Harlem club known for late-night jam sessions. An aspiration of bebop output was an inventive sound that could not be copied by "inferior white bands," which had benefited financially during the 1930s (Godbolt 1990: 119).

A model of bop sound is found in Dizzy Gillespie's "Salt Peanuts" recorded in 1945: the erratic melody and unforeseen vocal chants of "salt peanuts, salt peanuts" exclaimed a modernity as captivating as the exhibition of ragtime. By 1948, this sound had captured the attention of the *New York Times* with an article titled "Bop: Skee, Re or Be, It's Still Got To Swing." The writer contended that dancing was unthinkable with the "semicontrolled frenzy" of bop, thus compelling nightclubs and ballrooms to remove dance floors. "In these spots . . . no 'lavish' review, just tables and the shattering blasts of twenty-odd musicians" (*New York Times* 1948a). Supporting this scrutiny, originators of the New Orleans method drew few lines to bebop. Bechet recounted a concert where his ensemble battled a bop band: "the people didn't even move, they didn't move a hand for them . . . and then we came on . . . we had them going" (Bechet 2002: 192). In conciliatory contrast, Duke Ellington, who was still promoting swing in the late 1940s, stated in *Melody Maker* his opinion of Gillespie and bop: "It's stimulating and original, which is what I, personally, look for in music" (Feather 1946: 3). Thus, jazz began to fissure along lines of classic and avant-garde improvisations. Amid the latter technique, black culture progressed in the spectacle of inequality, violence and discontent. Charles Mingus, in his abstract narrative of life, disclosed this displeasure of being inside the music, yet oppressed by the profit-driven industry. "He owns the magazines, agencies, record companies and all the joints that sell jazz to the public. If you won't sell out and you try to fight they won't hire you and they give a bad picture of you with that false publicity" (Mingus 1991: 188).

Following the Second World War, African Americans realized that the liberation obtained overseas had little impact on their secondary status regardless of the contributions of black soldiers such as the Tuskegee Airmen and black workers in defense factories. The inventive output of bebop merged a denunciation of mainstream swing music and dissatisfaction with American segregation. Cornel West, in assessment of Afro-American music, argued that the bebop style expressed "the heightened tensions, frustrated aspirations and repressed emotions" of the community (West 1999: 475). These musicians faced criticism from their own and outsiders. Albeit late in life, Louis Armstrong wittily critiqued the new sound and objective of "modern musicians." "All they want to do is scream. And if they don't watch out, I'm gonna scream, right along with the public" (Armstrong 1999: 174–5). With harsher criticism, mainstream media debated the hazards of bebop through an association with adolescent insurrection and drug use. The *New York Times* branded the sound as "strange new jazz" (*New York Times* 1949a). In an article titled "Bebop Doesn't Make Child Musical Moron," the *New York Times*, covering an American Music Conference, assured parents that their children would progress to musical forms with a more tolerable and harmonious content. Such hostility was partially attributed to the fact that the music had a white youth following. In *Twentieth-Century American Fashion*, Welters and Cunningham discussed the Beat Generation's adoption of bebop as a signifier to their "discontent of the 1950s" with its patterns of suburban living, corporate conformity and political coercion (Welters and Cunningham 2005: 146). The cool slang of black jazz musicians, born decades earlier, and the abstract compositions fit neatly into the anti-establishment message of "beatniks."

Alongside a white appropriation of black music was a fear of the related tendency towards drugs. The *New York Times*, in December 1951, explained the happenings at Kleinhans Music Hall in Buffalo, where testimony of odd behavior among attendees and the discovery of narcotics was noted. "Both marijuana and heroin had been found in the hall after the 'bebop' sessions" (Weaver 1951). Additionally, the manager reported the "fury of sound" that caused the spectators to "sway, turn, yowl and express their feelings." The transition from marijuana smoking to heroin injection in the 1940s was substantiated by the troubles of Fats Navarro, Charlie Parker, Billie Holiday and Anita O'Day. With a divergent and anti-mainstream repertoire, the art of bebop initiated a fragmentation in jazz and propelled the genre to an intellectual status as opposed to dance hall music.

Bebop era fashion

Fully established in the post-war years, the fashion of bebop was individualistic and dynamic in a time that was first impacted by garment restrictions. A photo, titled "Jazz Friends" (Hulton Archive), taken on December 31, 1944 equated the period. Featuring Duke Ellington, Billie Holiday and Leonard Feather, the image juxtaposed the contrasting influences of the period including pattern variation, engineered volume and masculine adaptations. Ellington wore an elegant tweed jacket with large glen plaid pattern. To his far left, Feather's double-breasted chalk stripe suit competed with formality and contour fit, while Billie Holiday projected a mannish approach with a cuffed slack suit, monogrammed blouse and front-knotted turban. The increase in women's trousers arose from wartime work and new trends in casual and sports attire (Milbank 1989: 140–2).

Like Holiday, O'Day modernized women's dress by adopting the male orchestra jacket for one-nighters. Paired with a matching skirt and shirt, the clothing avoided the laborious maintenance of gowns on road trips. O'Day affirmed the influence of fashion on attitudes of sexual orientation. "After I invented the idea of wearing the uniforms . . . the story went around that I preferred ladies to men" (O'Day and Eells 1989: 102). Similarly, Marlene Dietrich, as Amy Jolly, inspired this belief in *Morocco*, a 1930s Paramount Pictures release. Dietrich, dressed in coat-tailed tuxedo and top hat, performed a cabaret, mimicking the gestures of a man and concluding with a kiss on the lips of a female spectator. In the scene, Dietrich overturned the theory that women vie with one another for male sexual attention through her macho facade (Hurlock 1929: 42). Musically, the bebop period represented a movement of women from secondary bandstand singers to headliners of nightclubs and concert performances. Their fashion mirrored this change in economic muscle with robust, masculine and tailored styles.

Equally swaying this alteration in women's fashion was the introduction of Limitation Order L-85 by the War Production Board. This 1943 regulation placed restraints on garment manufacturing due to government needs and the war effort. Two major changes were listed by Milbank: "suit jackets were limited to twenty-five inches in length . . . just below the hip" and material reduction via "the narrow dress with broad shoulders and narrow skirt" (Milbank 1989: 133–4). For evening, the generous length of the bias cut gown was replaced by shorter dresses that were restrained from sweeping the floor. This modified quality was a match for the dense and intimate jazz venues along 52nd Street in New York City. Frequented by service men, the refined dress of jazz singers acknowledged the overseas war and provided glamour in a less grandiose manner. Anita O'Day epitomized this approach with tailored suits, pocket squares and short gloves.

The intimate nightclubs such as The Famous Door, Jimmy Ryan's and the Royal Roost were a proving ground for experimentation in bebop music, as well men's fashion. In this decade, there was greater opportunity to escape the rigidness of swing bands that promoted tuxedo conformity among members. Longer suit jackets and pattern diversity were significant changes in men's clothing. Bigelow noted that "men's business suits of the 1940s had very broad shoulders, heavily padded to add breadth" (Bigelow 1970: 271). Aesthetically, jazz establishments resembled corporate meetings with elite musicians dressed in pinstriped suits with high-peak lapels and geometric patterned ties.

Charlie "Bird" Parker was the quintessential figure of this genre. His alto-saxophone technique was described as "melodious beauty, mastery of the air, and quickness of flight" (Giddins and DeVeaux 2009: 301). Parker matched his artistry with bow ties, wavy coifs and check woven suits. The favored design of the bebop era was the glen plaid in medium or large scale. Properly known as the Glen Urquhart check of Scottish origin, its "pattern yields a refined play of vertical and horizontal lines that intersect at regular intervals over a houndstooth pattern" (Chenoune 1993: 180). This visual play of lines, known for producing a vibrating effect, fittingly signified the complex melodies and unanticipated rhythms of bebop. More so, the heritage of the tweed, which was worn by gamekeepers of Scottish estates, drew a line to high culture, thus furthering the art of bebop to an exclusive standing.

In the mid-1940s, for better or worse, an amplified manner of dress became attached to bebop. Ralph Ellison's 1952 publication of *Invisible Man* seized the youthful energy, adherence, and strength of this style:

A group of zoot-suiters greeted me in passing. "Hey now, daddy-o," they called. "Hey now!" . . . It was as though by dressing and walking in a certain way I had enlisted in a fraternity in which I was recognized at a glance—not by features, but by clothes, by uniform, by gait.

(Ellison 1995: 485)

The main character in Ellison's novel witnessed the garment's role, together with rhythmic stride and inventive language, in creating visibility for an individual unseen and buried by society.

Appearing around 1935, the zoot suit consisted of a jacket lengthened to thigh level with double-breasted closure and peg leg trousers (Figure 2.6).

Pleats with significant depth added volume at the waistline, plummeting into narrow hem cuffs. The original purveyors of this style were black youth, who frequented Harlem dance halls such as the Savoy Ballroom (Chenoune 1993: 208). Among Lester Young, Charlie Parker and Dizzy Gillespie, the adoption was a subtle extension to the already fashionable business suit featuring broad shoulders, peak lapels and tapered pants, thus differing from the extreme version

Figure 2.6 Jazz bandleader, Lionel Hampton, with his trumpeter in a zoot suit, 1942. © Bettmann/CORBIS

of the zoot suit. Gillespie corroborated that beboppers wore typical garments, in contrast to the exaggerated representations of "wild clothes and dark glasses." "I wore drape suits like everyone else and dressed no differently from the average leading man of the day . . . I became pretty dandified, I guess, later during the bebop era when my pants were pegged slightly at the bottom" (Gillespie and Fraser 2009: 279). In addition, Gillespie affirmed that his prominent beret, goatee and eyeglasses commenced from utility. The beret was inspired from his time in Paris, at times functioning as cover for the bell of his trumpet. Considering the triangular beard, it operated as a cushion to his instrument's mouthpiece. "I've always thought it allowed me to play more effectively" (Gillespie and Fraser 2009: 280). Finally, the horn-rimmed glasses stood up to frequent travel while the dark lenses were protection from harsh spotlights. This is proof that fashion when adopted by groups can take on unintended meanings, often falsifying origins and motives.

On stage and screen, Cab Calloway, the orchestra leader of Cotton Club fame, transmitted ostentation, notably in the 1943 film, *Stormy Weather*. This was the zenith of the zoot suit, displayed by Calloway in extravagant form with wide-brimmed fedora, stretched bow tie, knee-length jacket and lapels that skimmed the shoulders. A cartoon in the *California Eagle* promoted the creative efforts of zoot suit tailors. The 1941 caricature featured a young black man engulfed by a checkered suit with neck bordering trousers and matching newsboy cap. In the illustration, generational conflict was mitigated with an elderly tailor that eagerly applied finishing touches to the ensemble. Fascination with the style was conveyed in the African America newspaper by usage of the modified spelling. "The Zute Suit . . . is pictured here in all its tonsorial triumph."

Although possessing high entertainment value, the zoot suit experienced hostility on the streets of America and around the world. Naval servicemen and zoot-suited Mexican Americans clashed on the streets of Los Angeles in 1943. The *New York Times* on June 13 reported that the assault by sailors was in retaliation for previous attacks (Davies 1943b). This event ignited similar violence across the country. In Philadelphia, members of the Gene Krupa band were beaten on a subway platform, supposedly for resembling zoot-suiters (*New York Times* 1943). The *New York Times* ran several articles in 1943 that demonstrated the nation's negative characterization of the zoot suit. For instance on June 11, a men's fashion editor declared a link between "financially poor people" and zoot suit wearers (Berger 1943). An article on June 20 listing reasons for the riots suggested dense populations and slum conditions among Mexicans and Negroes (Davies 1943a). In 1944, a *New York Times* item titled "Zoot Suit Robbers" narrated that the thugs were "wearing zoot suits and brandishing pistols."

The cumulative attachment to criminal activities and the appropriation of the style by white adolescents bred contempt among mainstream society.

Furthermore, traditional stores and tailors pressured by the War Production Board's material regulations ceased retailing of the garment. Paralleling this reduction, the *Afro-American* reported that Calloway would jettison his famed Hi-De-Ho bravura. "Today he gives his customers more music, less Calloway, more show, less show-off" (*Afro-American* 1941a). This proposes that Calloway had pulled away from the flashy look, despite its Hollywood film emphasis two years later in *Stormy Weather*. Fashion shifts, cultural demonization and links to the rebelliousness of bebop contributed to the demise of the zoot suit. In sum, the 1940s demonstrated extremes where women adopted masculine design details and men altered traditional tailoring.

Modern jazz: Music and fashion

During the 1950s, a sudden loss of innovators including Fats Navarro, Charlie Parker, Art Tatum, Clifford Brown, Lester Young and Billie Holiday was impetus for a change in popular music across America. An indication of this shift was evident at the 1958 Newport Jazz Festival, where the stage attracted acts covering Dixieland style, bebop, rhythm and blues, gospel and cool jazz (Stern 2000). This period was a time of fragmentation within jazz; as such the audience's interest and financial support were divided along lines of age, geography and race. A younger generation was enamored by rhythm and blues, and rock and roll, whereas adults and college students were divided among nostalgia for swing bands, female soloists and modern jazz.

The modern genre consisted of west coast "cool jazz" and east coast "hard bop," as well as avant-garde and free forms that would proliferate in future years. Contrary to the assertive patterns of bebop, cool jazz embraced "a light, laid-back, reticent quality" (Giddins and DeVeaux 2009: 339). Cool jazz gained prominence in California among white musicians, who had previous memberships with swing and bebop groups. Gerry Mulligan, an acclaimed baritone saxophone player, founded his own quartet in 1952. He possessed a resume of collaborations with Gene Krupa, Miles Davis, Duke Ellington and Billie Holiday. Although invoking the casual, beach lifestyle of southern California, the cool school maintained a commitment to "experimentation, a distaste for conformity, and a view of jazz as an underground movement" (Gioia 1998: 280). Mulligan's hip style migrated towards casual—incorporating plaid patterns, seersucker textures, cardigans, short sleeve shirts and dark sunglasses (Figure 2.7).

A new crop of female vocalists was criss-crossing the country at this time, notably Anita O'Day, Dinah Washington, Sarah Vaughan and Carmen McRae. Having gained new-found appreciation, the ability to scat was growing among the women. Louis Armstrong introduced the habit of improvising

Figure 2.7 Gerry Mulligan playing saxophone in Black Watch tartan blazer with Bob Brookmeyer, Switzerland, 1956. © Gianni Cardani/ Riccardo Schwamenthal Archives/Cynthia Sesso, CTSIMAGES

"horn-like lines, built on wordless syllables, with his voice" with the 1926 release of "Heebie Jeebies" (Gioia 1998: 62) The title of modern or cool was a rite of passage for jazz women, equally necessary for relevance. In 1955, the *Milwuakee Journal* declared "Cool Jewel Anita Gives Something Extra to Notes," stressing both her feminine and artistic qualities. O'Day advanced bebop style and scat singing; admittedly, she avoided straight melodies preferring to "free-sketch jazz" (O'Day and Eells 1989: 167). Comparable to the men, this musical era was characterized by small club venues, overseas bookings and sabbaticals from the scene.

Following the overstatement of the zoot suit, the 1950s jacket was refined with fish-mouth shaped lapels in narrow width, low-hip length and conservative colors. These modern suits were accessorized with slender ties, often of knitted construction. Lee Morgan, a hard-bop trumpeter from Philadelphia, exemplified this smartness on his albums at the end of the decade. The cover of *Here's Lee Morgan* (1960) contains a photographic montage of Morgan posing with cigarette and trumpet in hand. With pant hem slightly above the ankle and jacket hitting at high hip, Morgan deliberately employs fashion and posits self-confidence. *Expoobident* (1960), released in October, features a slender Morgan sitting in a director's chair with legs spread and his trumpet resting upon his lap. With upright posture and his hands placed upon his knees, Morgan epitomizes cerebral jazz supplemented by his dark, slim-fit suit and argyle-patterned tie.

In the same year, *Ebony* magazine advised African American men that tapered suits had become outgrown and were troublesome for all but the slightest body types. "The extreme Ivy League, that made the average man look slightly undernourished, has gradually lost some favor. Similarly, the authentic Continental—moulded on the skimpy lines of Italian tailoring—has receded in popularity" (*Ebony* 1960). The slim silhouette, contrary to the editor's forecast, flourished in the decade. By the mid-1960s, the mod style of the Parisian minets, youngsters that favored rhythm and blues and English rock groups, was influential. Their uniform, according to Chenoune, consisted of "crested blazers, twin-vented tweed jackets, boat-neck sweaters, plus the cuffed, wide bottom trousers" and penny loafers (Chenoune 1993: 264). *Ebony*'s depiction of fall styles in 1960 revealed comparable trends. In the editorial spread, male models displayed crew, boat and shawl neck Scandinavian pullovers, cuffed trousers, poplin car coats and buck chukka boots. Pointedly, the editor declared that the clothes were more flattering to the average man, lighter in weight and the utmost in comfort.

Embodying the coolness of the new music, sport shirts provided a casual option for studio sessions and intimate club engagements. The shirt retained the formal qualities of a tailored garment with straight collar and cuffs; however, loose flap pockets were added to the chest for detailing and function. Be it plaid or solid, Mulligan of the west coast school adopted this trend with a boyish flare. His grown-in buzz cuts nodded to the youth interest produced in Hollywood by James Dean and Elvis Presley. Not ready to pass the torch, the older generation of jazz faithfully wore suits that had added volume. Festivals, such as Newport and Monterey, featured Duke Ellington, Louis Armstrong and Jack Teagarden of 1930s swing fame.

Greater diversity occurred within women's fashion, where silhouettes varied from hourglass shapes to straight waistless styles. The introduction of the "new look" by Christian Dior in 1947 reached mass-market appeal in America during the decade. "Skirt hems plunged from knee length to within twelve inches from the floor" (Bigelow 1970: 257). To support this expansive material, designers utilized layers of tulle or crinolines for rigidity. Billie Holiday, Sarah Vaughan and Dinah Washington dressed in full-skirted gowns that added aristocratic glamour to their performances. In *Queen: The Life and Music of Dinah Washington*, Cohodas detailed Washington's dress transformation around the late 1950s that boosted her stage routine: "Her new wardrobe featured dresses with a fitted bodice and full skirt that twirled when she danced" (Cohodas 2006: 259–60).

Succeeding the "A-line silhouette" for day and evening was the rise of the chemise dress in the late 1950s. With sleek and modern aesthetics, the design complemented the avant-garde style of jazz proceeding into the next decade. The extreme versions of this trend were sack models, defined by Bigelow as "straight dresses with bodices slightly bloused over a low waistline" (Bigelow 1970: 257). Dinah Washington acquired her gowns and sack dresses from a personal designer, Mabel Page, and at Wilma's dress shop located at 4 West 57th Street in New York (Cohodas 2006: 296, 302). At the Newport Jazz Festival of 1958, Washington wore a voluminous, white sack dress, embellished with rhinestone brooch affixed to a large bow. The fabric, resembling softly crushed paper, created an airy, shapeless silhouette. Milbank noted that although women purchased these dresses in large quantities, to the contrary "men hated them" (Milbank 1989: 175).

Accessorized with the chemise and sack was the ubiquitous stiletto-heeled shoe of Italian influence. "For years hordes of the young—and not so young— teetered about their business on four-inch heels that narrowed almost to a point" (Ewing 1986: 172). In 1955, a Red Cross Shoes' advertisement in the *New York Times* revealed a modification to the footwear. "The smooth pump with a wonderful secret . . . for its pretty ribbon top is actually elasticized to mould to your foot a gentle, unsurpassed fit" (*New York Times* 1955a). Hence, a comfort limitation in fashion introduced design alteration.

The 1950s represented a volatile time of political and economic strife. White Americans departed cities for larger homes in the suburbs, where they shopped stores for modern-living conveniences. In contrast, black Americans continued to struggle against inequality in employment, education and housing. Real estate developers such as Levitt & Sons, Inc. of the Levittown communities restricted race mixing. In 1949, the *New York Times* informed controversy related to a Levitt prospectus that barred Negroes. "No dwelling shall be used or occupied except by members of the Caucasian race, but the employment and maintenance of other than Caucasian domestic servants shall be permitted" (*New York Times* 1949b). Other properties utilized racial steering, a "practice of real estate agents refusing to show or rent homes in white neighborhoods to blacks" (Kushner 2009: 49). Furthermore, conflicts in Korea and Vietnam added to frustration of war and inequity. A response came through a fresh black music known as rhythm and blues that was positioned to dominate and provide entry into higher ranks of the entertainment industry. The path of Quincy Jones, producer and musician, signified this achievement. His collaboration with jazz artists, especially Dizzy Gillespie, cemented a leadership role to be realized in the 1960s.

Conclusion

Scholars of jazz distinguish between the various genres according to musical orientation including technique, composition and style. This chapter surveyed the aesthetic totality produced in sound, appearance and behavior that defined a cultural legacy. The adornment of standardized clothing, the magnification of popular music and dance, and the construction of subcultural style validate the fashion themes of conformity (1900–1920), influence (1920–1940) and defiance (1940–1960).

3

A NARRATIVE OF JAZZ MODERNITY

Postmodern identity in jazz

In popular culture, jazz is situated in an environment beyond the 1960s stage of fusion, divergence and division, where it is now elevated, revered and presented as a nostalgic art form that conveys an ingenious past. Music scholars of the twenty-first century have applied numerous definitions to this period. Banfield used the title "Jazz Urbane" to represent a creative jazz culture that engages progressive ideas, live performance, autonomy from corporate enterprise and avoidance of the smooth jazz market (Banfield 2010: 179). In contrast, Giddins and DeVeaux define this stage of jazz as its classical status, when musicians navigate new techniques, audiences long for past genres and limitations in the domestic market exist (Giddins and DeVeaux 2009: 606). Two theatrical jazz performances in 2014, "Lady Day at Emerson's Bar & Grill" and "Satchmo at the Waldorf," reflect postmodern concerns. The shows capitalize on a sentimental mood, artistic liberty and simplification requiring contemporary musicians to compete with the legacies of Billie Holiday and Louis Armstrong (Chinen 2014).

Kenneth Gloag argued the difficulty of postmodernity in music. In his writings that reference the work of Jean-Francois Lyotard, he situates the movement from the late 1970s when global changes reshaped "the condition of knowledge, culture and experience after modernism" (Gloag 2012: 7). Gloag posits qualities of postmodernism in music including fragmentation, difference, synthesis, weight of the past and impact of technology that are useful in this jazz inquiry (Gloag 2012: 2–24).

These traits were notable in Sony BMG's *Legacy Remixed* series that reimagined the recordings of Billie Holiday and Nina Simone with contemporary instrumentation. The releases united dance music disc jockeys such as Tony Humphries and Charles Feelgood with famous jazz recordings to produce "groove-worthy" remixes (Berkowitz and Schlachter 2007). Symbolic of a postmodernist stance, these tracks retained the intuitive delivery of the bygone performance, merging it with an electronic melody, lyric repetition and overlapping vocals. The effect, particularly on songs like "Spreadin' Rhythm Around," was blues storytelling fashioned in a contemporary form of lyrical rapping. This concept was achieved by integrating the spoken word of Lady Bug Mecca, formerly of 1990s alternative, hip-hop group Digable Planets. Effortlessly, the track alternates between Holiday's vocals and Lady Bug's present day lyrics that explain to "disperse the jazz sound" and "Holiday celebrate" (Berkowitz and Schlachter 2007). The reinterpretation of Holiday's music into a modern composition absent her artistic judgment is compelling, enough for the producers to state that Holiday, if born in 1985 instead of 1915, "would have totally dug" the sound (Berkowitz and Schlachter 2007). Holiday's performance ritual, which catered to a post Second World War environment, was altered for a modern audience through reconstruction of vocal and melodic output. The legacy series acknowledged the swing era of jazz and its iconic performers, equally referencing 1980s hip-hop and house music, to that end, the union was true to postmodernism.

Equally, transmission of this experimental concept took place on a visual level. A depiction came from cover art of the Billie Holiday *Remixed & Reimagined* compact disc, where a black and white vintage image of Holiday, featured in a 1940s broad shoulder gown, singing in front of a microphone was layered onto an optical graphic with vibrating circles. The merger of old and new was further communicated through small boxes containing graphic images of a turntable, headphones and profile of Holiday prepared in the style of Apple, Inc. iPod advertising, where silhouettes are enhanced on brightly colored backgrounds. This modification of the music raises the theme of modernity in jazz during the mid-century.

Generally, modernism calls to mind that which is forward thinking, innovative and seeking to move beyond a current doctrine. Elizabeth Wilson, in relating the movement to fashion, describes "its questioning of reality and perception, its attempt to come to grips with the nature of human experience in a mechanized 'unnatural world'" (Wilson 2003: 63). Jazz inventors, such as W. C. Handy and Scott Joplin, finding solid ground at the start of the twentieth century, embodied modernist ideals. Analogous to the genres of rap and hip-hop that flourished in the 1980s, the style of ragtime and blues emanating from marginalized populations was unyielding to artistic control, eventually populating 1930s mainstream culture in the form of swing bands. The African American motivation, using the writings on modernity by Wilson, was "the restless desire for change characteristic of cultural life in industrial capitalism" (Wilson 2003: 63).

Qualities of modernism in jazz

Five qualities in the foundation of jazz that support modernism are freedom, struggle, bonding, narration and heritage. At the core of the music, there is freedom of expression. In 1903 W. E. B. Du Bois framed the ambition of the

American Negro that being "freedom of life and limb, the freedom to work and think, the freedom to love and aspire" (Du Bois 2010: 12). Drumming, spiritual chants and body movements were the earlier vehicles through which slaves conveyed this message, while post-slavery expression was evident in "fostering and developing the traits and talents of the Negro" (Du Bois 2010: 12). Second, a struggle for liberty, humanity and social status was present. In 1895, a *New York Times* review took notice of this effort by "Black America," an all-black theatrical show. "The whole entertainment . . . is interesting, as showing what the colored race is capable of doing in a comparatively untried field" (*New York Times* 1895). In other words, the all-Negro troupe performing melodies and movements of black origin at Madison Square Garden for a white audience was transforming the traditional model of popular entertainment. Black theatrical groups represented the essence of community connection and bonding that permitted a measured advancement of black people. Albeit employment for amusing people, these performers had achieved a social status and were recognized by mainstream newspapers. Here, an article divided along race lines in the *Washington Post* concerning the "Negro's Part in Music" published on August 14, 1904:

Time was when "coon songs," whether of the old plantation variety or the modern ragtime kind, were written by white men, but a great change has come about in the last few years, says a writer of the *New York Sun*. The negro composer has now almost a monopoly of ragtime and is reaching out into more classical work, and there has hardly been a musical play in the last two or three years which hasn't contained one or more songs of negroes.

(*Washington Post* 1904)

The fourth quality of storytelling through instrumentation and song allowed for the history to be carried forward. In *Blues People*, Baraka attested to the origins of this exchange where Africans used drumming for communication and developed the art to "phonetic reproductions of the words themselves" (Baraka 2002: 26). This custom present in the spoken word of blues documents a general ideology of a period. Alberta Hunter and Trixie Smith recorded songs like "Down South Blues," "Experience Blues," and "Railroad Blues" in the 1920s that give notice to this effectiveness. Last of all, the moans, cries, and exaltations that are expressed through jazz symbolized the heritage of early Africans and the path from persecution to liberation in America. With reflections on being "Human, Modern and American," West declared "to be modern is to have the courage to use one's critical intelligence to question and challenge the prevailing authorities, powers and hierarchies of the world" (West 1999: xvii). Early jazz, especially ragtime and blues, possessed modern traits and an impetus of cultural transformation.

Modern ideals in fashion

This forward attitude in jazz was equally signified through the clothing worn by performers. Costume scholars identified modern ideals in fashion at the dawn of the twentieth century. In *New York Fashion*, Milbank phrased it as a "new professionalism of women's lives" exposed through roles in philanthropy and the workplace (Milbank 1989: 48). Women's dresses became more streamlined and manageable through the removal of the hoop skirt that flourished prior to 1870. Charles Fredrick Worth, English couturier, was associated with the success of the polonaise gown that instituted "a new figure shape." These gowns elongated the frontal view by flattening the skirt drape and "consisted of outer dresses swept up and back over bustle frames, revealing a decorative underskirt" (Bigelow 1970: 212).

As well, the silhouette for men was simplified during this same period, realized through the width reduction of the collar and lapel, and departure from nipped-in waistcoats. The philosophy of contemporary men's dress being distinction by way of discretion proliferated, free of flamboyance and exaggeration (Chenoune 1993: 178). These aesthetic transitions symbolized a shift from fashion of the wealthy to dress for the people. Hurlock defined this action as the abandonment of "extremes and over-elaborateness of dress which were characteristic of ages when the nobility determined fashion" (Hurlock 1929: 125). In America, fashion designers began to focus on functionality necessitated by employment, travel and leisure. The field of art including traveling theater, popular music and moving pictures had a profound influence on social advancement. "Fashion arbiters will be recruited from the men and women of the world who have attained prestige and power through their ability to accomplish great things" (Hurlock 1929: 126); accordingly, the stage, comprised of musicians, singers and dancers, will be the setting for attaining these individuals. Through visual appearance infused with newness, jazz performers were elevated in stature and poised for attainment of fame, wealth and influence.

Visually modern

Around 1900, characteristics of modernity were palpable in the images of early jazz entertainers through a method of distinguished adornment and presentation. This moment was significant for black performers, who participated in a social revolution that led to ragtime and blues gaining in popularity. For instance, Baraka stressed the way blues singers entertained formally, "an external and sophisticated idea of performance had come to the blues, moving it past the casualness of the 'folk' to the conditioned emotional gesture of the 'public'" (Baraka 2002: 82). Many photographs prior to the twentieth century contained images that recorded an individual, family or significant event. Thereafter, images with music themes served as commodities for promotion of performers and bands, constructing the idea of celebrity and eccentricity.

During an era of minstrelsy that lampooned plantation life, primitiveness and cultural customs, a way of being and dressing in the jazz field was vital in asserting a dignified identity. This practice opposed old-fashioned ideas and challenged the obstruction to ragtime. On September 30, 1900, the *Washington Post* acerbically put forward the disapproval of ragtime and ragtime dancing. "It is too jerky and lacks the grace necessary for dance music . . . to righten this evil they have set themselves to the task of retiring rag-time music from the ballrooms" (*Washington Post* 1900). The choice of "evil" was pungent, connoting great harm and destruction. Implications of this language were heightened from the direct association to African Americans in the creation of ragtime. Here, early satire printed in the *New York Times* concerning the piano style: "it's a sort of syncopated arrangement of the notes, invented by the negroes . . . we top-raters have agreed to boycott it as it were" (Vivian 1902). Perhaps holding animosity for transitioning to a modern method, certain musicians sternly provided resistance to ragtime. The *New York Times* published succinct resolutions by a music federation on May 15, 1901, pledging members to cease playing and publishing ragtime, which they branded as "unmusical rot" and "musical trash" (*New York Times* 1901a). This is not to say, of course, that all commentary was against ragtime. Several articles demonstrated the public's demand for this variety, such as the *New York Times*' highlight of entertainment at a New Jersey resort, "cakewalks and vaudeville entertainments are furnishing mirth for all who enjoy ragtime" at Point Pleasant (*New York Times* 1904). On June 17, 1901, readers were enticed with "Wide-Open Sunday at Coney Island," where it was reported that colored troupes "indulged in all manner of ragtime songs" (*New York Times* 1901b).

These accounts contextualized the cultural attitudes concerning ragtime and its related dance the cakewalk, providing rationale for modernism through formal dress, styling, symmetry and posture. In totality, these visual details would confront the negative minstrel and blackface representations that utilized disheveled coifs, tattered clothing, shabby shoes and ripped stockings. Take, for example, this apparel description by the *New York Times* of a black troupe performing the famed dance: "led by the champion cake walkers . . . the men were in evening dress, and wore tall hats . . . the women were in evening dress" (*New York Times* 1896). Photographs from the Rudi Blesh collection at the Rutgers Institute of Jazz Studies illustrated this sharp styling of ragtime performers. An image, around 1903, of the Musical Spillers contained four men in long coats of sartorial workmanship with coordinating top hats, high straight collars and pointed-toe oxfords with white spats. Each man displayed individual distinction through posture. Centered among the men and providing stylish balance is a well-groomed woman, outfitted in a morning dress of the period.

The Edwardian accents consist of a wide-brimmed hat, high-collar, puffed short sleeves and vertical pleats that draped in bell formation on the skirt. Each vaudevillian player holds a different sized saxophone, perhaps suggesting diversity and magnitude of entertainment. Later, William Spiller, the founder of the group, garnered international recognition as a pioneer in the theatrical profession (NYPL 2000). Professionalism via dress, individualism through stance and talent by way of instruments are symbolized in the photo. Equally of a modern agenda was the absence of racial stereotypes that were abundant at the time. The ensemble with confidence determined their depiction. Regarding this representation, Hall emphasized a traceable point where the present day goal has been for black entertainers "to put their own interpretations on the way blacks figure within "the American experience"' (Hall 2012: 257).

Another photograph from the Blesh collection, with a date of 1901, exhibited this modernity transmitted by ragtime. The image includes two couples in a structured pose, where the implied leader of the ensemble is sitting. Placed forefront center, the man is flanked by the remaining team dressed in the finest of early century garb. Notable are the immense hats worn by the ladies that give them a towering stature over the men, seemingly challenging the subordinate role of women. As described by costume scholars, these hats "were monumental in size and trim," and "demanded that ladies stand erect in a haughty pose" (Bigelow 1970: 228). This composure, with a sense of racial pride and acknowledgment of talent, was evident in the picture. The clothing of the players encompasses formal suits and ties, and high-neck morning dresses, heavily accessorized with bows, brooches, earrings, lapel pins, bracelets and rings. Collectively, the artifacts and symbolic character of the image announced an authentic level of self-discovery. As Barthes resolved in his chapter on fashion and the social science:

> The wearing of an item of clothing is fundamentally an act of meaning that goes beyond modesty, ornamentation and protection. It is an act of signification and therefore a profoundly social act right at the very heart of the dialectic of society.

> (Barthes 2006: 97)

Ragtime performers contributed to the legitimacy of the music and their heritage through positive representations of their art. Coalescing the concept of modern individual, artist and celebrity was an image of Ferdinand "Jelly Roll" Morton discovered in the Blesh collection. Morton, of Creole origin, was raised in New Orleans during the growth of ragtime and blues; however, the 1920s cemented his skills as a pianist and composer, and prominent figure in jazz. Accomplishments during this period included "one hundred recordings or piano rolls of his compositions . . . and his most famous ensemble, the Red Hot Peppers" (Gioia

Figure 3.1 Ferdinand Jelly Roll Morton wearing a Norfolk style jacket in a publicity photograph, 1915. © CORBIS

1998: 40). In a studio portrait of 1921, Morton faces the viewer while imitating performance at a raised-top piano (Figure 3.1).

His dress is categorized as "casual" with a Norfolk style jacket with two side pleats, half back belt and hip patch pockets with inverted pleats. Morton's angled torso reveals a shirt and tie, and wide-leg cuffed trousers; more so, the body position signifies a routine openness that draws the viewer to the talent on display.

The concentration on these visual details cannot satisfy the complete description or meaning of the photograph as argued by theorists. Rather, the aim is to understand the role of dress among musical performers, when they were persuasive. In analysis of the photographic message, Barthes issued that the press photograph "is not only perceived, received, it is read, connected more or less consciously by the public that consumes it to a traditional stock of signs" (Barthes 1978: 19). Hence, Morton was instrumental in creation of a mechanical message through dress, posture, expression and use of objects. A secondary code in the form of written text was applied to the photograph. At the bottom right of the image, Morton inscribed "with success" followed by Morton's signature. Examination of this photograph reproduced in other publications revealed the varied location and style of signature, thus indicating multiple productions of this image that constructed modern celebrity.

Communicating modernity

Textual language was documented as a method for expressing modernity in the jazz era. Akin to visual representation, the written word defied negative labels placed upon the music that were rampant in the early jazz period. One area that transmitted caustic meaning was song titles and text published in the nineteenth century. Eventually, these songs served as comedic tools in minstrel shows that entertained whites with skits about cotton plantations and primitive African heritage. Commencing around the early 1800s with white men, the minstrel form of entertainment expanded to black performers by the end of the century. Suthern, in his writings on "Minstrelsy and Popular Culture," indicated that the white performance in competition with all-black productions had "degenerated into a vicious garble of hatred and diatribe" (Suthern 1989: 79). Antebellum and post-Civil War song titles promoted epithets and vernacular linked to slaves, such as "The Sensitive Coon" (1851), "I'se Gwine Back to Dixie" (1874), and "Where Am Massa" (1879). These songs narrated scenes of idyllic servitude, bliss of harvesting cotton and childlike courtship among adult slaves, in consequence swaying the mainstream judgment about African Americans.

Negative text regarding black culture continued into the twentieth century and the Jim Crow era, when ragtime and jazz evolved. "Ev'ry Darkey Had a Raglan On" (1901), "Oh How I Miss You Mammy" (1920), and "Short'nin Bread" (1939) focused on women as mammies and social activities, especially dating and the performance of dance. Occasionally, the antagonism derived from international newspapers. This bitter quote reduced the history of African Americans to a simple experience. "A couple of generations removed from the jungle, the American negro brought a great deal of his natural rhythmic vitality into his spirituals" (*Daily Express* 1937).

A resistance to these narratives was printed in periodicals that elevated the importance of jazz performers, thus diminishing the dated stereotypes. Clippings and ephemera at the Archives Center of the National Museum of American

History demonstrate that leading singers and musicians were given trademarks of high social standing and celestial being. Commencing in the 1920s, "prima donna" and "goddess of song" were bestowed on Bessie Smith and Billie Holiday, respectively. For the men, Duke Ellington was labeled "aristocrat of jazz," while Joseph Oliver, cornetist and bandleader, received the classification of "king." Often individuals invented monikers to amplify their identities. William James Basie enhanced his persona while seeking traction in 1920s Kansas City. "I decided that I would be one of the biggest new names; and I actually had some little fancy business cards printed up to announce it. COUNT BASIE. Beware the Count is Here" (Basie and Murray 2002: 17). Parlaying regal titles placed meaning within and outside their communities, fueling a defeat of barriers and prejudiced views. Favorable assessments were noted in mainstream periodicals, such as "smart modern music is being offered by Benny Carter's new seven-piecer" and "bebop . . . does have something new to offer and something worthwhile to say" (*Melody Maker* 1947; Tanner 1947).

As described by Anna Marley, Curator at the Pennsylvania Academy of Fine Arts, artists of the period crafted "a cosmopolitan, global version of the black aesthetic" (Marley 2012: 85). African American painters rebuffed the negative representations of their culture and popular jazz. Such as the painting *Blues* (1929) by Archibald Motley, Marley specified that the "study of a Parisian nightclub portrays musicians and dancers as elegant and multifaceted" (Marley 2012: 85). In the artwork, expressions of glee, romantic embraces and friendly exchanges radiate from the dancers enthralled by the jazz ensemble. Equivalent to this modern interpretation was Palmer Hayden's *Bal Jeunesse* (1927), where a youthful couple exemplifies buoyancy and stylishness in dance as a jazz band plays for their delight. In the ballroom setting, cocktail-length dresses, floor-length gowns, tailored suits, chandeliers and a mural reminiscent of *Dance (I)* (1909) by Henri Matisse are flaunted. The work of Motley and Hayden depicted the modern ideology of the Harlem Renaissance through urbanity, fashionable dress and genteel posture. Too, William H. Johnson's canvases of bold color during the jazz era articulated allure through unique color combinations, tossed prints, stripes and plaid patterns. For instance, *Café* (1939–40) contained a male subject wearing a brown and yellow check suit with a harmonizing yellow fedora. His facial expression embodies confidence matched by his crossed legs and upright posture advancing refinement. In *Harlem Renaissance: Art of Black America*, it is declared that Johnson's bonds with modern artists, his expression of simplicity and "his documentation of Black life make him a fascinating figure in modern American art" (Campbell et al. 1994: 35). A similar attitude is found in the work of Aaron Douglas. His series of murals titled *Aspects of Negro Life* (1934) boldly combine aspects of African American history, industrial landscapes and jazz culture; Douglas through geometric shapes, muted tones and silhouettes emphasized modernist themes. As with other artists, the "jazz musician" was a leitmotif in his work signifying human freedom and cultural identity (Campbell et al. 1994: 29).

Modern practices of jazz performers

Jazz entertainers exhibited a sophisticated, freedom-seeking attitude through practices of style and career development. McCracken in *Transformations: Identity Construction in Contemporary Culture* described the process as a reformulation of "the individual in relationship to the group" that "creates a more robust individualism" (McCraken 2008: 85). Hence, this perspective addressed the role that modernity played in stressing the merit and muscle of the African American performer. During her early years of singing and dancing on the black vaudeville circuit, Ethel Waters shifted from a low-wage secondary act to the star of the show. Waters, in her autobiography, disclosed that a larger salary generated more personal expenditures. "As a headliner I had to buy plenty of expensive clothes . . . I really dressed in beautiful gowns for that act of ours" (Waters and Samuels 1992: 156). In the same manner, Alberta Hunter identified her strategy of ensuring stage success. "I gave them something else they weren't used to, beautiful dresses . . . I had me a slew of them, and I changed several times during the show—the audience loved it" (Albertson 2003: 28). The fashion routines of Waters and Hunter during the 1920s can be defined by the work of scholars in the field of psychology. Essentially, the dress motive was to garner approval from the audience with a distinguishing and aspirational appearance (Flügel 1950: 15; Hurlock 1929: 26).

Through the presentation of their talent, the aesthetics of jazz were evolving from cultural roots to a stylized craft with increasing profit potential. Bessie Smith alluded to this concept with her amusing comments to Langston Hughes in 1926. Hughes revealed in a personal letter that Smith was planning a return to Alabama to "make a few more thousands" and "her only comment on the art of the Blues was that they had put her 'in de money'" (Bernard 2001: 35–6). With the first jazz recording in 1917 and an ensuing urgency to record bands and singers, the 1920s commercialization of jazz was established. Smith's remarks, along with other vocalists' commentary, constructed an image that signified popularity and star status, and more so the realization of blues performance as cultural capital. This concept of social identity is explained as "the configuration of attributes and attitudes persons seek to and actually do communicate about themselves" (Davis 1994: 16). These women were confronting racial and gender barriers through modern philosophies, fashion management and spectacle. Ethel Waters drew large crowds at Negro theaters and curtailed the flow of blacks to white theaters. "I kept the colored patrons out of the balconies of the white theaters where the Negro revues were playing and damn near starved some of those shows to death" (Waters and Samuels 1992: 156). Waters' civil rights action in the 1920s demonstrated the economic and political power of black performers.

The recognition of social identity and performance as commodity was apparent among the men. Miles Davis articulated his evolution during the year of 1944. "I was making about $85 a week playing in Eddie Randle's band . . . buying myself some hip Brooks Brothers suits" (Davis and Troupe 2011: 47). In his memoirs, Louis Armstrong recalled his esteem regarding the style of Bill "Bojangles" Robinson, famed tap dancer. "I personally Admired Bill Robinson because he was immaculately dressed—you could see the Quality in his Clothes even from the stage" (Armstrong 1999: 27). Armstrong exuded this laser-like attention to dress and formality throughout his career with tailored suits and his graceful interactions with the audience. Although having common usage during the period, Armstrong's utterance of "ladies and gentlemen" during performance was stylized to his unique brand. Earl "Fatha" Hines, an acclaimed pianist and bandleader who played with Armstrong in the 1920s, accessorized his fine dress with cigars and tobacco pipes (Figure 3.2).

Figure 3.2 Earl "Fatha" Hines in sharp dress conducting an orchestra session, 1940. © Bettmann/CORBIS

With an association to dinner jackets used in smoking rooms, these lighted instruments, especially when stylized in hand, announced sophistication and a degree of self-importance. Armstrong cited that Earl Hines "kept the Big Fresh Cigar in his mouth everyday" during their fledgling period (Armstrong 1999: 99). Seemingly, roll size and quality of tobacco were badges of distinction. Gelly inventoried Lester Young's eccentricities, "the private language, the padding gait, the aloofness, even the broad-brimmed pork-pie hat," that established his "personal style" and intensified his reputation as a prominent tenor saxophone player (Gelly 1984: 10). These men altered modern ideals of American male dress by offering positive black viewpoints accented with jazz finesse.

Conclusion

A shared set of modern beliefs and practices flourished during the development of jazz at the beginning of the twentieth century. Also, the prevalence of the genre's output through phonograph, film and media ushered in a conversion to a postmodern technique realized by the 1950s. The image and performance of early ragtime and blues was rooted in cultural expression and untouched by commercial hands. As noted, newspaper coverage was often hostile, while favorable reports allowed the music to exist freely, perhaps believing it was a whim.

Redhead, in explanation of Jean Baudrillard's writings about the twenty-first century of non-postmodern condition, conceived "that 'the real' has become transformed in such a way in this era that as the virtual takes over, the real, in its simulation, has hoovered up its own images" (Redhead 2008: 11). As in the Sony BMG legacy series' manipulation of Billie Holiday's music and image in 2007, the outcome was an artifact where the real and reproduction are merged, resulting in a new artistic sound. The nostalgic references aided by mid-century recordings of Holiday are constrained to virtual technique. Baudrillard, according to Redhead, characterized this process where "the real can no longer be thought separately from the image" (Redhead 2008: 11). As with urban rhythmic creations in the late 1970s, this freedom of expression in synthesized music flowed from the youth in society. The Giant Step website, in promotion of the Billie Holiday *Remixed & Reimagined* release party, described the target market as "an audience more inclined to a modern club environment" (Giant Step 2007). Hence, the technicians established "nostalgia for the unattainable" and "impart a stronger sense of the unpresentable" (Lyotard 2011: 362), that being the sublime performance of early jazz. Compelled by yearnings of the genre, the retooling and reimagining of jazz positions it beyond its cultural and spiritual birth, manifesting postmodern approaches to the image, text and feelings of the music.

4
ASSESSING ELITISM AND BRANDING IN JAZZ

Qualities of elitism were an aesthetic means employed by African American jazz artists to navigate a challenging music and entertainment industry in the early twentieth century. This elevated manner of behavior has significance with distinctions applied among blacks in the eighteenth and nineteenth centuries. In writings on the black aristocracy in America, Gatewood noted that elite individuals adhered to social hierarchies and evidenced wealth, culture, refinement, family pride and formal education (Gatewood 1990: 8). Such distinguished status was outside of the white sphere but lodged and observed within the black community. In these efforts, the black upper class pursued fairness, racial progress, assimilation and access to quality employment.

The practice of superiority and highfalutin comportment had been associated with slavery, economic disparity and racial inequality. For instance, the cakewalk, a comical dance that exaggerated the formal dance routines and salutations of plantation owners, flourished in black and white popularity at the turn of the century, eventually separating from its low opinion of affluence becoming a trend of modern dance. Also, the African American population commonly used the term "dicty" to refer to both white and black upper class people with snobbish ways. Waters recollected that "Harlem's dictys" (Waters and Samuels 1992: 138) had classified her as an upcoming star around 1919, when she appeared at the Lafayette Theater. The term was given legitimacy with the 1923 recording of "Dicty Blues" by the Fletcher Henderson Orchestra, a black band known for polished style and symphonic compositions. Adding support to the experience of elitism, W. C. Handy described the influential of black society that looked down on vaudevillian performance. "In traveling around with the minstrel company we bumped into society folks too dicty to buy tickets for our show . . . we were invited to their functions only when we brought our instruments along" (Handy 1969: 130). Grandness in jazz was musically expressed in the composition "High Society," recorded by King Oliver and Louis Armstrong during the 1920s and 1930s. The arrangement melded formality, through the pompous salutations of drums, with the humorous flare of a trumpet and trombone exploiting uninhibited style.

Black performers continued the transition from the margins of society to popular icons through varied techniques. McCracken furnished a formula for this status transformation, necessitating "change in speech, gesture, posture, dress, and material culture and in patterns of thinking, feeling, and acting" (McCracken 2008: 71). Along with success in the music profession was the desire to erode the negative images that thrived in the Jim Crow environment. In support of this strategy through dress was Flügel's analysis of the social value of decoration, that being "the more elaborate and decorative the costume, the higher the social position of the wearer" (Flügel 1950: 138). Dress was an unlikely ploy. Yet, the influential apparel and accessories that were displayed equated to youthful aspirations, organized music tradition, upper-class lifestyle and wealth. Count Basie recalled his acquisition of a pinch-back suit in 1924 that settled one requirement for his progression. "We had some few doubts about being ready for a big-league city like New York, but I must say we were also pretty excited about all of the things we were going to have a chance to be around" (Basie and Murray 2002: 48). This construction of identity through prestige was crucial, as mainstream institutions had initiated a crusade of demonizing the music.

Societal opposition to jazz

Early on, jazz experienced modes of disdain, streaming from religious institutions, black societies and majority tradition. This conflict commenced with the intersection of gospel and secular music. The latter was associated with music performed in saloons, nightclubs and theaters. Around the early 1900s, Du Bois explained the magnitude of the church in black communities: "the church often stands as a real conserver of morals . . . and the final authority on what is Good and Right" (Du Bois 2010: 117). This superior role stemmed from a forefront effort against slavery and racial segregation. Within a "hostile environment," the church was a safe space for African Americans to worship and socialize (Gatewood 1990: 281). The strict boundary between religious and secular function was born. However, there was opposition to this binary division dating to the slave dances in Congo Square and on numerous plantations, where a fusion of spiritual celebration and social mixing occurred.

Ragtime, a pre-form of jazz dating to the 1890s, was played within social mediums, such as parades, sporting events and afternoon concerts (Gioia 1998: 32). This framework placed it outside of spiritual worship into a realm of amusement. Erroneously, jazz became associated with unrespectable "good times," as a consequence of the piano's performance in prostitution houses and dens of alcohol consumption. Armstrong discussed the plentitude of this music around the red light area of New Orleans: "any place you should go in the District, whether it was a Café—Cabaret or Saloon—or if you should just stop in some place for a few drinks and listen—you heard the best in Jazz" (Armstrong 1999: 24). Religious protocol obliged musicians to decide between a presence within the church or public entertainment. Contextualizing this edict, Mary Lou Williams, pianist and arranger, informed that "she was nearly refused from childhood baptism for playing 'devil's music'" (Mousouris 1979: 84). Also, W. C. Handy upon carrying his violin or cornet into church choirs heard elders emit, "Yonder goes de devil" (Handy 1969: 130). As an adolescent, Dizzy Gillespie witnessed religious classifications that disregarded the sanctified church due to its open expression of spirituality and music (Gillespie and Fraser 2009: 31). These accounts demonstrate music's culpability for community anxiety.

Second, black elite societies of the nineteenth century contributed to the antagonistic vision of jazz. These organizations prided themselves on class differentiation by means of pedigree, wealth, profession and skin color. Women were expected "to devote much attention to social graces, fashionable dress, and canons of good etiquette" (Gatewood 1990: 244). Furthermore, these factions rejected visceral responses of African American performance for orchestral tradition. Gatewood described, in *Aristocrats of Color*, a choral society's mission: "to diffuse among the masses a higher musical culture and appreciation for the works that tend to refine and cultivate" (Gatewood 1990: 223). Endeavoring to transform publicly from post-Civil War identities to modern individuals, they rejected African cultural characteristics and adopted "snobbish behavior." Joseph Willson, author of *Sketches of the Higher Classes of Colored Society in Philadelphia* (published in 1841), illustrated the competency of young ladies that "perform on the piano-forte, guitar, or some other appropriate musical instrument . . . with singing and conversation on whatever suitable topics that may offer" (Winch 2000: 99). This description reinforced class structure and appropriate musical choices for the privileged groups. Ragtime, considered a "ragging" of classic arrangement, was the antithesis of parlor music. The rhythmic sound attracted a young African American audience that was distant from elite traditions. In response, upper class black society implemented "cultural change," defined by Hall as "forms and practices" of popular culture that are extracted and marginalized (Hall 2011: 72).

Majority tradition, as the third mode, was ensconced in a history of slavery and Jim Crow laws, where African Americans experienced systemic segregation. These rules of conduct carried forward an environment of cultural dominance among the mainstream. Early jazz born of African traditions and driven by black Americans was provocative. Contributions to mainstream culture were often received with hostility. The music, with increased tempo and improvisation, contested the rigid dance styles of waltzes, quadrilles and mazurkas (Gioia 1998: 35). An article in the *New York Times* on May 21, 1905 demonstrated a qualitative comparison of classical and jazz techniques:

The success of the past season has taught that the public at large is taking a real interest in operatic musical forms as contrasted with the art of tuneful airs. It would seem that Wagner is driving out the ragtime . . . it is evident from past experiences that the American public will continue to patronize grand operas in the vernacular of the highest class and good American light operas.

(Savage 1905)

In addition, the commentary denoted the clash occurring within the white mainstream related to proper entertainment. Subtleties involving class structure were summoned in the critique through language such as "educated theatregoer," "intelligent and pictorially pleasing musical," and "need not be buffoonery, horseplay, or indecency" (Savage 1905). The latter were traits of vaudevillian and minstrel performance.

As examined in Chapter 2, minstrel shows where white men and women performed in black face became a strategic vehicle to undermine racial advancement. The theatrical model institutionalized the condition of African Americans performing in blackface or acting in a manner that nourished stereotypes. Perpetuated by Hollywood, black face was applied to major film stars such as Fred Astaire in *Swing Time* (1936) and Judy Garland in *Everybody Sing* (1938). In the second picture, Garland sings a jazzed-up version of "Swing Low, Sweet Chariot," while adorned in short gingham dress, sagging stockings and plaited hair with ribbons. These jazz era films employed the makeup in musical scenes where the lead satirized African American appearance, servitude, dance and spiritual songs. In major form, this entertainment style thrived for one hundred years until the Civil Rights Movement overthrew the practice in America. Religious organizations, affluent groups and mainstream media set forth embellished attitudes regarding the art of jazz, prompting a behavioral response from performers.

An elite identity

Born of improvisation, jazz demonstrated ingenuity through sound, behavior and image for societal pleasure and recognition. Flügel argued that the main purpose of clothing decoration was "to beautify the bodily appearance, so as to attract the admiring glances of others and fortify one's self-esteem" (Flügel 1950: 20). This theory has supported the conduct of performers, who espoused dress, vernacular and manner that constructed a jazz elite. The outcome was a subcultural movement, where the jazz community represented art and aesthetics that signified influence and transformation. Hence, the visual depiction had a primary role in classifying players as an elite among their people. Fletcher Henderson, Louis Armstrong and Ella Fitzgerald were a few among many performers that elevated the status of jazz through technique and appearance. Each figure held a unique identity in popular culture due to style representations, negotiated by means of conformity, attraction, class distinction and eccentricity. Hurlock submitted the practice of these motives in dress and fashion as "an effective medium of expression" (Hurlock 1929: 42).

Male dress conformity

Among African American male musicians, conformity in dress developed from a few stimuli including Romantic period influences, gracious rivalry and economic advancement. The sack suit and tuxedo were garments that jazzmen wore to match contemporary fashion, and likewise to suggest formality. Photographs of bands and orchestras from 1900 to 1920 illustrated an adoption of the two silhouettes. As described by Bigelow, the sack suit had a "looser fit of the coat . . . it hung on the male figure like a sack" (Bigelow 1970: 223). Kid Ory's Woodland Band and Buddy Petit's Jazz Band adorned this baggy style in photos, while the Buddy Bolden Band and The Original Creole Orchestra adopted tuxedos. The latter garment dated to the 1880s, revolutionizing eveningwear by removing tails from the coat (Bigelow 1970: 225). In his memoirs of 1920s Chicago, Louis Armstrong noted his opening night at the Lincoln Gardens:

> I was getting dressed, putting on my old "Roast Beef"-P.S. that was what we called an old ragged Tuxedo; of course, I had it all pressed up and fixed so good that no one would ever notice it, unless they were real close and noticed the patches here and there. Anyway-I was real sharp at least I thought I was anyway.
>
> (Armstrong 1999: 49)

Armstrong's comment revealed the desire to conform to formal dress standards within the band, as well as "the pursuit of beauty" (Figure 4.1).

Fashion scholars Roach and Eicher affirmed that the individual will "faithfully follow standards for beauty in his own society or modify them for idiosyncratic reasons" (Roach and Eicher 1973: 78). Many of the black musicians originating in New Orleans came from backgrounds of poverty. Consequently, the suit and tuxedo suggested work that was a departure from physical labor; it also signified an edict of band membership. Agreements between leader and member could be stringent with dress and behavior. For example, the contract for Ridgley's Tuxedo band detailed specific formal wear requirements; in addition strict regulations related to smoking, arguing, solo performance, rehearsal attendance, instrument repair, tardiness and talking were enumerated (Ridgley 1928c). Throughout the 1920s and 1930s, the tuxedo was cemented as the aesthetic

Figure 4.1 Louis Armstrong at the piano and his Hot Five members adorned in tuxedos with Lillian Hardin in a chemise evening dress, 1926. © JazzSign/Lebrecht Music & Arts/ CORBIS

standard of dress for jazz bands, particularly among the musicians of Fletcher Henderson, King Oliver and Duke Ellington, where elite venues equated to greater pay scales. Count Basie of his time with the Blue Devils emphasized this expectation:

> In those days you had to have a uniform. Bands that didn't have their own special costumes didn't look professional . . . you had to be pressed and clean with everything shined up. All you have to do is look at some pictures of the orchestras in those days and you'll see how well they were dressed. All of the orchestras were like that.
>
> (Basie and Murray 2002: 19)

Like the monarchs that influenced court fashion in the sixteenth century, this directive of formal dress demonstrates that orchestra leaders formulated, approved and publicized style, thus wielding authority in men's clothing and generating economic demand.

An examination of the tuxedo establishes items of the costume that designate favorable attributes of a professional man making a living through skilled work. For instance, the winged collar with its rigid and high formation around the neck prompted musicians to elevate their posture, akin to the sixteenth-century ruff, a detachable collar with numerous folds that were starched or crimped. This symbol of aristocracy became elaborate in scale by the end of the century. It impeded freedom of movement, thus signifying an individual of a leisure class without daily toil (Black and Garland 1975: 158). The tuxedo collar through crisp form and white color endorsed the regal element when displayed by a jazz ensemble. Also contributing to this notion were fabrications and closures of the garment. The satin-faced lapels that reflected light in black and white photographs of early jazz bands suggested richness of quality and luxury, while the buttoned placket of the shirt and vest intimated precision and order. Nestor Roqueplan, a French writer and journalist, is credited with covering his trouser seams with a strip of silk (Chenoune 1993: 60). This detail utilized in tuxedos camouflages an uneven seam edge with a lush fabric, in similar manner to how the garment can visually disguise a person's modest social status. A correlation between men's dress and status is evidenced in *A History of Fashion*. The "fashionable materials" of the early nineteenth-century waistcoat are stressed to be velvet, satin and cashmere; likewise the preference of black or white for formal occasions was "considered proper" (Black and Garland 1975: 248). Photographs of Don Albert's Orchestra (1933), Armand J. Piron's Society Orchestra (1923) and the Camelia Dance Orchestra (1918) reveal that jazz musicians wearing suits and tuxedos projected authority, refinement, seriousness of expression and a stalwart composure with hands held to the side or rested on their limbs. These performers, through dress and posture that contained meaning, transformed class and race constructs.

A direct correlation to gentry is found in the naming of a 1920s African American band. Paying homage to George Bryan Brummell, Englishman and fashion arbiter of the Romantic period, the jazz group was labeled Zach Whyte and His Chocolate Beau Brummels (Godbolt 1990: 50). Brummell, who was associated with dandyism, gave considerable attention to elegant dress, cleanliness and gentility (Bigelow 1970: 198). The legend of Brummell's style was publicized in major newspapers during the 1920s. "The Beau Brummel of wartime prosperity redolent with hair tonic, and with manicured nails and "sporty" clothes, who was wont to spend $2.50 every ten days in improving his appearance . . ." (*New York Times* 1921), remarked the *New York Times* on August 17, 1921 concerning men's fashion during the First World War. By means of the "Brummell" moniker, Whyte adopted standards of refinement equivalent to the elite benefactor. A 1929 photograph of the band showed the bandleader in tuxedo and black tie commanding the attention of his well-mannered orchestra in formal evening suits (Godbolt 1990: 50). This trademark challenged negative attitudes of jazz by referencing a notable cultural leader.

On September 22, 1926, the *New York Times* published an article titled, "Fashion's Edict Bans 'Jazz' Attire for Men." A meeting of the National Association of Retail Clothiers and Furnishers resulted in the declaration to men that "oxford bag trousers" and "exaggerated jazz clothing" were to be discarded. The organization reported that "attire that does not express the period of the day, or the occupation, recreation or formality in which the wearer is engaged is absolutely incorrect" (New York Times 1926a). Also opposing such disapproving jazz-related regulations was the naming of Buster Bailey and his Seven Chocolate Dandies, which gave reverence to well-dressed men of the nineteenth century. Whyte's and Baileys' ensembles through text and image represented strategic moves to craft positive visions of jazz. Bechet suggested competitiveness as another motive: "every band was trying to find some name that was one higher than the next one" (Bechet 2002: 88). The name of groups with value references including "original creole," "all-star," "hot five," "original Dixieland," "aces," and "rhythm kings" were prolific. Often, the label "orchestra" was substituted for "band" and imparted authority, structure and convention. Using Hurlock's description of the lower class mimicking high society, "this process of identification" allowed the group "to gain some of the pleasure of prestige which is generally accorded that set" (Hurlock 1929: 39).

Evolution of feminine attraction

In analysis of attraction, the women of jazz provided a solid foundation, commencing with the white gardenia worn by Billie Holiday (Figure 4.2).

This symbol of beauty was adopted by the legendary jazz singer, and transformed into a medium of desirability. Holiday's embellishment of the tropical blossom was a signal to primitive ornamentation suggesting innocence, raw femininity and exotic appeal. Barthes' sociology of clothing distinguished the flower in the hair as "pure and simple adornment" (Barthes 2006: 7). When the floral application became socially ordered, it transformed into a methodical and synthetic act. Holiday's repetition of wearing the gardenia was a performance practice with fetish-like meaning. "Fetishism takes us into the realm where fantasy intervenes in representation" (Hall 2012: 266). Late in life, Holiday recalled: "I thought I couldn't sing if I didn't have a gardenia in my hair and it had to be fresh" (Holiday 1956). The white, airy and multi-layer flower signified the magical object that ensured a quality vocal performance, compelling audiences to associate the flower with the performer's sophistication and talent. "Hairstyles can also signal the wearer's endorsement or commitment to a particular role, status, or course of action" (Arnoldi and Kreamer 1995: 14). Applying the flower to the hair constructed a persona that of Holiday as stage celebrity with prosperity and influence.

The last few years of Holiday's career evidenced the diminished practice of the gardenia, mounting drug charges and a thinned vocal range. A report in the New York Times on September 15, 1958 announced "Billie Holiday Sings With

Figure 4.2 Billie Holiday wears the iconic white gardenia in a publicity photograph, c.1940. © Bettmann/CORBIS

Old Magic." "This magic has been hard to come by for Miss Holiday in recent years" (Wilson 1958b). The author's comments merged the concept of a forbidden force and brilliant singing that Holiday had attached to the flower. Highly regarded into the twenty-first century as iconic, the voluminous gardenias that were worn during the 1940s catapulted Holiday into a unique social standing coded with beauty, grace and uniqueness. Hurlock described the pursuit of approval through dress: "it enables people to advertise themselves in a way that will win the attention and admiration of others" (Hurlock 1929: 27). As one of the prominent female singers, Holiday was instrumental in establishing a posture of prestige in jazz.

Considerable appraisal derived from media that inflated appearance in assessing female singers. "Ivy can really wear clothes with that stylish figure . . . never smokes or drinks, but is a great success in being the life of the party," declared the *Pittsburgh Courier* of Ivie Anderson, songstress in Duke Ellington's Orchestra (Nelson 1931). Twenty years later, the treatment was consistent, when Sarah Vaughan launched her career (Figure 4.3).

"She was dressed tastefully, her hair and makeup had been worked out to give her a pleasantly glamorous touch, and she handled herself on the floor" (*Down Beat* 1950). Dispensing potent criticism in the jazz industry, the *Down Beat* article projects a scrutinizing eye of the white male gaze, "fixing very specific

Figure 4.3 Sarah Vaughan in a one shoulder, tiered gown mesmerizes at microphone. Los Angeles, 1950. © Joseph Schwartz/CORBIS

notions of what is desirable in women" (Sawchuk 2007: 481). Female jazz artists that had toiled in the business received a more technical observation. As *Down Beat*'s update of Billie Holiday in 1952, "a new Lady Day calmly conquered the jazz-oriented citizenry of Boston in the course of a rewardingly successful week at Storyville recently" (Hentoff 1952).

An outcome of sharpened appearance among women was a leveling with male musicians. "Singers were paid less than musicians, reflecting their status in the band's hierarchy," wrote Nicholson (Nicholson 2004: 48) about Ella Fitzgerald's start in the big band era. Fitzgerald as well Bessie Smith and Ethel Waters came from economically disadvantaged backgrounds, where the ability to entertain provided undreamed wealth and influence. These women began their careers as youngsters with little knowledge of pay scales and contracts, learning the business on the road, one city at a time. Here, Waters' description of exhibition rituals experienced on a tour in the late teens:

> They would frantically look over their clothes as they unpacked, run out to buy something new and resplendent, press the clothes, and then promenade down the main drag of the Negro section. They talked of nothing but this big shot here, that big shot there.
>
> (Waters and Samuels 1992: 78)

A dignified presence became essential to the exhibition of their art, equally to attain regard from the audience. The media participated in this exchange through colorful narratives that focused on the exterior of black and white vocalists. Such as this description of Anita O'Day recorded in the *Milwaukee Journal*: "a tall, willowy specimen who dresses like a schoolteacher and sings cool bop with a very special style" (*Milwaukee Journal* 1955). Also, *Variety* declared: "Miss O'Day, her fine figure draped in a floor-length beige-and-white gown . . . Miss O'Day's scratchy, small voice has a wonderful authority" (*Variety* 1960). These articles evaluated body form and artistic talent with skillful avoidance of the performer as pure object. Susan Kaiser, cultural scholar, put forward the feminists' concern, where there is a "tendency for females to be objectified by this relative focus on the importance of appearance" (Kaiser 1997: 419). However for African American performers in all-white venues, magnetism facilitated visual and musical achievement, in the long run breaking down barriers of racially segregated entertainment. Basie recalled this enhancement in Boston during the late 1930s. "Billie Holiday was in the band when we went up to the Ritz Carlton that first time, and that was also a big plus for us because her repertoire and her style were just great for a place like that, and she just had so much personality as a performer" (Basie and Murray 2002: 204).

At other times, the singer was instrumental in maneuvering the music for recognition of wealth and beauty. *Our World* printed a depiction of Dinah

Figure 4.4 Dinah Washington projects affluence in beaded gown and textured shrug, Newport Jazz Festival, 1955. © Burt Goldblatt Estate Archives Cynthia Sesso, CTSIMAGES

Washington in August 1951. "She's earned as high as $150,000 a year. Dinah still gets a kick out of buying expensive clothes, fancy shoes and big cars . . . next to singing, Dinah loves shoes. In 200 pair collection, she can match any costume change" (Figure 4.4).

Regardless of the splendor and affluence projected, these women still experienced racial discrimination. Josephine Baker, dancer, singer and actress of Parisian triumph, ignited a picket line boycott of the exclusive New York Stork Club, when she was refused food service. *Jet* covered the NAACP (National Association for the Advancement of Colored People) protest that included Bessie Buchanan, former showgirl, in mink coat, representing the practice of resistance through esteemed identity. Further demonstrating her authority and influence, Baker wired President Truman the following note: "I implore you to destroy this horrible discrimination disease that exists in this great land, and, with God's help,

I am confident you will succeed" (*Jet* 1951a). In addition, Billie Holiday recalled the constraints of 52nd Street and its numerous jazz clubs. "We were not allowed to mingle any kind of way. The minute we were finished with our intermission stint we had to scoot out back to the alley or go out and sit in the street" (Holiday and Dufty 2006: 110–11).

Furthermore, performers experienced segregation in Las Vegas. Dinah Washington while playing at the Casbar Lounge was required to stay in a trailer attached to the kitchen. Direct access to the hotel and use of the facilities was not permitted (Cohodas 2006: 220). In 1955, *Down Beat* reported that the interracial Moulin Rouge had opened in the black district of Las Vegas, opposite the almost 100 percent Jim Crow casino strip (Emge 1955). Segregation established demeaning accommodations and treatment for black performers; contrary to the social mixing that occurred on stage and off. Also fledgling bands and vocalists would find indifference or hostility if booked in "unsuitable venues" (Gelly 2007: 45). Aesthetics of artistic and visual means challenged these barriers, in effect, according to West, "responding in an improvisational, undogmatic, creative way to circumstances . . . that people still survive and thrive" (West 1999: 544).

Signifying class distinction

"Wealth has always been associated with social position, and the higher the individual ranked in the social scale, the greater was the wealth he possessed" (Hurlock 1929: 36). As the third means of prestige, class distinction was exemplified through clothing. This visual display had historical relevance from the headdresses of Ancient Egypt to the high ruff collars of the Renaissance era. Fur coats were frequently employed among female jazz artists to convey affluence. Markedly in the twelfth and thirteenth centuries, "a definite hierarchy emerged in the use of furs . . . the pelts of finer, rare and smaller creatures were only within reach of the very wealthy," inclusive of sable, fox, marten and ermine (Black and Garland 1975: 104–5).

Female performers embraced fur coats as ostentatious signs of their mounting wages and status as celebrities (Figure 4.5).

In the biography *Bessie*, Ruby Walker Smith, niece of Bessie Smith, recounted to Albertson the function of fur one evening: "It made us feel like we were very important and loaded . . . she wore a white ermine coat and looked like a million bucks" (Albertson 2003: 141). Ruby Smith listed five fur coats in Smith's ownership at the time. Of comparable routine, Dinah Washington, celebrated as the Queen of the Blues, was often photographed in fur coats. Cohodas, author of *Queen*, discussed Washington wearing a mink during a Los Angeles engagement despite the warm weather (Cohodas 2006: 128). All three

Figure 4.5 Billie Holiday robed in a fox stole during a recording session for "Strange Fruit", New York, 1939. Photo by Charles Peterson. Courtesy of Don Peterson

performers commanded over a thousand dollars per week in their prime; therefore, the display of wealth was not atypical. In 1957, Washington's inventory included "ten fur coats, among them a black diamond full-length mink jacket, a stole, a breath-of-spring mink jacket, a silver blue mink jacket, and a white mink scarf" (Cohodas 2006: 265). Washington infused in her identity the prestige associated with acquiring and wearing fur. Articulating her ascension to fame in 1952, *Down Beat* declared "This Washington Mink is On The Up and Up" (*Down Beat* 1952), concerning her signing bonus of a mink coat from Mercury Records. Further distinction of luxury was achieved through the hue of wigs and furs. "Red-haired Miss Washington showed up for the hearing in a green beaver coat over a two-piece white suit and a white mink fez hat," reported the *New York Post* on October 23, 1961. The chemical revolution in fur fashion, contrary to exclusivity, endorsed imitation of articles possessed by the affluent class. Hurlock posited: "even fur . . . dyed so skillfully that a fur coat costing one hundred dollars closely resembles one many times as expensive" (Hurlock 1929: 86).

On January 4, 1914, the *New York Times* prognosticated an enthusiasm for pelts when it declared "Fur is Now All the Rage in the World of Fashion" (*New York Times* 1914). A testimonial within the article likened the offering of peltry to a divine feat. "Fur appeared as though the human animal were in need of it, and it was a special dispensation of Providence to provide it." The trend of fur grew from trimmings on gowns and wrap-front coats segueing to full-length, boxy silhouettes by the 1930s. In her memoir, Waters divulged the purchase of a mink coat valued at twelve hundred dollars for half the amount. "Then I had just fifteen dollars left in my savings account. And I wore that mink coat for years" (Waters and Samuels 1992: 144–5). Waters was just starting to record for companies like Cardinal and Black Swan that targeted black consumers. With her name on marquees and phonograph discs, the coat was symbolic of this newfound success.

This adulation for fur was communicated through periodicals to white and black consumers. By the 1950s, fur coats were within reach of more African Americans than during the depression and war years. "Today anyone with the 'right approach,' even an office girl who has the right credit standing and salary, can obtain a mink coat," declared *Jet* magazine in a 1951 editorial (*Jet* 1951a). The story humorously provided "Ten Ways to Get a Mink Coat." Here, a sampling of the top three: one, "save your pennies and buy one;" two, "marry a rich man;" and three, "catch your husband cheating and as a pacifier — 'get a mink.'" On November 8, 1951, *Jet* magazine covered a society event in Chicago, where an extreme display of fur was observed. "A bombshell was dropped . . . when pretty divorcee Virginia Garner walked into the Parkway Ballroom in a $12,000 mink dress and cape ensemble–and stole the show" (*Jet* 1951b).

In addition, the editor of the *New York Amsterdam News* disclosed in *Jet* magazine the power of the fur garment.

> There comes a time in every woman's life when she realizes that a mink coat represents a certain kind of security. That's the reason every woman wants a mink. It's a badge of having successfully arrived.
>
> (*Jet* 1951a: 47)

Aimed at working class audiences, this quote claimed that the act of wearing fur goes beyond admiration to a sign of marital and womanly achievement in society. *Jet* and *Ebony* magazines recognized that regular African American women were drawn to these sensational stories about fur dresses and haute couture evening gowns. "The budget-minded housewife will not have to worry. Copies of many of the finest are available for less than $50," declared *Ebony* (*Ebony* 1959: 177) regarding the designs of French couturiers. Equally, *Jet* appeased readers with a smug declaration: "women not fortunate enough to have affluent husbands . . . are not neglected by the fur industry which uses the magic word 'mink' rather loosely" (*Jet* 1951a: 45). Smith, Washington and Waters crafted prestige in the jazz discipline by embracing and flaunting a wealth-encoded object to working class fans. The style and conduct was aspirational whereas the music was innate, otherwise stated as the high and humble traits of jazz. For jazz vocalists, the wearing of fur supported the dress functions of attraction, class distinction and wealth display, as put forth by traditional scholars (Hurlock 1929: 32–7, Flügel 1950: 20).

For the audience, it was the mere novelty of an African American escaping common hardship and discovering fame by singing the blues. This thought was summarized in the recollection of Ruby Smith on Smith's behavior, when wearing fur. "But she never put on airs, not Bessie. She wasn't going to change for anyone, she just wanted people to like her for what she was—a real person" (Albertson 2003: 171). Fred Davis explored this idea through the conflict of the "garment's status" (Davis 1994: 73). In detail, Smith's philosophy and mink coat habit were polarized by reinforcement of "distinction and hierarchical division" (Davis 1994: 73), at the same time, attempting to suggest that she had not forgotten her "abject poverty" roots in Chattanooga. Smith's illustriousness was preserved following her untimely death in 1937. At the funeral, an audience of seven thousand paid their respects to the blues belter. The *Afro-American* described Smith's body as "garbed in a low cut peach lace gown which harmonized with the casket lining" (*Afro-American* 1937). Further enhancing this prominence, pallbearers, dressed in "morning coats, white vests, striped pants, black shoes and white spats," carried Smith's $500 silver metallic casket. The occurrence of celebrity instills devotion from the totality of an individual's existence contrary to momentary possessions of wealth. Beyond death, Smith's identity is continually revived through prominent jazz recordings that inform a daring and stellar life, while moderating artifacts of class.

Exhibiting an eccentric manner

Unconventional traits developed among entertainers that assigned them iconic reputations. Outsiders idolized this engineered behavior. For instance, Lester Young utilized slang from his experiences that became jazz vernacular. "To 'feel a draft' was to sense racial prejudice; to have 'eyes' for something was to approve of it. 'Bells' meant enjoyment" (Gelly 2007: 55). Hall classified this "system of representation" as spoken and written words that permitted the exchange of "concepts, ideas and feelings" (Hall 2012: 1). "Louis Armstrong himself invented a lot of slang words, like 'dippermouth' and 'cats,' during the late twenties and thirties" (Wilson, Ligthart and Van Loo 2001: 26). Through ambiguous methods, Young and others restricted the comprehension to select black musicians, subsequently influencing a broader market of jazz hipsters.

Eccentricity was practiced by means of dressing. Dizzy Gillespie accentuated his trumpet playing with dark-rimmed glasses, bow ties, berets, impeccable suits and a goatee (Figure 4.6).

This styling, along with the music, was criticized for being an extreme departure from the danceable swing period (Godbolt 1990: 119–29). Gillespie and other bebop innovators were signifying through practice and appearance their reclamation of a genre, which had become distant from the birth of jazz.

Figure 4.6 Dizzy Gillespie sporting a striped suit, goatee and dark-rimmed glasses with Charlie Parker at Birdland, New York, 1951. © Burt Goldblatt Estate Archives/Cynthia Sesso, CTSIMAGES

This division grew when the art form became profit driven during the 1930s. Illustrating this idea, Bechet argued: "back in New Orleans . . . before all this personality stuff, all this radio and contracts and 'attraction'—the music it was free" (Bechet 2002: 218). The new style of bebop was not sheltered from commercialization as described by Gillespie:

> Then they diluted the music . . . added "mop, mop" accents and lyrics about abusing drugs . . . this synthetic sound was played heavily on commercial radio everywhere, giving bebop a bad name. No matter how bad the imitation sounded, youngsters, and people who were musically untrained like it, and it sold well because it maintained a very danceable beat.
>
> (Gillespie and Fraser 2009: 279)

Fredric Jameson's analysis of high culture's stigmatization, "as a status hobby of small groups of intellectuals" (Szeman and Kaposy 2011: 60), can be related to the retort of bebop musicians. Their development of a complex and coarse sound was restrictive to mass audiences, requiring attentive listening and scrutiny of technique. Consequently, jazz became further withdrawn from popular tradition into a realm of specialization and indicative of an elite group.

Branding jazz in advertising

> Branding: the means by which names, logos, symbols, trademarks, or product design endow goods or services with a recognizable presence and a set of associated values or expectations on the part of the consumer. Its origins lay in the literal branding of vagabonds with a "V" . . . making the bearers of such brands instantly recognizable to society at large.
>
> (Woodham 2004)

As the preceding designation, the concept of branding has undergone transformation, progressing from a means of severe identification to a strategic method of consumerism. The current definition places emphasis on a message that creates sensation. In *Beyond Design*, the brand process is described as "the direction, inspiration, and energy . . . that immediately implies value to the customer" (Keiser and Garner 2008: 54). The receiver's high opinion is the end goal, where "emotional connection" to the product is essential. Comparably, the representation of jazz has been used to brand products, signifying attributes of nostalgia, sophistication and exclusivity flowing from elite traits. The modes of jazz advertising can be classified in two eras: pre-1980s classic, when jazz was primary subject matter, and post-1980s contemporary, when it was secondary and oblique in ads.

Classic marketing of jazz

In the late 1950s, Polaroid introduced its Land Film with an advertising image of Louis Armstrong, beloved trumpet player (Figure 4.7).

The company complemented the product's characteristics of "exceptional clarity and brilliance" with the musician's reputation and technique. In *Brand Story*, Hancock asserted that "branding is not just about individual products, but creates an identity for the company, for consumers" (Hancock 2009: 5). Polaroid employed a large image of Armstrong to represent the film's ability to capture vivid details. Together with his aged skin, Armstrong's suit, tie and jewelry transmit

Figure 4.7 Andrew Blakeney, Kid Ory and Louis Armstrong with roots in New Orlean's Dixieland sound exemplify jazz royalty, Los Angeles, 1956. © Cecil Charles/Cynthia Sesso, CTSIMAGES

affluence and wisdom. Modest posture is noteworthy in the ad comprised the cheery musician with head tilted sideways and hands resting on his partially visible trumpet. Roach and Eicher offered an outcome of this modification. "Changes in posture alter the visual impact of body and dress as do body movements" (Roach and Eicher 1973: 109). Coded from his stage persona, Armstrong's image is genuinely charming and non-threatening with a dose of humor.

The approach was tactical during a decade when advertising was largely segregated among white media. In African American newspapers such as the

Philadelphia Tribune, illustrations of white people were used to advertise clothing, entertainment and dining to the black community. Joe Krass, Truitts and Elaine's clothing stores near South Street in Philadelphia exhibited this artwork in the *Philadelphia Tribune* (1945). In addition, evidence of both races was shown in black newspaper advertising dates to the early twentieth century. Black consumer spending impacted white businesses located in or near their neighborhoods. Equally, the community was serviced by its own businesses including: "barbering and hairdressing, tailoring and dressmaking, catering and cooking, insurance and undertaking" (Summers 1998: 11). Certain retailers were obligated to publicize an amiable shopping experience. In 1943, Earlbrook Clothes, located at 1445 South Street, advertised "Staff Exclusively Colored" in the *Philadelphia Tribune*. The Dunbar Theatre communicated similar authority: "Owned and Controlled by Colored People" (*Philadelphia Tribune* 1920a). Through subtle qualities, classic marketing of jazz negotiated racial separation.

Also in the classic mode, a 1953 Coca-Cola advertisement features musician Lionel Hampton, known for his mastery on the vibraphone. Text and image in the ad persuade consumers to "Drink Coca-Cola in Bottles." Hampton, sporting a colorful plaid jacket and abstract patterned tie, playfully confronts the viewer by means of dress formality peppered with bold and modern accents. Legitimacy of his character was provided by the tag line of "Internationally Known Orchestra Leader," hence advocating that Hampton's distinction in the arts was motive for consumers to drink Coke. In consideration of the advertising image, Barthes concluded that "the text helps to identify purely and simply the elements of the scene and the scene itself" (Barthes 1978: 39). This structure or "right of inspection" was present in a Smirnoff Vodka advertisement featuring Benny Goodman. The 1950s ad unifies the enjoyment of jazz with the consumption of vodka through his quote: "it leaves you breathless!" Goodman displays sophistication with a warm expression; equally his navy suit, French cuff shirt, horn-rimmed glasses and gold watch amplify prestige. Smirnoff accessed the admiration of jazz by juxtaposing Goodman's upright clarinet to a bottle of vodka thus linking the desirability and richness of the artifacts. The traditional ads utilizing Armstrong, Hampton and Goodman signified a direct correlation to jazz achievement and aesthetics, thereby creating societal beliefs in the product narratives and establishing "chains of meaning" (McFall 2007: 133).

Contemporary marketing of jazz

In 1989 designating the contemporary marketing of jazz, American Express, a financial services company, promoted its credit card with a scene featuring Ella Fitzgerald posed in front of an open-door, 1940s style Cadillac convertible. Primary qualities of the ad are wealth references including a tailored suit with pillbox hat, leopard fur coat and vintage automobile, balanced by the tag line, "Cardmember since 1961." Despite Fitzgerald's recognition as a jazz singer, direct markers of music such as a microphone, instrument or studio environment were not harnessed, indicating that celebrity eclipsed the artistry.

Conforming to this practice in 2009, CHANEL, the Parisian luxury brand, promoted its Chanel No. 5 fragrance with a Billie Holiday song, exclusive of direct references to the singer. Holiday's affecting tone provided intimate mood to a television commercial, emphasizing the romantic pursuits of an upper class woman. By selecting "I'm a Fool to Want You," CHANEL implied through language the woman's anxious, albeit refined desire for the gentleman. Affluence was conveyed through dress and accessories, mode of travel and marina locale, at the same time being reinforced by the song's orchestral string arrangement. Even more, CHANEL constructed value through the application of jazz melody to magnify the fragrance. McFall categorized this advertising practice, where "ads are free to harvest any attractive referent systems" to produce meaning (McFall 2007: 134).

Last of all, Honda Motor Company, a Japanese automaker, released vehicles under the "Jazz" nameplate. The correlation, with an innovative music form, was deemed apropos for the target market that included Europe and the United States. Its 2011 issue, the Honda Jazz Hybrid, used the genre to connote an innovative, flexible and boldly colored electric car. Honda recognized the protracted European appeal to jazz, which had developed from the sojourns of American musicians at the beginning of the twentieth century. Sidney Bechet recalled the dissemination of 1920s jazz in Europe:

> We all sailed in the old Berengaria mid-September and opened the Revue Nègre soon after at the Théâtre des Champs Eylsées. The show was a great success. Josephine (Baker) and Louis, I remember, danced the Charleston and nobody in Europe had seen that dance before, and that really started something. That show really had Paris going. All the critics and all the papers were writing it up, and the house was full every night.
>
> (Bechet 2002: 147)

Honda accentuated this fascination and energy in Europe, as well the improvisational nature of jazz with the slogan: "One Life. Why So Serious?" Like American Express and CHANEL, Honda's ad espouses showmanship, free expression and elevated standing comparable to jazz qualities.

Conclusion

In classic and contemporary marketing of jazz, the depiction of the genre was instrumental in communicating prestige: the quality of being influential, respected and prominent. Performers had gained this recognition through decades of skilled technique and attractive display. For this meaning to take root, jazz had been "encoded" with elite elements of virtuosity, esteem and affluence, dating to the 1900s. Four signifying concepts were applied in both periods of promotion: (1) jazz as an American treasure; (2) presence of genius; (3) freedom of expression; and (4) high social status. Advertisers accessed this value through visual, aural and textual means. The placement of jazz instruments, casting of older musicians, incorporation of dynamic text and exhibition of formal dress composed an image of jazz that paralleled the brand's desired standing. It is notable that the modern imagery placed less direct jazz elements in ads, plausibly due to the elite rank the genre had previously secured and circulated in society.

The continued implementation of these signs through advertising, "where techniques and innovations can rapidly take on the status of established knowledge" (McFall 2007: 136), have transmitted a global ideology of jazz.

5

GENDERED IDENTITIES, IDEOLOGIES AND CULTURAL DIFFERENCE

Functions of published sheet music

Prior to the 1920s dominance of phonograph records and radio, a dominant American aesthetic was disseminated into households via illustrated sheet music covers. These booklets contained descriptive cover art, music, lyrics, dance instructions and photographs of performers that stimulated popular interest in songwriters, publishers and entertainers. Homes, schools and churches in possession of pianos, organs, mandolins and guitars provided demand for sheets (Viator 2011). Notably, this was a key moment when the commerce of music was directed towards a broader market instead of solely to the wealthy class. Ethel Waters documented the additional function of this musical trade in the early teens, when singers sought authorization from song publishers to perform copyrighted and printed sheets. "I wanted to sing a new number that I'd once heard . . . and I'd have to get permission from the copyright owners, Pace and Handy . . . before I could sing it on the stage" (Waters and Samuels 1992: 73). Later having achieved star status, these singers would appear on the covers to advance the retailing of published music and lyrics. "Sales of sheet music was the bottom line. People had to buy sheet music to make a song a success" (Scheurer 1989: 88). With the proliferation of recorded music in the 1920s and 1930s, the published sheet trade utilized publicity photographs from singers and musicians on covers accented with graphic artwork and text. Many of these booklets supplied the recording company number for a consumer to purchase the song on phonograph disc. At this juncture, the performers became instrumental in the marketing and popularity of song titles, thus altering the established production system of composer, lyricist and publisher.

Imagining black culture

African American themed cover art from 1840 to 1940 depicted an affinity for black mores and fashion within a racially charged framework. Images stood out through graphic text, panoramas of everyday life, comedic narratives about love and promotions of well-known entertainers. The techniques during this time period included metal plate engraving, five-color lithography and photographic printing. Commencing in the nineteenth century, popular songs, as well as published sheets, gave "form and substance" to "stereotypes of minorities and women" (Scheurer 1989: 45). The provocative visuals interpreted the music, dance, religion, values and relationships of black Americans against the backdrop of slavery, segregation, wars and economic turmoil. Hall identified these cultural signs as "popular representations of racial difference," where themes of subordination and primitivism were emphasized (Hall 2012: 244). A critical ideology of African American culture and style was generated, exclusive of primary black contribution and historical context.

This chapter will evaluate the gendered identities present in art covers from the Sam DeVincent Collection of Illustrated American Sheet Music housed at the Archives Center of the National Museum of American History. Dating from 1840 to 1941, a total of eighty-five covers were examined that included artwork or photographic images of African Americans or Caucasians in blackface. Artists contracted by different publishing houses prepared noteworthy illustrations. "Although most covers weren't signed, a number of known and notable professional cover artists produced them" (Viator 2011). A prominent commercial artist was Albert Wilfred Barbelle, born in 1887 he reached adolescence at the turn of the century, when malicious attitudes and restrictions were placed upon African Americans. Thus, societal constructs impacted the tone of illustrations, as did the aim of publishing companies to profit with creative and conceivably shocking cover material.

The popularity of black music including spirituals, folk melodies, blues and ragtime was crucial to this representation, as such necessitating the likeness of African Americans on the covers for genuineness. An article in the *New York Times* on August 18, 1859 begrudgingly established the existence of "patrons of the Black Art:"

> For even at this day there are certain souls which find delight in the awkward exhibition of brute endurance known as negro dancing – wherein an individual will, for twenty minutes, incessantly perform, with his feet and legs, a variety of antics in which there is not the remotest approach to anything like beauty or grace—to say nothing of the poetry of motion—and this to a strumming on the banjo which, being an utterly unmeaning noise, is quite as barbarous as anything in or out of a veritable Congo or Dahomey.
>
> (*New York Times* 1859)

The narration posited antagonistic judgments that would thrive for a hundred years regarding the traditions of black Americans. Repulsive, uncultured and vulgar impressions that were conveyed about black art were replicated in published sheet music covers, where the fabrication of caricatures spawned gendered identities. Embedded in these characters was the shrewd portrayal of African American fashion and etiquette, divulging an attentiveness by the white majority into the facets of black culture and the circumstances that led to such practices. In 1895, this focus was apparent in a *New York Times* critique of "Black America" at Madison Square Garden, which was previously mentioned in Chapter 3 regarding the entry of black Americans into white entertainment venues: "The audience much enjoyed the entertainment afforded by 300 negroes . . . it was noticeable that the most appreciated numbers were such old-time melodies as 'Carry Me Back To Old Virginia' and 'Old Black Joe'" (*New York Times* 1895).

Female representations: Mammy, highbrow and temptress

Three gendered identities, including mammy, highbrow and temptress, were distinguished in the cover art of the DeVincent collection of sheet music, where feminine characteristics erected contentious personality types. Within the assortment, subclasses were noted that stressed positive and negative qualities influenced by race. The mammy identity was featured on song covers with themes concerning lullabies, food preparation, plantation life and jubilees. In *Clinging to Mammy*, McElya asserted that this archetype is "the most visible character in the myth of the faithful slave, a set of stories, images, and ideas that have been passed down from generation to generation in the United States" (McElya 2007: 4). Jacket artwork with titles using "mammy" or "Aunt Jemima" had common traits of female posture and attire. For example, "Mammy's Little Kinky Headed Boy" (1926) contained an elderly black female sitting in a rocking chair with a boy of the same race clinging to her torso. The woman's upright posture, child nurturing and stoic expression symbolized her prominent position in the family. Also her clothes consisted of the typical headscarf, polka dot dress, apron and fringed shawl that denoted southern traditions of antebellum servitude.

A decade earlier similar qualities were documented in "Mammy Jinny's Jubilee" (1913) comprising an elderly black woman at the entrance of a log cabin receiving enthusiastic relatives. Adorned in a polka dot headscarf, apron and floor sweeping dress, the respected woman's identity was enveloped in domestic service and restricted of individual, scholarly and political ambition. A chicken and watermelon held by two characters in the scene dispensed stereotypes that flourished during the period. The entry of African American composers did not initiate favorable artwork from publishing houses. From 1899, "Aunt Jemima's Cake Walk" written by James Weldon Johnson followed the mammy type in its cover. It exhibited a wide-eyed woman with monkey-like facade in polka dot head wrap and long dress. Johnson, who would later serve as poet, civil rights activist and author of the black national anthem, "Lift Every Voice and Sing," was immersed in ragtime compositions, along with his brother Rosamond and partner Bob Cole. "The 1890s were the era of the so-called 'coon song' and its companion, the cakewalk" (Levy 1989: 94). Hence, the lyrics and the cover art of this era applied crude stereotypes of African American women through the reduction of beauty markers. In these illustrations, cloths of simplistic patterns including circles and polka dots were attributes of domestic workers who buttressed the black family in a non-threatening way. Markedly, the kerchief scarf was stripped of its historical association to West African headties and headscarves, where it was an expression of tradition, status and modesty. "Among the Yoruba, where women's headties are considered a key element in formal dress ensembles, the practice of wrapping and decorating the head relates to critical Yoruba beliefs about the sacredness of the head and its role in defining aspects of personhood" (Arnoldi and Kreamer 1995: 127). The American depiction of the red and white dotted headscarf with double winged tails on black women suggested a southern tradition of subjugation. Hence, applying Calefato's terms, the covering of the body with satirical and uninformed material was a "carnivalesque protuberance" and "parodic second skin" (Calefato 2004: 30).

Second, the image of a highbrow woman was emphasized in these covers, where the complex image has continued to inform the modern interpretation of black femininity. Within this category, a dichotomy established a progressive portrayal of the prideful aristocratic woman and an undesirable display of the snobbish uncompromising female. For instance, "Eli Green's Cake Walk" (1896) presented a couple performing the dance that necessitated a degree of arrogance. The woman's gown is fashionable with low neckline emphasizing the bust, leg-of-mutton sleeves, allover floral print and border hem, balanced with upswept coif and gloves. Resisting harsh racial attitudes, the illustrator put forth a sophisticated ideal of the black woman through a look that exudes sincere preeminence. "Lucinda's Ragtime Ball" (1913) continued this refined and exquisite image. On the cover, a female flaunts high style with a golden yellow Empire gown with floral embroidery, flowing tulle train, center front floral ornament and elbow-length gloves. The artist replicated the fashion precisely as the Empire silhouette was a "short-lived revival" declining with the 1910 death of King Edward VII (Milbank 1989: 54–6). Alongside the dress and accessories, a favorable interpretation is achieved through the subject's expression of delight and acknowledgment of personal beauty. These reflections of the black female were aligned with the modern white woman, where self-expression, independence and respect were intensified by high fashion. Also, their adoption of Oriental and Grecian details signified liberation from the corset and an exploration of new identities.

Completing the prototype of the prideful highbrow woman is "At the Coffee Cooler's Tea" (1918) (Figure 5.1).

It features polished couples dancing and mingling at a well-decorated garden party where formal attire and demeanor suggest upper-class rank. This signed cover sheet is attributed to William and Frederick Starmer, who were born in Leeds, England. The illustration is an admiring glance at the leisure activity of black couples, supported by the exhibition of gaiety and tangible prosperity.

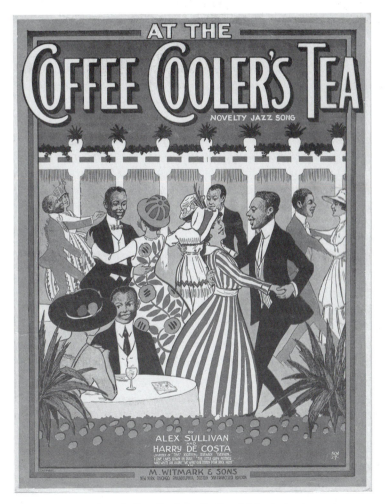

Figure 5.1 "At The Coffee Cooler's Tea" published sheet music cover emphasizes a positive representation of African American jazz culture, 1918. Photo by Transcendental Graphics/Getty Images

Noteworthy attention was taken in rendering fitted suits on the men, as well applying unique patterns to the above ankle summer frocks. Among the women, the floral and stripe accented fabrics are accessorized with belted waists and compact hats trimmed in conservative plumes. The resistance to caricature, feasibly due to the Starmer brothers' distance from American Jim Crow, positions this cover as a flattering and modern reflection of black culture with "the ideal of gentility and religion set before the perfect lady" (Coolidge 1912: 161). In addition, an egalitarian perspective was communicated by these images that complimented the beauty of African American women, tearing down the mammy stereotype and rejecting the "white supremacist ideology . . . that black people, being more animal than human, lacked the capacity to feel and therefore could not engage the finer sensibilities that were the breeding ground of art" (hooks 1990: 105).

The alternate branch of the highbrow woman fed on minstrelsy that counteracted the gratifying image circulated in the late teens. Illustrations distorted the black female through qualities of narcissism, snobbishness, obstinacy and high-handedness signifying emasculation of the male. Concerning the idiom of male castration, bell hooks in *Yearning* argued that "embedded in this assumption is the idea that black women who are not willing to assist the black men in their efforts to become patriarchs are 'the enemy' " (hooks 1990: 76). This flawed image of the black female transformed her from submissive nurturer of white and black children to an unappealing disobedient individual. Primarily occurring in the 1920s, these adverse compositions were born in an environment of increased migration of African Americans to northern cities for opportunity and exposure to a renaissance of black culture through music, literature and fine art. The latter, defining the modern negro, was referenced by the *Washington Post* on July 31, 1927: "the rich imagery and musical sense of this race direct its genius into singing channels for which the world of literature already has had cause to be most grateful" (*Washington Post* 1927b).

The merger of fashionable dress, coarse stereotypes and domineering song titles constructed a grotesque image of the modern black woman. In 1917, "The Darktown Strutters' Ball," with words and music by Shelton Brooks, was published portraying cover art of this nature (Figure 5.2).

The dancing scene features African American couples in elegant dress including tailcoat tuxedos and summer tea frocks. Song lyrics reinforce affluence by mentioning "Paris gown," "new silk shawl" and "high-toned neighbors." Regarding the illustrated dresses, the Parisian trend of fuller skirts with accented waists and above the ankle hemlines suggested easiness, freedom of movement and feminine modernity (Ewing 1986: 81). Even so, the caricatured faces of the women in thick red pouting lips and fastened eyes oppose the positive qualities of dress. The artist employing posture and demeanor submits the women as domineering and strange reinforced by surrendering male partners in blackface. Regardless of the early graphic image, the iconic song by a black composer was

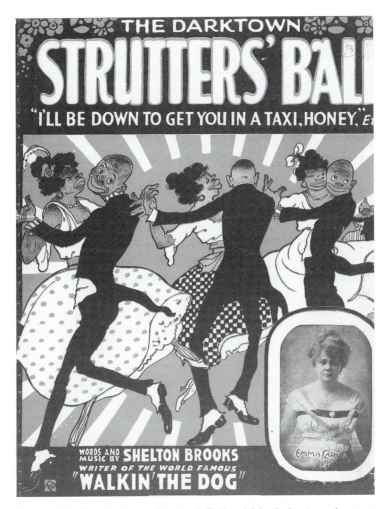

Figure 5.2 "The Darktown Strutters" Ball' published sheet music cover reinforces racial stereotypes of the Jim Crow era, 1917. Photo by Transcendental Graphics/Getty Images

recorded by many jazz legends including Teddy Wilson, Alberta Hunter and Ella Fitzgerald.

Also, "How Come You Do Me Like You Do?" (1924) presents a stylish woman in a red flapper dress and matching headband imparting a stern glance to her partner. The male repudiates this message that infers his philandering conduct. In the woman's appearance, a balance of coolness and irritation is demonstrated. Posture was essential to this meaning, transmitted by crossed legs, hand on hip, upward sloping shoulder and head tilted. These twisted body movements disrupt space, directing the viewer to the sharply dressed gentleman in check suit and contrast collar shirt. Chenoune, in analysis of the roaring 1920s, asserted that new male identities comprising film stars, gigolos and the nouveau riche became highly visible (Chenoune 1993: 143). In this sheet cover, the male, sporting a corsage and cigar, personifies the freewheeling, hedonistic temperament of the new trendsetters. An obstruction was applied through the assertive black woman drawn as the antithesis of the nineteenth-century lady occupied by "passive virtues of subservience" (Coolidge 1912: 187).

Providing an even more jarring vision of race and culture is "Mean Papa, Turn in Your Key, You Don't Live Here No More" (1923), where blackface, kinky hair and red lips are employed in the artwork. Traits of non-compliance are observed through the female subject's posture illustrated by one hand perched on the hip and the other reaching for the sporting man's household key. Chic clothing, specifically the vibrant-colored tea frock of the 1920s, elevates her attitude. Bigelow noted such "dresses had loose fitting bodices, rather full skirts, and a waistline slightly lower than the normal waist . . . trimmed with a large sash" (Bigelow 1970: 236). Contrasting an acute focus on fashion, the artist disfigures the woman's beauty in grotesque minstrelsy. The look comprised of an ornate hair comb, strands of pearls, multiple bracelets, striped stockings, and a polka dot patterned dress that clothes the body in exaggerated details. In *The Psychology of Women*, Deutch classified this type of feminine woman as a stalwart protector of her "erotic and emotional life" (Deutch 1944: 193). The defense put forth by the female has a male translation of her being conceited, intolerant, unmanageable and demanding (Deutch 1944: 197). Even though this new social ideal was evident among white women of the 1920s as film parodies in *Why Change Your Wife?* (1920), *Our Dancing Daughters* (1928) and *Dance Fools Dance* (1931), this depiction isolated the challenge within the black female giving her culpability for upsetting Victorian era notions of decorum and modesty.

Exploitation of the color red was instrumental in cover illustrations of the highbrow woman. Historically, red had been associated with royalty as well political revolution. Hurlock detailed that "lower classes were limited to the use of dull hues . . . and higher classes, who could afford to pay for expensive dyes, were permitted to use the brighter colors" (Hurlock 1929: 34). By the nineteenth century, the hue had adopted a moral association with its display. A loose manner of conduct and "a freer play of the emotions" began to define the color red (Flügel 1950: 76). For instance, the title "Red Light District" indicated the availability of prostitution among cabarets and saloons in American towns including New Orleans. The color suggested show and exhibition, as corroborated by Ethel Waters concerning her teenage dress to attend a "semi-red-light district" in Philadelphia circa 1911. "For cheek rouge I rubbed the red dye from crepe shelving paper into my face, topping it off with talcum powder . . . I hung whores' hoop earrings in my pierced ears, for a last touch of class, tied a black velvet ribbon around my neck" (Waters and Samuels 1992: 41–2). Waters' habit of dress utilized velvet material that signifies affluence and modesty to balance the stigma of red makeup. Evenly, W. C. Handy noted the dress of prostitutes in the red light district of Clarksdale, Mississippi around 1903. "These rouge-tinted girls, wearing silk stockings and short skirts, bobbing their soft hair and smoking cigarets in that prim era . . . were among the best patrons the orchestra had" (Handy 1969: 78).

In "Phoebe Snow (That Anthracite Woman)" (1925), the hue is pronounced through the mature subject's red suit of white polka dots, displayed as she saunters down the street. Mannerisms including the suspension of a purse with pinched fingers and an upward tilted head accentuate a prideful upper-class woman of repute. Her clothes are precisely coordinated from the crimson feather in her straw hat to the scarlet pumps on her feet. Relating inferiority and smallness of position, a black railcar attendant with bulging eyes and a clownish smile is shown gawking at the stylish spectacle. Here a matricentric view of the black family is symbolized, and so, with this structure differing from mainstream society, the relationship between the woman and man was unusual. The abnormality of roles was related in the 1923 sheet music cover of "Ignorant Mama, Papa's Gonna Educate You," where a towering man holding a bat threatened to correct his insolent woman dressed in red. Hence, a black woman's assertiveness and modernity is mitigated through "male aggression or violence" (hooks 1990: 76), then returning her to a subordinate gendered identity.

Last of the female representations is the temptress, rendered in a style where desire is stimulated through exhibition of skin and sexual zones. This flamboyance was apparent in the 1941 cover of "A Zoot Suit (For My Sunday Gal)," provided by the exaggeration of the woman's bust with a snug fitting dress and décolletage. More so, the boastful, wide smile declares that her contemporary attitude rejects the relegation of love to docility. This feminine type, tied to sexual objectification, is present in religious-themed song sheets, such as "Oh Death Where Is Thy Sting" (1920) and "Hold Me Parson, Hold Me, I Feel Religion Comin' On" (1910). In each illustration, women are projected as erotic stimulant through posture and dress. Cabaret style dresses raised about the thigh and hand-held wine glasses represent the toxin of indulgence in "Oh Death." Equally, the embrace by the female subject in "Hold Me Parson" is aberrant by means of a low-cut neckline, a hand on the minister's chest and a suggestive gaze. These instances of insubordination, akin to the images of the highbrow type, contradict the passive feminine role programmed in society, threatening male authority and religious tradition. In analysis of labeling women deviant, Schur concluded: "it is the perception of a threat, regardless of whether that perception is well founded, that triggers the efforts at systematic devaluation" (Schur 1983: 44). The portrayal of black feminine types in sheet music covers mirrored a hegemonic conflict in society concerning the culture, morality and familial relationships of African Americans.

Male representations: Servant, buffoon and sport

Resembling the black woman's portraiture, three male characters, including the servant, buffoon and sport, were given manifestation in the cover illustrations. Among the sheets examined, few representations were of a favorable nature with the notable ones occurring prior to the Civil War in 1850. These early nineteenth-century pictures were placid, thereafter during reconstruction morphing into literally darker reflections that satirized the humanity of black men. A modern assumption of the "representations of black men in mass media" by bell hooks (hooks 1990: 71) provides a rationale for this treatment one hundred years earlier, being that such "images appeal to white audiences, who simultaneously fear them and are fascinated by them."

From 1840 to 1880, published sheets took an acute awareness of the behavior, spirituality and relationships of slaves in the form of text and image. The earliest booklets of this time period were ornate with fancy lettering, simple vignettes and intricate detailing of garments and scenery (Viator 2011). "Techniques employed by nineteenth century fashion illustrators involved the massing of dark and grey areas by crosshatching or a series of small dot patterns" (Bigelow 1970: 292). Case in point, the covers with text only, including "When the Cotton's Gathered In" (1850), "Old Pine Tree" (1850), and "Where Am Massa" (1879), incorporate finely drawn botanical elements and graphic lines that emphasize the plantation themed titles. The black male was given primary focus over the scarce female characters that appeared in these illustrations. A softer tone and less caustic hand are evidenced in the depiction of the black man, substantiating his status as a non-threatening servant. Also known as Sambo, this distortion, often an older man, expressed contentment with a life of servitude (Pilgrim 2000). On May 1, 1894, the *Washington Post* printed a fictional story labeled "Our Only Blackman," which recited the arrival of a former slave into northern territory. The following excerpt matches the depiction of the contented black servant in early sheet music:

> Uncle Eph was perfectly black and had a mighty chest, though his legs were less powerful. His head was well shaped, his face was grave and his eyes unusually keen for a negro. He could read a little, Wesley said, and he was very religious. He was far from being a white man painted black, however. He seemed rather to be a very superior negro . . . the big black man was dazzled by his reception in the North. Everybody seemingly took a friend's interest in him.
>
> (Garland 1894)

In mid-century sheets, this treatment of the agreeable, obedient and banjo playing servant was abundant, placing emphasis upon entertainment skills opposed to black man as chattel. "Old Bob Ridley," "Sally Come Up," and "Fred Wilson's Clog Dances," all circa 1850, followed this formula with the addition of finely tuned dress. Although the clothes were slightly tattered in some artwork, great attention to style was apparent by bow ties, vests and pants of stripe and check patterns. Minstrel performances had been in documented existence since the 1800s, as a response some of these early covers, like "Sally Come Up" feature a restrained parody exclusive of blackened skin and subordinate body position. In the "Sally" illustration, the white man portraying the black man has elaborate dress hearkening to the Romantic period. The composition of a wide neck cloth, broad collared shirt, cropped vest, waist-length coat and awning striped pants, as well a theatrical pose, execute an influential fashion plate. This image equates the drawings in Godey's Lady's Book, where "the representations of the garments were extremely realistic, with only a small amount of exaggeration or proportional adjustments to give emphasis to unique details" (Bigelow 1970: 292–3). Thus, sheet music covers disseminated fashion in a similar mode as Godey's, in addition Peterson's and Harper's magazines.

By the 1880s, the moderate display of the servant yielded to bitter pictures of the black man as a buffoon. This alteration commenced at the end of the Civil War continuing through the failed attempt at reconstruction of the south. Newspaper articles accounting for southern lynchings revealed the opinion of black men in society. "Hunting For a Negro," "Vengeance Upon a Negro," "A Negro Burned Alive," and "Lynching in the Center of Town" published in the New York Times and the Washington Post during the late 1800s positioned a vicious attitude that sheet covers would adopt. The barrage of headlines following the ratification of the 13th, 14th and 15th Amendments promoted a racist belief that black men were a threat to white authority, equally a danger to white women; thereby the legislative optimism from the abolishment of slavery, the recognition as United States citizens and the right to vote was severely damaged. "If I Was What I Ain't, Instead of What I Is" (1922) signified the image of the black man as an ineffectual person. In the artwork, two blackface versions of the man are as follows: the slothful, poorly dressed individual and the happy, stylishly clothed male. The song text and layout of the illustration imply that the languid character desires to be the refined urban gentleman. Fashionable details represent class division including top hat, tuxedo and corsage contrasted with suspenders, patched trousers and felt hat of the rural type. Likewise, an emphasis of tasteful dress merged with ill-mannered behavior epitomizes "That's What Makes a Wild Cat Wild" (1920). In the artwork, six members of a jazz band perform riotously, from blowing the saxophone on the top of a piano to trumpet playing on floor boards. The improvisation of music and chaos of the jam session is lampooned by domestic cats running for safety. Even with facial stereotypes, high fashion is employed as recognition of the formal traits of black jazz musicians that had been ritual for two decades. The mature players adorn white tie dress including black tailcoats, white waistcoats and white spats.

Fifty years earlier, a similar treatment of the buffoon identity was published on sheet covers. Sheets including "When the Band Played" (1868) and "Shew Fly" (1869) exercise distorted facial qualities and comedic postures that eliminate the subjects' finesse. Awkwardly performed actions of drumming and waving away an insect are identifiable in the scenes. Formal dress attributes worn by the black men consist of bow ties, dress slippers, snug-legged trousers and claw hammer coats that are waist level in the front cutting to tails in the back. This close attention to the dandy details of the Romantic period designates an African American affinity for style and good appearance. However, the identification is mocked by way of ill-fitting footwear, patched garments and above the ankle trousers. By the 1850s, long trousers that broke over the shoe at the instep were established fashion for gentleman seeking to be less flamboyant (Bigelow 1970: 194). The grotesque exhibitionism of the buffoon type through behavior and sartorial dress endorsed non-conformity in society, reduction of masculinity and established an otherness of the black male. An entertainment review in the *New York Times* confirmed the existence of this approach:

A blackened face, a ragged coat thrown off the shoulder, and a pair of elaborately patched trousers, with a shocking bad hat, first introduced Ethiopian minstrelsy to a New York public . . . the thing took at first, though it was voted low, and it continued to take and to be low for some time.

(*New York Times* 1859)

Last, narcissistic tendencies of the black male received great attention in the third classification of sport. Unsuccessful endeavors at fashion and clumsy manners were omitted in these illustrations that project a vain, unruffled and cultivated man. In analysis of counter-hegemony where opposition to being dominated by a group was evidenced, bell hooks related an outcome among contemporary black men, that being "manifestations of cool as aesthetic style and as subversive response to adversity" (hooks 1990: 180). The sport character personified this suave resistance, even though traits of caricature were present. As with "Sweet Henry, The Pride of Tennessee" (1923), the artist with subtlety colors the lips red and darkens the skin curbing the extreme overstatement of blackface that was expressed in "Struttin' Jim," of the same year. The sort is given vernacular handling in the cover of "Crappy Dan De Spo'tin' Man" (1890). In addition, a measure of vice is presented with dice fixed on seven (Abbott and Seroff 2007: 18). Walking canes, top hats, corsages, jeweled stickpins and gloves are accessories that embellish the sport type. Further, a lit cigar with gently rising smoke in "Sweet Henry" and "Crappy Dan" calls attention to a smooth and audacious man. In *Louis Armstrong's New Orleans*, Brothers identified this bold clothing and flashy display in the early jazz setting. He asserted that this facade, most associated with the hustler, demonstrated a brushoff of tradition (Brothers 2007: 200).

Far from original, this identity was produced on Broadway in 1902 by the act of Bert Williams and George Walker, black vaudevillian performers. "Walker was the dandy, the sporting Negro, dressed a little too high, spending generously whatever he was able to borrow or filch" (Suthern 1989: 81). Also, traits of the flashy sport were produced among white minstrel performers in the 1830s that displayed "peacock habits" of eighteenth-century men's dress on black characters. On August 25, 1895, the *Washington Post* narrated the theatrical style of Thomas Dartmouth Rice considered the "father of negro minstrelsy:"

> The street attire of this jolly fellow was most picturesque and eccentric. His costume of bright plaid trousers, corn satin waistcoat, and blue "claw-hammer," topped off with shining silken beaver was at first a startling, but soon a very familiar, sight in the respective towns in which he played. His display of jewels was most ridiculous. In the folds of his cravat would nestle a cluster pin, containing eight or ten costly gems . . . his fingers were ever as beringed as possible, and he invariably carried a huge cane, the gold top of which was studded with rubies, sapphires, and emeralds.
>
> (Quinn 1895)

Rice was credited with the introduction of the "dandy darkey" character on stage, where lavish clothing distinguished the character from the servant type. Although Rice limited his performance to the feeble Jim Crow slave, he incorporated the "fancy coon" that he fashioned into the minstrel program. Scholars have set forth the dress motives of attraction and approval that have existed throughout time, taking on varied expression in cultures and histories (Coolidge 1912: 137, Flügel 1950: 15, Hurlock 1929: 26). Thus, the fundamental practice of clothing display, self-promotion and dress distinction were social norms painted with grotesque qualities and ridiculed on black male bodies.

Conclusion

Spanning a hundred years, the reflection of history, culture and style was evidenced in American published sheet music. Products of these representations were sartorial details, social ideology and gendered identities witnessed from the time of slavery through the Second World War. Here, the advancement of African American humanity experienced great turmoil coinciding with a formulated threat by the white majority due in part to black influence on mainstream culture. In account of this volatility, Hall asserted that "cultural struggle arises in its sharpest form just at the point where different, opposed traditions meet, intersect" (Hall 2011: 78). Emphatically, this crossroad emerged when ragtime music was born and flourished alongside mass lynchings, Jim Crow laws and minstrel entertainment. The black struggle for race pride, modernity and equality was communicated in sheet illustrations with hostile displays of white hegemony.

The salient images of African Americans appearing in covered sheets seized dress, posture and behavior to create and defy stereotypes of minorities and women through scenes of conformity and insubordination. These images were the impetus of music promotion, signifying on a single page the comedic, dramatic, festive and tragic sentiment of the lyrics. Fundamental to this communication was the interpretation of fashion and accessories to express inferiority and superiority of African Americans in society.

6

SUBVERSIVE REPRESENTATION: VERNACULAR, DRESS AND MORALITY

Radical notions of jazz

Early jazz, including ragtime and blues, found fruition at a time of social, political and economic change in America when the turbulent interfaces between blacks and whites were intensifying. W. E. B. Du Bois articulated this reality in 1903:

> Through the pressure of the money-makers, the Negro is in danger of being reduced to semi-slavery, especially in the country districts; the workingmen, and those of the educated who fear the Negro, have united to disfranchise him, and some have urged his deportation; while the passions of the ignorant are easily aroused to lynch and abuse any black man.
>
> (Du Bois 2010: 39)

Among African Americans, the pursuit of an improved status received impetus from the church, civil rights activists, elite societies, academic institutions and the arts. Influential black leaders, like Mary Church Terrell, championed race pride and "right principles of living" while condemning immorality, especially amid the youth (Terrell 1897). In this conviction, refined art and class were least associated with ragtime and its companion dance, the cakewalk. Du Bois warned of the contamination of Negro spirituals made into popular entertainment as old time melodies. "Caricature has sought again to spoil the beauty of the music, and has filled the air with many debased melodies which vulgar ears scarce know from the real" (Du Bois 2010: 152).

Black aristocrats of the late 1800s rejected ragtime and plantation songs by linking their musical penchants to "Wagner, Mozart, or Coleridge-Taylor" (Gatewood 1990: 192). Their yearning to be distant from Negro music received justification through biased commentaries in leading newspapers. On May 3, 1903, the *New York Times* published a review of a black choral society's performance of "Hiawatha," a classical piece composed by Coleridge-Taylor. "It is notable that the only African relation of this work is the paternity of the composer. The work itself shows no trace of Africanism, but is marked with the characteristics of modern music as written by an educated cosmopolitan musician" (*New York Times* 1903). Even with the practice of conventional compositions, black performers were scrutinized for possessing Negro qualities. Here, a declaration from the same *Times* article, "although the soprano was herself almost white, her voice had the peculiar African metallic quality already alluded to" (*New York Times* 1903). A cynical assessment was planted in white and black society, dependent upon beliefs of inferiority, garishness and vulgarity with references to antebellum songs and ragtime. Such hostility of this syncopated sound was evidenced among white society, as printed in the *Washington Post* on September 30, 1900.

> The first action to be taken . . . was one of disapproval against rag-time music and rag-time dancing . . . The hopping which is now done in the ballroom is, they say, not at all keeping with good taste. There are none of the graceful, easy motions of the waltz, none of the gliding, sweeping motions of the old two-step in the popular dance step of to-day.
>
> (*Washington Post* 1900)

Key to the denigration of ragtime was the removal of artistic qualities that signified creativity, admiration and authenticity as a type of music.

A subversive attitude towards early jazz was born and thrived until the 1950s, steeped in recollections of and affiliations with slavery, plantations, minstrel blackface and immorality. The early demoralization of music with African American origin occurred by way of power institutions including the church, media, entertainment industry and social groups. In *Subculture*, Hebdige argued that "violations of the authorized codes through which the social world is organized and experienced have considerable power to provoke and disturb" (Hebdige 2009: 91). The manifestation of a distinctly Negro aesthetic was judged to be deviant in post-Civil War America, where blacks were regarded as inferior to whites.

Representations of jazz surfaced in the form of spoken word, written word and visual image, primarily generated by performers or associates of jazz style. An emphasis of dress and behavior registered in the analysis of these products. As societal consumption took place, the elements were perceived as artistic or rebellious according to group meanings and traditions. In support of this idea, Dewey's implication of the merger of creative work and public sentiment is appropriate: "works of art once brought into existence are the most compelling of the means of communication by which emotions are stirred and opinions formed" (Dewey 1989: 16).

Spoken word of blues singers

The classic blues that prospered during the 1920s launched many female stars including Mamie Smith, Ma Rainey, Bessie Smith and Alberta Hunter, who earned significant salaries and contributed to a jazz aesthetic. On December 19, 1920, the *Washington Post* certified the influence of Mamie Smith, the first recorded blues singer:

> The Howard Theater next week will present Mamie Smith, the only colored girl who sings for phonograph records. She is the star for one of the largest concerns in the United States and the highest paid singer the firm employs. Her income next year will be close to $15,000 . . . it is said that she has been packing theaters to the doors wherever she appears.
>
> (*Washington Post* 1920)

Song lyrics expressed the difficulties of life, work and love, at the same time formulating an assertive femininity that departed from the mammy identity. To enhance their stage performances, blues singers wore elaborate ensembles that challenged older traditions and built magnitude over the men. The chemise frock was essential dress with its beading and fringed hemline accessorized with pearl strands, feathers, and elaborate headwear. Case in point, the following description of Bessie Smith during a 1923 promotional tour:

> She wore a plain dress with beaded fringes, a Spanish shawl loosely draped around her shoulders, a simple necklace, a skullcap covered with beads and pearls, and a wig of shiny black hair that ran down to her shoulders.
>
> (Albertson 2003: 42)

Particularly among the southern crowds the extravagant clothing and decorated sets provided uplift from poverty, inequality and Jim Crow rule.

Double entendre was utilized to posit sex in early blues recordings, matched by a comparable liberation in attitude, behavior and status among women. Songs with ambiguous connotations included "My Man Rocks Me (With One Steady Roll)" (1923), "You Can't Do What My Last Man Did" (1923), "I'm Wild About That Thing" (1929), and "Need a Little Sugar in My Bowl" (1931). In these lyrics, the practice of feminine sensuality transformed from primness to a frank acknowledgment of intimate relationships and metaphors for male genitalia. Lucille Bogan, designated Bessie Jackson by the American Record Corporation, recorded blues songs that are celebrated for being morally objectionable and rare examples of "early-recorded erotica" (Spottswood 2002). Although the lyrics are sexually explicit using profanity, the titles retain hidden codes such as "Till the Cows Come Home" (1933), "Shave 'Em Dry" (1933), and "Skin Game Blues" (1935). Bogan did not garner the fame or wealth of Smith or Rainey, possibly due to the narrow channels of distribution for lewd recordings and their creation following the 1920s blues enthusiasm.

Less shocking language was employed in promotional posters for Bessie Smith, where text advertised "a brown beauty chorus that won't behave" and "hip ha hip ha girls, men here is a chance for a good wife" (Albertson 2003: 16). Bechet suggested the strict entertainment value of these "dirty" lyrics that balanced out sorrowful songs about rural life, financial hardships and racism. "Lots of them, they're exhibition like, they're for show – a novelty to attract attention" (Bechet 2002: 54).

The ostentatious quality was palpable in live performance, as recollected by Maud Smith Faggins, Smith's former sister-in-law, to Chris Albertson. She revealed the audiences' reaction to Smith as "people screaming with delight as she accompanied her vocal tales with suggestive movements and subtle dance steps" (Albertson 2003: 42). At this occasion, melody, words and image stimulated feeling in the audience, embodying their happiness, pain and jubilee. Barthes identified this meeting of language and music as the "grain of the voice" (Barthes 1978: 181) where signification is achieved. More so, he asserted that "the 'grain' is the body in the voice as it sings, the hand as it writes, the limb as it performs" (Barthes 1978: 188). Within an environment of cultural and feminine boundaries, the take it or leave it mind-set of blues singers bred a calculated response. Here, an explanation of the sad, raucous music in the New York Times on September 26, 1926: "this lusty concoction of contemporary music, a blend of ragtime, jazz and the blues, reflects with blaring color and barbaric fidelity the gay, absurd and giddy world . . . and tribulations to which America's amazing population is heir" (Noble 1926). The daring style of the female blues supplied white opponents with material to define jazz as subversive and an "agency of the devil" (New York Times 1926b). For African American obstructionists, the music endangered social equality often at the risk of cultural assimilation.

Jazz themes in literature

A bounty of novels published during the era embraced jazz as a key component of their narrations where the genre was colorfully transcribed to intensify the plot. These writers were eyewitnesses to the era adding authentic meaning in their own idiom (Figure 6.1).

Figure 6.1 Count Basie and Richard Wright (r), author of *Native Son*, at recording session posit the intersection of jazz and literature, 1940. © Bettmann/ CORBIS

Hall defined this form of representation as an intentional approach, where the author "imposes his or her unique meaning on the world" (Hall 2012: 25). Take, for example, Claude McKay's description of a brownstone party in *Home to Harlem*: "a phonograph was grinding out a 'blues,' and some couples were dancing, thick as maggots in a vat of sweet liquor, and as wriggling" (McKay 1987: 14). McKay accentuated the eroticism of the music through connotations of bodies rubbing and twisting together, as well the reference to alcohol. An attempt to attach vulgarity received deflection from the writer's genius supported by a *New York Times* review on March 11, 1928. "Here is a book that is beaten through with the rhythm of life that is a jazz rhythm . . . it is lyric, a cry from the heart" (Chamberlain 1928).

While McKay reinforced the visceral human response of blues, Carl Van Vechten professed "exploitation of the exotic" (Chamberlain 1928) by infusing jazz rhythm into clothing. The following depicts a Negro socialite at a Harlem charity ball in his provocative 1926 novel *Nigger Heaven*:

> A robe of turquoise-blue satin clung to her exquisite body, brought out in relief every curve. The dress was cut so low in front that the little depression between her firm, round breasts was plainly visible. Her golden-brown back was entirely nude to the waist. The dress was circled with wide bands of green and black sequins, designed to resemble the fur of the leopard.
>
> (Van Vechten 2000: 163)

Van Vechten's text related anatomy, nudity and untamed fashion in the presence of a jazz orchestra playing a composition of "Sweet and Low Down." These elements proposed dress motives, including the pursuit of attention, the display of wealth and the challenge to modesty that have been issued by scholars (Flügel 1950; Hurlock 1929). Resembling the highbrow identity discussed in Chapter 5, the bareness applied in this narration suggested a narcissistic quality of the woman, manifested by "the tendency to admire one's own body and display it to others, so that these others can share in the admiration" (Flügel 1950: 86). The insertion of the song title with a shameful and tempting nature added to the subversion of jazz style. In 1926, the *New York Times* skillfully declared, "blatant, tender, sardonic, sentimental, poignant or pathetic, this musical medium of modern life has attained the proportions of a phenomenon worth attention" (Noble 1926).

In *Infants of the Spring*, Wallace Thurman demonstrated the aesthetic conflict of jazz in society with a character whose preference for classical compositions was scorned. "He must, it seemed, capitulate, although in his opinion there was a sufficient number of darkies already shaming contemporary Negroes by singing these barbarous, moaning shouts and too simple melodies" (Thurman 1992: 110). Thurman situated music within the African American effort seeking expanded definitions of culture and liberties during the Harlem Renaissance. Although the aforementioned character desired separation from spirituals and blues, Van Vechten's protagonist advocated the art. "To be sure, she, too, felt this African beat — it completely aroused her emotionally . . . this love of drums, of exciting rhythms, this naïve delight in glowing colour" (Van Vechten 2000: 89). Both authors demonstrated a dialect of jazz that polarized society by means of damaging adjectives and encouraging expressions.

Critical to the insurgency in jazz were signifiers of culture, dress and ideology. Barthes, in reference to the science of signs from Ferdinand de Saussure, asserted that "objects, images and patterns of behaviour can signify" (Barthes 1973: 10) with the outcome being "a mental representation" (Barthes 1973: 42). In the literary examples, jazz was contextualized as sexually, artistically and culturally rebellious juxtaposed to mainstream tradition. These writers were protesting the everyday reality through fictional storytelling that possessed qualities of difference and goals of transformation. In reasoning the revolution within the Jazz Age, Hurlock declared that "traditions and customs are swept away without the slightest feeling of remorse" (Hurlock 1929: 62). Central to the resentment towards jazz aesthetics was its opposition to black subordination and racial segregation. Here, Thurman's depiction of a rent party that challenged societal code:

> The lights in the basement had been dimmed, and the reveling dancers cast grotesque shadows on the heavily tapestried walls. Color lines had been completely eradicated. Whites and blacks clung passionately together as if trying to effect a permanent merger. Liquor, jazz music, and close physical contact had achieved what decades of propaganda had advocated with little success.
>
> (Thurman 1992: 186)

Visual image in films

In the form of moving image, film directors contributed to an abrasive vision of jazz through an improper partnership of music and vice. The latter term, generally suggestive of immorality or bad behavior, is linked with criminal activities including prostitution, gambling, and drugs. Starting in the 1920s, film themes of prostitution and gambling were presented alongside the genre. Jazz historians highlighted this fallacy. For instance, Gioia argued a true narrative was complicated by "the mythification of the role of jazz in New Orleans bordellos" (Gioia 1998: 31). The conflation of jazz and vice discarded a rich history of the Congo Square, African sacred tradition and a century of evolution. Bechet disputed the link with brothels. "The musicianers would go to those houses just whenever they didn't have a regular engagement . . . no party or picnic or ball to play at" (Bechet 2002: 53). The business of vice relegated an entertainment venue to a "low-down category" imparted Ethel Waters in recollection of a Harlem jazz spot circa 1925. "For entertainers, the last stop on the way down in show business was Edmond's Cellar . . . Edmond's drew the sporting men, the hookers, and other assorted underworld characters" (Waters and Samuels 1992: 124). Cinematic representations merged jazz and undesirable habits in lively accounts, where characters surrendered their morals even as religious salvation was proffered.

Produced by Metro-Goldwyn-Mayer with an all-black cast, *Hallelujah!* (1929) features Nina Mae McKinney as Chick, a character consumed with money, seduction and good times. Chick's manner coerces the protagonist, Zeke, away from his ministry and a promising marriage. By way of dress and behavior, the film narrated a transformation of Chick from vamp to reformed lady, returning again to a deceptive woman. Standards of personal conduct and decency have expression in manner of dress. "Morality, that close companion to religion, shows its presence or absence in the life of the nation through dress" (Hurlock 1929: 220). In two primary scenes with the component of jazz, Chick flaunts clothing that symbolizes a departure from modesty. The first display situated in a gambling den presents Chick dressed in a tight fitting, above the knee chemise with long fringe dangling from the waist and shoulders. Plentiful bracelets and necklaces signify excess matched by a dice appliqué with the sum of seven over her bust, perhaps symbolizing a lucky gamble. Here, exhibitionism is heightened by her performance of "Shuffle Along" accented with the black bottom and cakewalk dances that dispense body twisting.

In the final act of the film, Chick wears a plain, dark satin sheath adorned with a white heart silhouette over her left breast. The conservative dress, paired with a few bracelets and dark stockings, is an attempt to reflect her atonement. Also demonstrating piety is Chick's mournful delivery of "Saint Louis Blues." Color significations in clothing are notable by the high contrast of the white heart and the formal black dress. Flügel accounted for the way color can mean in society with a wearer operating it for a desired impression: "the universal connection of black with seriousness and white with innocence and moral purity, as distinct from the spectral colours . . . which signify a freer play of emotions" (Flügel 1950: 75–6). Chick's false redemption through clothing and behavior is nullified when she tries to skip town with her lover, subsequently meeting her death in a buggy accident.

The fashion shift of the late 1920s including longer skirts altered the guise of Chick from a carefree product of the flapper era to an insubordinate temptress. In 1927, the *New York Times* declared this new sensibility in "jazz dresses" that were designed with regular waistlines and bouffant skirts. "It is the return of genuine feminine charm, so long out of fashion!" (*New York Times* 1927). Milbank corroborated this style and attitude modification among women that took hold. "Aggressive, reckless behavior, like that which has caused stock market speculation to go awry, waned, and women stopped protesting the more modest, or conservative, silhouette and began looking more demure" (Milbank 1989: 86). In *Hallelujah!*, the occurrences of gambling and violence, the boisterous playing of syncopated music, the glitzy dress and the wild exhibition of dancing programmed the relation between jazz and indecency.

Continuing this cinematic plot was the release of *Rain* (1932) by United Artists, where the female lead, Sadie Thompson, juggles involvement with prostitution and a path to salvation. In a pivotal scene, Sadie, played by Joan Crawford, reveals through dress and behavior her deceit at conversion (Figure 6.2).

Visual attributes including ripped fish net stockings, numerous bracelets, heavy makeup and soiled pumps demonstrate a departure from the virtuous

JOAN CRAWFORD

Figure 6.2 Joan Crawford (as sassy Sadie Thompson) dressed in her provocative costume for *Rain*, 1932. © Bettmann/CORBIS

alter ego. A white shiny belt of broad width functions as a dazzling accessory. The extreme proportion of the band constricts Sadie's waist, partitioning the body into an elongated wasp silhouette, signifying boldness and intimidation. Belts on dresses and suits were trending in the 1930s, giving women "a little more leeway in adjusting" the garment to their shape (Milbank 1989: 102). In the film segment, a phonograph grinding out a slow and arousing version of "Saint Louis Blues" accentuates the sinful transformation, as well Sadie's sassy manner of twitching and dragging on a cigarette. Although the recording was non-vocal, the lyrics of Handy's 1914 composition described a woman jilted by her man and grieving in the blues. The song was positioned to intimate indecent behavior, in similar fashion to its placement in *Hallelujah!* when the female character walked out on her man.

A third film, *Cabin in the Sky* (1943), illustrated the waywardness of jazz employing a fast woman, gambling and violence to bait the male lead from a righteous way of living. The director, Vincente Minnelli, situated the temptation in a saloon, where the Duke Ellington Orchestra entertained. Sweet Georgia Brown, wearing a midriff top, high-slit satin skirt and lace undergarments, seduces Little Joe Jackson from his pious wife, Petunia. A battle for moral principles is demonstrated with agents of heaven and hell inducing the conduct of Brown and Jackson. The movie's climax occurs when Jackson upon winning the sweepstakes leaves his wife and spoils Brown with wealth. This outcome is exhibited in the nightclub where lavish dress and unruly behavior signify conspicuous consumption, elevated class status and sexual desire. Adorned in glittery jewels, ostrich feather wrap and a slinky cocktail dress, Brown wields these artifacts to entice the crowd, triggering a female admirer to declare that Georgia's dress "will be ahead of fashion a hundred years from today" (Minnelli 1943). Brown's sultry appearance and behavior are praised in the jovial surroundings of Jim Henry's Paradise. Men in zoot suits, women in flirty dresses and the gyrations of bodies to jazz melodies embellish the nightclub. Hurlock noted that "morality . . . is a variable thing, dependent upon the time and the people among whom this ideal has originated" (Hurlock 1929: 220–1). Fashions of the 1940s had departed significantly from the turn of the century dress with its neck to ankle coverage and refined decorations; thus this modern sensibility was not pure insurrection of decency but an element of shifting social ideals. At the conclusion of the film, Jackson learns that happiness, faith and respectability are found at home with his wife opposed to the gambling den and dance hall.

Consistent storylines around morality were evident in race films that featured black casts and were marketed to black theaters. These movies produced in great quantities between 1920 and 1950 allowed expanded involvement for blacks with content written, produced and directed by African Americans. Frequently narratives established conflict between jazz amusement and faith, also introducing nefarious men who advanced female exploitation, violence and blackmail. In agreement with Hollywood films, goodness was victorious in these tales indicative of the religious authority within the black community. Du Bois foretold of this ethical battle to be waged as blacks migrated from the south to northern cities. Families would have exposure to greater opportunity, equally access to temptation in the absence of provincial traditions and bonds. "Some sink, some rise. The criminal and the sensualist leave the church for the gambling-hell and the brothel" (Du Bois 2010: 123). Likewise, black cinema projected a cynical view of the industrial city with a focus on organized crime, henchmen and fast women. The emphasis of jazz in these films demonstrated its popularity and cultural influence in the community. Although the music and dance thrived in

Philadelphia, Detroit, Chicago and Kansas City, race films exploited Harlem as the prominent setting for story conflict.

Two leading directors of black cinema were Oscar Micheaux and Spencer Williams, who operated their own film companies that produced storylines around morality. In *Lying Lips* (1939) from Micheaux, the protagonist, a female cabaret performer, resists the pressure by club management for her service with entertaining men. The character is objectified in the film by reducing her talent and attractive appearance to a means for making money. When Elsie refuses these demands, she is labeled as "too high hat," which parallels the feminine type of highbrow as discussed in Chapter 5. Hence, the female is deemed narcissistic, uppity and insubordinate to male authority. The distortion of jazz continues with the assertion that customers consider "themselves slumming" when mixing in the music hall. Again, pointed language is instrumental in signifying subversion via references to paid acts of pleasure, haughtiness and low standards of amusement.

Spiritual context was applied in *The Blood of Jesus* (1941) from Williams, who employed representatives of heaven and hell to battle for a woman's soul. In the film, traits of jazz were exercised to steer the protagonist's soul from salvation. Satan's helper aims to corrupt Martha Jackson by employing an elaborate gown, flashy shoes and nightclub exposure. Here, clothing serves as a "visual metaphor for identity" (Davis 1994: 25) associated with good times and self-display. In a climactic scene, Jackson, finding no enjoyment in the vile den of the urban nightclub, flees the city and is confronted by a road post pointing "To Hell" and "To Zion." A rowdy group engaged in drinking, gambling, fighting and jazz delight represents purgatory, while individuals of a serene nature denote rapture. Similar moral narratives were transmitted in *Sunday Sinners* (1940) and *Go Down, Death* (1944) that present religious institutions in conflict with juke joints and their undesirables. Hall expressed this process of meaning as "the 'system' by which all sorts of objects, people and events are correlated with a set of concepts or mental representations which we carry in our heads" (Hall 2012: 17). The negative reflection of jazz that prospered in white and black cinema was sustained by religious values. In analysis of the Negro church, Du Bois emphasized the potency of its ideology: "Depravity, Sin, Redemption, Heaven, Hell, and Damnation are preached twice a Sunday after the crops are laid by; and few indeed of the community have the hardihood to withstand conversion" (Du Bois 2010: 117).

Even with a skewed identity, jazz remained an influential genre throughout the 1940s due to its visceral emotion and origins in liberating a marginalized culture, too being a voice for young people fenced in a segregated society. Aesthetics of jazz were functional in these pictures by filling space between dramatic scenes and mimicking vibrant entertainment that moviegoers would experience in their communities. Hence, its placement in film had a motive of promotion and profit.

The portrayal of jazz as corruptor of morals had strong visual appeal; however its legitimacy as a gene of indecency eventually faded. Ambivalences surrounding jazz and morality were complex taking into account views of race, class and gender, more so the tensions within these divisions.

Conclusion

Directors, costume designers, actors and musicians created powerful visuals that merged jazz and vice with inflated struggles of good and evil. The dress and ornamentation in these films mocked gentility with unrestricted movement, disrupted space through noise and light reflection and challenged morality in the exhibition of bare skin. Jazz music, in cultivation since the late 1800s, served to influence, not govern, this aesthetic change. Hurlock interpreted the style transformation as an escapism factor that shaped the 1920s zeitgeist:

> Almost immediately women's dress became very exaggerated to compensate for the enforced simplicity of war time. With jazz dances and jazz music came jazz clothing. Very likely one reason for the vogue of all of these was the widespread desire to keep from remembering and thinking . . . extremes verging on immodesty made their appearance among the women of social classes which formerly had been the most conservative.
>
> (Hurlock 1929: 219–20)

Jazz influenced popular culture, signaling a new, youthful spirit that defied outdated traditions. Consequently it was vilified through mythical and debasing representations from institutional powers. Signifiers of provocative dress, vice, alcohol consumption and violence characterized jazz culture as evil, untamed and immoral. However, within a decade, the genre's style eclipsed this subversive image through elite qualities and a maturing demographic. Hebdige, in consideration of this cycle noted: "from opposition to defusion, from resistance to incorporation encloses each successive subculture" (Hebdige 2009: 100). The caustic attitude towards jazz was not static. Media and community institutions discovered more youthful forms of music, namely "rhythm and blues" and "rock and roll" to criticize; while the transformed aesthetics of jazz including melancholy, remoteness and erudition were exposed in films like *Young Man with a Horn* (1950), *Paris Blues* (1961) and *A Man Called Adam* (1966).

7

NARCOTICS AND JAZZ: A FASHIONABLE ADDICTION

From the early days of legalized marijuana to the heroin years of bebop, drug use was an obtrusive companion of jazz performance. The addictive power of romance and reasonably illegal substances found intimation in popular song titles of the 1940s, such as "What a Little Moonlight Can Do," "I Got it Bad and That Ain't Good," and "Groovin' High." As cited in Chapter 1, the pursuit of musical brilliance and stylish image aimed to liberate artists from social and political margins. Jeopardizing such advances was the possession and consumption of drugs by Billie Holiday, Charlie Parker, Anita O'Day and Chet Baker to name a few. Refined dress and appearance were employed as resistance to narcotic penalty and stereotypes associated with being a junkie, one addicted to drugs.

Narcotic effect

There has been a narrative of narcotics in American popular culture. Narcotics are one of the five classes of drugs regulated by the Controlled Substances Act (CSA) in the United States. Classified as a Schedule I substance under the CSA, 21 U.S.C. § 812, heroin has "a high potential for abuse, no currently accepted medical use in treatment in the United States, and a lack of accepted safety for use under medical supervision" (Drug Enforcement Administration 2012a). The consumption of heroin was shrouded by users and demonized by the law. Jazz performers, particularly of the modern school, navigated a decade of heroin popularity during the 1940s bebop and 1950s cool jazz movements (Spencer 2002: 124). "There was a lot of dope around the music scene and a lot of musicians were deep into drugs, especially heroin," asserted Miles Davis (Davis and Troupe 2011: 129) in his autobiography. Media headlines named and shamed. In 1954, *Variety* declared "Federal Agents Arrest Anita O'Day," and the *Philadelphia Tribune* announced on their front page "Lady Cop Exposes Billie Holiday's Dope Cache" (1956a). O'Day described the enduring label: "Once you have the reputation of being an addict, it's hard to shake" (O'Day and Eells 1989: 124). Equally, the surveillance targeted male performers, including Gerry Mulligan and Chet Baker. On April 15, 1953, the *Los Angeles Times* reported "Night Spot Musicians Taken in Dope Roundup" with the twenty-six year old Mulligan's quote of innocence: "But when I do use it I get it when somebody gives it to me. I never buy the stuff" (*Los Angeles Times* 1953b).

Those convicted of drug offences were subject to supervision, which threatened their ability to perform. In the *Washington Post*, Gene Krupa was compelled to issue "a personal campaign against marijuana smoking" (*Washington Post* 1949), after his band members were arrested for possession of narcotics. Krupa faced scrutinizing publicity, since his jail time for a marijuana charge. After his orchestra's ban from a Detroit dancehall, he affirmed "that marijuana or any drug can ruin a musician" (*Washington Post* 1949). A second guilty plea for possession and use of narcotics forced a judge to admonish Billie Holiday. "It is a shame that such a talented singer as you had to become involved in a habit that can result only in heartbreak" (*Philadelphia Tribune* 1956a). The early regulation of heroin in the United States created a stigma that was intensified by the legal system and media coverage. Artists utilized visual style and the admiring qualities of formal dress to thwart heroin association. Regarding the adoption of fame and prestige as protection, Hurlock postulated: "when a man or woman has reached 'stardom,' the world opens its doors to them in much the same way it would have to high-ranking nobility" (Hurlock 1929: 115).

Demonizing drug addiction

In 1949, following confiscation of narcotics on airplanes and ocean liners, the *New York Times* declared "Seizures Reach Peak in Heroin and Cocaine" (*New York Times* 1949c). This headline summarized the outcome of governmental laws that commenced at the start of the century. The Smoking Opium Exclusion Act of 1909, the Heroin Act of 1924 and the Marihuana Tax Act of 1937 were instrumental in curtailing drug practice in the United States (Keel 2010). These laws controlled or banned the manufacture, distribution and use of specific substances. Prior to the 1900s, a less regulated period demonstrated the circulation of opium and cocaine with little federal oversight. These substances were included in patent medicines that offered cures for numerous ailments. Around 1899, Bayer, a German pharmaceutical company, manufactured diacetylmorphine and sold it under the brand name heroin (Askwith 1998). Heroin was advertised to relieve and sedate coughs in Bayer product materials. This benefit came from the chemical's ability to depress the respiratory system (Moraes 2000: 6). It is acknowledged that consumers were not fully educated on the "potentially addictive and deadly ingredients" contained in these formulas

(Smithsonian 2010). The regulation of narcotics and the restriction of certain substances for medical purposes contributed to a negative association of heroin by designating it harmful.

Societal fear around substance addiction was strongly contextualized by President Franklin D. Roosevelt in the 1930s. Warning of America's crime problem that was leading to social disorder, Roosevelt explicitly commented on weak laws that were unable to impede the trafficking of illegal drugs (*New York Times* 1934). This danger was emphasized to organize state support for uniform anti-narcotic legislation. Roosevelt invoked the words "narcotic drug evil" (*New York Times* 1935). The letter read over the radio described a nation that was not being fully protected from the illegal drug trade. Roosevelt argued that legislative support would prevent the nation's "ravage" from narcotic drugs. In 1936, the film release of *Reefer Madness* directed by Louis Gasnier heightened the drug peril, equating marijuana to "a violent narcotic, an unspeakable scourge." Heroin was mentioned in the propaganda-loaded introduction as one of the drug menaces. These occurrences added to the nervous tone of narcotic discourse in America.

Even with legislative restrictions, by the late 1940s, heroin had become a drug of choice with a number of modern jazz performers. Davis (Figure 7.1) recalled in

Figure 7.1 Miles Davis, Roy Haynes and Charlie Parker in wide lapel suits at Birdland, New York, 1952. © Marcel Fleiss/Cynthia Sesso, CTSIMAGES

his memoir, "all of us, started to get heavily into heroin around the same time" (Davis and Troupe 2011: 129).

Music venues, style of dress and exclusive slang fortified the habit of drugs. "Works" was a nickname for needles and tie-offs; likewise "pop" and "hit" intimated the practice of raising blood vessels for injection (Davis and Troupe 2011: 132). Davis confessed that this period was the start of his "drift" from self-discipline and control of his life (Davis and Troupe 2011: 129). The culmination of labeling drugs "evil" and aggressive enforcement resulted in the arrest and confinement of several jazz artists. In 1947, Holiday served a year's sentence in prison after pleading guilty to receiving and concealing a narcotic drug. Reports released by the Federal Bureau of Investigation illustrated the incessant surveillance that was placed upon jazz performers. For example, this teletype letter addressed to Inspector John Mohr from Harry Kimball, special agent in charge of the San Francisco FBI office:

> The source states that because of the importance of Holiday it has been the policy of his bureau to discredit individuals of this caliber using narcotics. Because of their notoriety it offered excuses to minor users. Source states that raid was a legitimate raid based on above and that claimed quote frame up unquote was as much for publicity purposes as it was to avert the suspicion of guilt from her inasmuch as she was caught in possession of the makeshift pipe.
> (Federal Bureau of Investigation 1949)

Such haste to find narcotics and arrest users negatively impacted the reputations of performers. Davis cited the reason for his aloofness during his years of addiction: "when I was a drug addict, the club owners had treated me like I was dirt and so had the critics" (Davis and Troupe 2011: 180). This declaration proposed that a change in behavior, including isolation from others, was a response to being associated with narcotics. A decade earlier, Louis Armstrong recalled being busted by detectives outside the Cotton Club in Culver City. Armstrong intimated that the arrest for smoking reefers was achieved through a ruse (Armstrong 1999: 116). The date of 1930 placed the event prior to the banning of marijuana. Unlike other musicians, Armstrong did not use heavier drugs like cocaine or heroin that he considered "unGodly" (Armstrong 1999: 114). The assault on narcotics and the demonization of addicts planted an ideology that drugs were evil and parasitic, prompting a reaction in society among users and straights.

Part of this palpable response was to equate the practice of bebop and narcotics. The New York Times printed several articles that negatively indicated an association. In 1945, the paper reported on the arrest of jazz players from a nightclub dope bust. "While it would be unjust to say that marijuana addiction was typical of jazz or jive or other band men, many musicians have become addicted, feeling that they were 'hot' after smoking 'reefers' " (*New York Times* 1945). The conflation of the two variables was cautioned, albeit slightly by the United States Attorney. On July 25, 1949, the *Times* continued the effort relating compulsive habits and musical interests among adolescents. "Their addiction to this strange new jazz (bebop), if encouraged, should develop naturally into appreciation for more . . . bearable forms" (*New York Times* 1949c). Also, an article on hearings of proposed drug clinics stated: "instances of narcotics used had been detected in the hall during the past year when concerts of 'bebop' music were held there" (Weaver 1951). The reputation of jazz and its New York epicenters of Midtown and Harlem were at risk. On April 26, 1955, the *New York Times* reported that a member of a Commission on Narcotic Drugs "remarked that there seemed to be a definite connection between increased marijuana smoking and 'that form of entertainment known as bebop and rebop'" (*New York Times* 1955b). These accounts dodged the underlying circumstances triggering drug consumption.

Concealing addiction with fashion

With the assault on narcotic use, jazz artists developed behaviors around dress that would lessen identification as a user. Dress is defined as "an assemblage of body modifications and/or supplements displayed by a person in communicating with other human beings" (Roach-Higgins and Eicher 1992: 1). According to Barthes, dress is "a strong form of meaning" that informs a "relation between a wearer and their group" (Barthes 2006: 10). Miles Davis described how his use affected his clothing during his years of heroin addiction: "where I used to be a fashion-plate dresser, now I was wearing anything that would cover my body" (Davis and Troupe 2011: 143). Concealment was essential for the addict: "policemen routinely would make me roll up my shirtsleeves, looking for fresh needle marks" (Davis and Troupe 2011: 163).

Since the nineteenth century, tuxedos, suits and elegant evening gowns were established stage fashion for entertainers. Such formal attire reflects that "clothing could signal social distinctions" as practiced by aristocrats, who altered their dress to distinguish them from the middle class (Barthes 2006: 23). Pre-Code Hollywood films, swing orchestras and Harlem nightclubs heightened the fashionable dress of the upper class. From 1910 to 1950, "wearing one's wealth on one's back" became an elite status aesthetic imitated by less affluent segments of the population (Davis 1994: 58). Formal dressing among jazz artists negated the drug addict media representations. In recounting his appearance on stage, Davis alluded to the desire for admiration, also the requisite of formal clothing. "We were up there in our processes (chemically straightened hair) and I had my suits out of the pawnshop, so you couldn't tell me we weren't doing it"

(Davis and Troupe 2011: 158). This statement demonstrates Hurlock's idea that recognition from the stage offers "widespread popularity and prestige" (Hurlock 1929: 115), especially when buttressed by fashion.

Billie Holiday wore long gloves during the 1940s—it is commonly believed the gloves concealed heroin track marks (Kliment 1990: 77). An additional concealment tactic was described in *Billie Holiday: Wishing on the Moon*: "She carried a kerchief on stage, chiffon in a colour to match her gown, to cover the needle marks in her hands; and then she wore long gloves to cover her hands and her arms" (Clarke 2002: 391). In performance, kerchiefs were typical among men like Louis Armstrong, who tactfully wiped his mouth and trumpet with the cloth. Thus, the gloves and kerchiefs were disguise, utility artifact and affluent fashion trimmings. In support of an ascribed class position, the gauntlets of early Renaissance nobility extended to the forearm with accents of colored embroidery and slits at the knuckle that revealed decorative rings (Black and Garland 1975: 157). These leather accessories having distinction in the Middle Ages protected and accentuated the limb in select material, fit and ornamentation. Hurlock cited the strategic manner that royals of this era utilized dress to shield physical defects (Hurlock 1929: 104–5). Long coats to conceal unflattering limbs, wigs to mask baldness and high collars to exaggerate the neck were fashionable practices. In parallel, Holiday was meticulous in her appearance. She wore fur coats, turbans, embellished gowns and ornate jewelry for attraction, moreover diversion. Carl Drinkard, her pianist during the early 1950s and fellow drug user, commented in interview that Holiday's skin was scarred from injections (Clarke 2002: 391; Blackburn 2005: 231). Hence, the expensive and striking adornments reinforced a jazz star's status, distancing them from the tag of addict.

On January 22, 1949, following an arrest on narcotics charges, Holiday was photographed at the San Francisco booking wearing a shawl collar mink, high-knotted turban and aviator sunglasses (Kliment 1990: 89). This representation included two components of a sign established by Swiss linguist Ferdinand de Saussure, according to Roland Barthes (Barthes 1973: 35). The signifier or material thing in the photograph consists of Holiday's fur coat. Affluence and refined behavior are the "mental representations" or signifiers of this item (Barthes 1973: 42–7). The sophisticated appearance of Holiday contested the drug arrest and exhibited the merger of celebrity-fantasy and narcotic involvement. When Holiday was recorded in the mid-1950s with her arms visibly marked and her face bloated, the perception of fame and glamour was directly challenged (Clarke 2002: 148–9). The peak of heroin trouble for Billie Holiday was perceptible in a photo of her leaving a Philadelphia jail in February 1956 (Kliment 1990: 97). In the image, Holiday, with a leashed Chihuahua leading the way, exits a holding area with her head hung low. A cigarette accents the hand that camouflages her anguished face. Holiday wears a stylish suit with poet sleeves, shawl collar and

Figure 7.2 Anita O'Day performing at Club Starlite following a
five-month jail term for narcotic possession, Los Angeles, 1954.
© Bettmann/CORBIS

narrow skirt; all have been rumpled during the detention. In the background, an
official traces her footsteps. The photo demonstrates the concept of heroin chic,
where unnatural glamour is presented in a shadowy setting and the subject
expresses drug-related distress.

Through colorful quotes in her autobiography, Anita O'Day (Figure 7.2)
exemplified a comparable approach: "Going the glamour route—long white
gloves, champagne-blonde hair, etc.—was my way of countering my reputation
as a user" (O'Day and Eells 1989: 160–1).

O'Day's dress method to conceal attributes of drug addiction prevented
social disapproval from her peers and the audience. More so, the singer's

statement attests to the deception necessary to perform in music venues of the 1940s. O'Day declares: "I may have looked straight to casual observers, but three quarters of the time I was higher than a kite" (O'Day and Eells 1989: 160–1). By the 1950s, O'Day's habit resulted in a five-month jail sentence and condemnation. "I had this big mark on me now—drug addict—and it wasn't true" (O'Day and Eells 1989: 207). O'Day and Holiday were users of heroin, an opiate that "is processed from morphine, a naturally occurring substance extracted from the seed pod of certain varieties of poppy plants" (Drug Enforcement Administration 2012b). For efficiency, heroin is injected into the circulatory system for quick delivery to the brain. Its effects include euphoria, constricted pupils and respiratory depression (Moraes 2000: 3–6).

Male musicians such as Charlie Parker, Miles Davis, Dexter Gordon and Gerry Mulligan experienced the narcotic trend that influenced modern jazz. In the 1940s, Parker, an innovative alto-saxophone player with a well-known heroin habit (Giddins and DeVeaux 2009: 317), and other male members of the Earl Hines band observed the law of clean and tidy dress (Gourse 1994: 23). With particular attention to fashion, Parker sported a wavy coif, bow ties and stylish business suits—as documented by the photography of Herman Leonard (Houston and Bagert 2006: 130–3). Made in stripe or glen plaid patterns, his suits had broad shoulders, peak lapels and tapered pants. Parker, despite his heroin addiction, attempted to maintain the integrity of traditional men's dress. This led him to borrow a suit from Miles Davis, when he had pawned his attire for heroin funds (Davis and Troupe 2011: 65). As McDowell (1997: 158) ascertained in *The Man of Fashion*, the striped suit was a "symbol of reliability and conformity." Reasonably, the wearing of the suit on stage cloaked Parker's action of forfeiting clothes related to his heroin addiction. Attractive and formal fashion had the ability to shield artists from drug demonization. On the other hand disheveled hair, messy clothes, bruised limbs, excessive sweat and nodding were markers of dependence. Spencer, in *Jazz and Death*, succinctly notes that "the thread of substance abuse is inextricably woven into the fabric of jazz" (Spencer 2002: 247). Regardless of the appearance techniques that artists used to conceal addiction, the dangers of heroin and alcohol were unavoidable, as evidenced by the deaths of Fats Navarro, Charlie Parker, Lester Young and Billie Holiday in the 1950s.

Performing addiction in film

In 1972, Diana Ross, starring as Billie Holiday, performed heroin addiction by exhibiting fantastical looks and unrestrained gestures in the Academy Award nominated *Lady Sings the Blues*. The opening scene features Ross twitching from withdrawal while forcefully being led into a padded jail cell. Upon grasp of the confinement, the character falls into a fit of madness, pounding the walls and emitting gut-wrenching wails. The director resolves this early introduction of the conflict—heroin addiction—with Ross knotted in a straightjacket brandishing a glossy eyed, hypnotic gaze accented with perspiration and tousled hair. Simplistically drug dependence was reduced to dramaturgy through the body reinforcing societal ideas of illness. Later in a less bleak setting, Ross demonstrates the climax of Holiday's addiction with a full-body collapse on stage in glamorous evening gown. The shocked orchestra leader mollifies the audience using speech that corroborated upper class status and repudiated a disorder. "Ladies and gentlemen, uh, Miss Holiday has been experiencing some, uh, dizzy spells" (Furie 1972). In each scene, the use and cessation of narcotics stimulates "the body to misbehave in various painful ways" (Moraes 2000: 58), eroding the fashionable tendency of heroin.

Contrary to such colorful visions, Holiday's bearing on stage following years of drug consumption was extremely distressing. The television series *Art Ford's Jazz Party*, taped on July 10, 1958 in Newark, evidenced the merger of fashion and addiction. Holiday, wearing a strapless evening gown with embellished floral bodice, exhibited an emaciated frame, weariness and a downcast bearing. Nevertheless, she pulled through the renditions of "Easy to Remember" (1935) and "What a Little Moonlight Can Do" (1934) made popular during her peak years. Steve Allen, television star and comedian, recalled Holiday's dire health at a 1959 Phoenix Theater concert: "we finally got her to the mike and we left her there, and she sang terribly of course, her voice was all scratchy, no vitality, no volume, nothing" (Clarke 2002: 432).

Years earlier, provided that the negative characteristics of substance use were obscured, the merger with jazz artistry was tolerated as fashionable and endearing. Memry Midgett, Holiday's pianist in 1954, interpreted the outcome of a Carnegie Hall concert: "'The people laid their hearts out and showed their love for her,' and everyone agreed it was a triumph, and never mind if Billie was drunk or high or what the problem had been at the beginning" (Blackburn 2005: 258). Holiday's lustrous ponytail, jewelry and elegant gowns worn up to her passing created an illusion for society that eventually conceded to her conflict. In this equation, the disease of addiction transfigured dress and body with grotesque meaning. Barthes argued that the language of clothes being conditional with other sciences involves cause and effect. "The garment . . . is at every moment a moving equilibrium, both produced and undermined by determinisms of nature, function and amplitude, some internal, others external to the system itself" (Barthes 2006: 14).

Also exhibiting the act of addiction were the affecting visions of Forrest Whitaker as Charlie "Bird" Parker in *Bird*, a 1988 film directed by Clint Eastwood. In a studio scene, Parker is shown fixed while playing the saxophone. His perspiration, unsteady movements and sporadic awakenings from a trance merge with a virtuosic solo. Max Roach substantiated this reality, when Parker's addiction initiated an intervention at the Three Deuces. "We were telling him how much he meant to us . . . how much he meant to black music . . . and for him to just throw away his fucking life like that was ridiculous" (Gillespie and Fraser 2009: 235). Further in the incarnation of Parker, Whitaker, during a piano interlude, takes a gulp of a brown-bagged drink, superficially providing fuel to stay animated and accomplish the recording. The band members, who are disinclined to intervene although cognizant of the prophetic sign, witness addiction that is fashionable. Truly, fashion can be severe, repulsive and melancholic in its demonstration of a romanticized coolness. During the final frame, the inventiveness is brought to a crashing end when Whitaker tosses the saxophone through the studio's window, signifying Parker's collision of public and private identities. Periodicals documented the decline of Parker. "The leading exponent of the re-bop style, has been placed in a sanitarium suffering from a complete nervous collapse," alerted *Down Beat* in its foreboding article, "Parker in Bad Shape" (*Down Beat* 1946).

The destabilization through psychological and physiological forces was profound in many performers. In defense of a heroin arrest, Gerry Mulligan's explanation to the judge was delivered in the *Los Angeles Times*: "he was induced to use narcotics because he was overworked in getting his own combo into the groove, and that he rehearsed and played 12 hours a day and then arranged music for hours additional" (*Los Angeles Times* 1953a). The artistry was incriminated as impetus and justification for drug use. Likewise, Chet Baker alluded to the paradox of making large sums of money that supplied his habit. "At one time, I was spending $800 to $1000 a week on heroin . . . I worked and every cent I made went for drugs" (Micklin 1973). Baker professed to the enticing nature of heroin that persuaded consumption. "So many musicians I got to know were using it, and it seemed like an interesting idea at the time. You know, drugs were part of the scene, and like everybody I met was using it" (Micklin 1973).

Dinah Washington's untimely death at the age of 39 disrupted the beauty that she adhered to with skillful jazz, furs, extravagant dresses and blonde wigs. While accidental, "an overdose of barbiturates" as cited by the medical examiner was reported in *Jet* on January 2, 1964 (Still 1964). Washington's use of prescription pills to reduce weight and regulate sleep nourished her career, evenly jeopardizing her wellbeing. In Washington's biography, Cohodas outlined the numerous broadcasts that stressed the singer's size, "reinforcing the notion that for female entertainers looks were as important in getting attention as talent" (Cohodas 2006: 233). A spread in *Jet* contextualized the tone with the proportional descriptions, "Dinah lands on Sunset Strip" and "hefty blues chirper Dinah Washington" (*Jet* 1955). Adding favorable testimony, the magazine revealed that Washington was "smartly-gowned . . . in white tulle" and "served up the blues and Hollywood loved it" (*Jet* 1955). Finally, the value and quality of dress and appearance were terminated at Washington's funeral as she lay in state as "Queen." "At the funeral, a diamond and pearl tiara-set jauntily atop the Queen's red-tinted head. She was dressed to kill in her tough $200 rhinestone shoes. And all about her was her royal court of admirers and the old Dinah Washington crowd" (Britton 1964: 50). Perhaps with sarcasm, *Jet* employed the text "dressed to kill" signifying the enduring life of popular style despite the wearer's death from pursuing it. Valerie Steele in *Gothic: Dark Glamour* presents this theme, the externality of fashion to life. "The human body may age and die, but by celebrating novelty and artificiality, fashion promises seasonal renewal and eternal youth" (Steele and Park 2008: 65).

Conclusion

An affiliation with the performance of jazz and the addiction of narcotics prospered in the 1940s from proximity, actuality, propaganda and exclusivity. The artists that indulged in heroin exhibited the traits of being hip, fixed, troubled, victimized and sick, consequently altering their identities through the sciences of psychology and physiology. This examination has shown five definitive motives that stimulated drug use. First, there existed a communal climate in the art of music making that endorsed the shared experience of techniques, vernacular and recreational substances. Although not unique to musicians, the expectation of repetitive nocturnal performances that exhilarated the audience certainly had an impact on wellbeing. Third, the genre of jazz possesses innate traits of risk taking and freedom seeking that grasped artificial contrary to spiritual means in this decade. The final two causes relate to mental and physical health. Narcotic drugs are habit forming with the ability to raise tolerance dictating greater use. "People use more to get the increasingly allusive euphoria, risking an overdose" (Moraes 2000: 31). Lastly, personal histories influenced by social, economic and behavioral variables suggested motivation.

Addiction within jazz is not fashionable in the conventional meaning of the word. It is fashionable, because it emphasizes performance, exhibition and branding that attract, entice, shock, create sympathy and posit an emotional response. As evidenced in jazz history, substance abuse among performers altered the aesthetics of dress, appearance and behavior, ultimately leading to the entertainer's descent from eminence.

8
BEYOND THE GARDENIA: BILLIE HOLIDAY

Billie Holiday's iconic image has been branded in popular culture as the solemn jazz singer, who wore a cluster of white gardenias perched above her ear accented by impeccable jewelry and fluid evening gowns. This singular vision, by way of repetition in mass media, obscured the path of her transformation from an adolescent of meager beginnings to an American style icon. Over a thirty-year period, Holiday's style was given birth evolving through the Harlem Renaissance, Great Depression, Second World War and the Civil Rights Movement. Dress orientations that alluded to designers including Madeleine Vionnet, Elsa Schiaparelli, Christian Dior and Cristobal Balenciaga are discernible in her appearances over the years. Modifications of appearance and behavior spawned the icon that would be immortalized as "Lady Day," known for her elegance and stillness on stage that concealed a troublesome and frantic career. McCracken, in analysis of identity construction, articulated this conversion from unknown to famous. "The objective is to expunge the markers that identify them as 'outsiders' and to take on the appearance of 'insiders.' Doing so demands thoroughgoing change in speech, gesture, posture, dress, and material culture and in patterns of thinking, feeling, and acting" (McCracken 2008: 71).

Early on, Holiday began her status transition with changing monikers as Eleanora Fagan, Eleanora Gough, Madge, Billie Halladay and Billie Holiday, suggestive of a volatile family tree and diverse identities that would yield to shifts in visual image (Nicholson 1995; Clarke 2002). The nickname Madge came from a stint at a Catholic reform institute where the label, as concluded by biographer Blackburn, "was to protect their identities, although it seems more like a way of making them forget who they were" (Blackburn 2005: 26). O'Meally in *The Many Faces of Billie Holiday* posited a related aspiration of these evolving identities. "She sought the power to free herself from the narrow set of expectations offered her as a poor black girl born into a family where being a 'bastard' child was considered an embarrassment" (O'Meally 1991: 14). This chapter will categorize the key periods of fashion in Holiday's time, analysing the historical and personal circumstances that brought the design elements to fruition. Holiday's style transcended the gardenia embellishment into a significant record of evolutionary fashion images and silhouettes that continue to resonate.

Plain dame

On April 7, 1915, Eleanora Fagan, who would later become known as Billie Holiday, was born in Philadelphia to Sadie, a single mother. This simple event did not foreshadow the star that would suddenly shine bright and burn out within a few decades. In Baltimore, Fagan's early years included a laboring mother, an absent father, truancy, rape by a neighbor and time at an institution for troubled adolescents (Nicholson 1995: 18–27). This was a life of hardships, where education took a back seat to odd jobs, fast streets and survival in Jim Crow inequality.

A relocation to Harlem in 1929 represented the first significant period of Holiday's style. Freddie Green, a childhood friend from Baltimore, described her style circa 1925 as plain dress including "gingham cloth skirts and blouses" with hair pulled back and cut short (Blackburn 2005: 20). This style was evidenced in two early photographs. One image, circa 1932, featured Holiday at a beach with a prominent Seagrams' sign in the background (O'Meally 1991: 65). Despite an age of 17 years, she projected maturity in body size and demeanor, specifically the cigarette that rested casually in her left hand. Holiday showed off a floral printed bathing suit of dressmaker style with narrow shoulder straps and thigh-length skirt-effect, typical of the early 1930s. Exemplifying the homespun wardrobe, the second photograph taken in 1935 behind the Apollo Theater in Harlem presented her clad in a simple check patterned dress with hip patch pockets and matching belt (O'Meally 1991: 56). Also called a shirtmaker style or modified shirtwaist dress, it flourished in the early 1930s with short sleeves, small width collars and belted straight skirts. This silhouette, occurring during the Great Depression years, was heightened in movies, like *Possessed* (1931), to establish a class of lifestyle to escape. In the film, factory worker Marian, played by Joan Crawford, wore a printed shirtwaist dress with contrast Peter Pan collar, patch pockets and cuffed sleeves. Her dialogue affirmed a desire to leave the "godforsaken" town, sip champagne and live prosperously. "There's everything wrong with me. My clothes, my shoes, my hands, and the way I talk, but at least I know it" (Brown 1931). Akin to the movie plot, Holiday soon jettisoned this simple frock and unglamorous appearance segueing into more elaborate dress.

Lost in Hollywood

Around 1930, Eleanora Fagan created her stage name, Billie Holiday. The first name was inspired by either Billie Dove, a famous screen star of the period, Billie Haywood, a singer in Harlem dives, or Bill, a childhood nickname, while the surname was adopted from Clarence Holiday, her presumptive father (Clarke 2002: 49–50). Holiday's dress and appearance had not rivaled the actress with whom she was smitten; however her natural beauty and passion for jazz fame was apparent. Subsequent to appearing in a Duke Ellington film short and touring with the Count Basie Orchestra, the panache of Holiday was amplified in 1938 with publicity shots for a tour with the Artie Shaw Orchestra. These images, emulating Jean Harlow, presented Holiday as a Hollywood bombshell with pencil thin eyebrows, smoky eyelids, contoured lips, shimmering coif and lucent skin. On September 4, 1938, the *Washington Post* confirmed the ascending reputation: "Billie Holiday, will be the featured songstress with Artie Shaw and his orchestra . . . Billie has built her fame with many famous name bands as one of the most exciting blues singers in America" (*Washington Post* 1938). However, the glamorous appearance of Holiday was ineffective with evading Jim Crow treatment and hostility surrounding a black woman performing with an orchestra of sixteen white men. In her autobiography, Holiday recalled the intolerable practices:

> I got so tired of scenes in crummy roadside restaurants over getting served . . . some places they wouldn't even let me eat in the kitchen. Some places they would. Sometimes it was a choice between me eating and the whole band starving. I got tired of having a federal case over breakfast, lunch, and dinner . . . but the biggest drag of all was a simple little thing like finding a place to go to the bathroom.
>
> (Holiday and Dufty 2006: 84–6)

Holiday's unsung crusade in the Shaw Orchestra challenged segregation policies by demonstrating equality of appearance, dress and performance on stage. The placement of an elegant African American singer on the bandstand altered the social facade of a black woman as inferior, in so doing modestly symbolizing "a position not far below that which the men hold" (Hurlock 1929: 221). Shaw's actions to limit Holiday's time on stage suggested either an avoidance of Jim Crow issues or intimidation from having an attractive female singer garner attention. Following her departure from the Shaw group, Holiday remarked in a *Down Beat* article: "Pretty soon it got so I would sing just two numbers a night. When I wasn't singing, I had to stay backstage. Artie wouldn't let me sit out front with the band" (Dexter Jr. 1939). Although her tenure with Benny Goodman and Artie Shaw was short-lived, she participated in the progression of integration in the studio, on stage and within venues. Her gaining notoriety was palpable by the *Afro-American* newspaper in 1938 with commentary on a sold-out Chicago performance: "It is felt that the extra big drawing is entirely due to Billie Holiday's popularity, since Artie Shaw is not well known in this section" (*Afro-American* 1938). The close of the decade brought solo opportunities and more freedom, allowing Holiday to create an enchanting style minus the rigid Hollywood makeover.

Lady's day

Lester Young's issuance to Holiday the nickname "Lady Day" secured a mark of distinction that has remained beyond her death. "The giving of names had long been Lester's specialty" (Gelly 1984: 41). For instance, Holiday's mother reigned as "Duchess," while Count Basie was "The Holy Man." These authority infused labels had been practiced a decade earlier with the classic blues singers, providing levels of excellence with "Mother," "Queen," and "Empress" of the blues. Hurlock argued that professional titles were revered in American society; also "the longing for distinction which could not be satisfied by any other means" was pursued through the accessibility of dress (Hurlock 1929: 35). In the black community, such brands likened terms of endearment, internal hierarchy and competitive rivalry, as examined in Chapter 4 with elaborate orchestra names.

The "Lady" title signified respect, sophistication and beauty, evenly harkening to Victorian traits of modesty and measured behavior. In spite of her troubled childhood and arduous rise to fame, Holiday merged graceful behavior and elegant appearance on stage to maximize the revered designation and obstruct race restrictions. Such agency provided a degree of resistance, defined as "action which impeded or subverted unequal power relations" (Barnard and Spencer 2012: 615). Although the brand of "lady" may simply represent a flattering title, recognition of the positive context was profound in jazz venues where segregation and inequality thrived. Holiday, in possible adaptation of Louis Armstrong's stage practices, often uttered the phrase "thank you very much ladies and gentlemen" at the conclusion of a song that put forth formality and authority. This conduct merging with appearance symbolized the practice of class distinction, when performers differentiated themselves socially from the audience.

1930s: Draped in tradition

In the late 1930s, Holiday's style matured as substantiated in photographs taken at Café Society. This West Village haunt with the motto "The Wrong Place for the Right People" was innovative for providing a downtown venue where the audience was integrated (Nicholson 1995: 111; Giddins and DeVeaux 2009: 213). In 1939, Holiday, standing erect at a microphone, was photographed in a white column gown that swept the floor in tiny flounces, possibly of silk crepe. The halter neckline and accessories including a metallic bracelet and leaf-motif buckle put forth a pattern of influence between fashion and jazz. Here, Holiday embraced a trending style and added to the garment's identity through exhibition on the jazz platform, where qualitative measures of vocal talent and physical appearance were registered into the costume's impression.

A clear resemblance of this Holiday image was discovered in a 1939 photograph of Claire McCardell, an American fashion designer, who modeled her own halter jersey design cinched at the waist with a studded belt and accessorized with coordinating bracelet. McCardell was known for her work that referenced the "design genius" of Madeleine Vionnet and Madame Grès, Parisian designers who perfected the drape of fabrics cut on the bias (Yohannan and Nolf 1998: 24–5). The image of Holiday and McCardell paid homage to the Vionnet halter dress that was heralded in the *New York Times* on March 8, 1938. "Vionnet produced a completely backless dress of superb cut, the high front secured by a halter neck and the princess line of the white satin flaring gently to the floor in graduated narrow pleats" (*New York Times* 1938). The Paris trend of straight gowns with narrow waists and lengthy full-skirts was debuted at Saks Fifth Avenue. As indicated in the *Times*, such looks were "destined to lend glamour to late hours" for the American woman.

Another elegant snapshot of Holiday at Café Society revealed a streamlined gown of velvet material with leg-of-mutton sleeves, high-front neckline and long skirt that widened below the hip line. On September 10, 1937, the *New York Times* forecasted this style following an autumn fashion presentation at Bergdorf Goodman. "A predominant number of gowns . . . are plastered against the figure tightly as a wet bathing suit, above the hip line. Below, they may swirl and flare and ripple in voluminous yardage, floor length, or cling about the knees" (*New York Times* 1937). Holiday accessorized her dress with an elaborate metallic coin necklace and the same foliage buckle mentioned previously. The set of the sleeves, fabrication and Surrealist accessories that accented the busts were reminiscent of Elsa Schiaparelli's creations. These details were highlighted in the *Times* article: "strategic shirring . . . as in Schiaparelli's dignified black velvet with deep décolletage and darted brassiere top, the skirt long and full" (*New York Times* 1937). Additional looks of this period that Holiday was photographed wearing included a polka dot belted halter dress at the Apollo Theater, a belted lace gown at Café Society, and a short-sleeve shirred décolleté at the Off-Beat Club (O'Meally 1991). Perhaps offering a bit of optimism in a time of inequality and economic depression, Holiday began wearing the iconic gardenia in small scale. Teddy Wilson certified that her ability rivaled her blossoming glamour. "Billie was in her prime then: you only have to think of such numbers as 'What a Little Moonlight Can Do' and 'Miss Brown to You,' with Benny Goodman on clarinet, Ben Webster on tenor sax, Roy Eldridge on trumpet, John Kirby on bass, and Cozy Coles on drums" (Wilson, Ligthart and Van Loo 2001: 22–3).

1940s: An icon emerges

Entering like a lion, the 1940s was a decade of drastic change in fashion and culture. Modern techniques spawned from jazz musicians experimenting with non-traditional riffs, vocals and harmonies that often seemed incoherent to audiences that were acclimated to the structured and danceable swing genre. This new music, fathered by Gillespie and Parker, settled into the category of bebop. During this genesis, the United States of America entered the Second World War with the bombing of Pearl Harbor in 1941. Restrictions on garment construction, limitations on industrial materials and shortages of provisions were necessities of the war effort.

Specifically related to apparel, the 1943 application of Limitation Order L-85 had a considerable impact on women. Dress hemlines were shorter, skirts and pants had narrow circumferences, and jackets terminated at the hip (Milbank 1989: 133–40). Frustration in fabric conservation and the straight silhouette as interpreted by designers was passionately noted among women. On March 27, 1943, a fashion editor opined in the *Washington Post*. "It's all very well to extol the narrow silhouette but the fact of the matter is . . . the female figure is simply not constructed like a pencil. Most of us have unmistakable hips to say nothing of derrieres" (Contini 1943). A year earlier the *New York Times*' fashion editor foretold of this extreme with the warning that a collection featured "midcalf-length dresses of barber-pole slimness . . . he drapes the scant fabric up in the front so that the hemline is uneven" (Pope 1942). Notwithstanding the sentiments, the slim silhouette flourished and received fashionable treatment in war-themed films such as *Casablanca* (1942) and *Pillow to Post* (1945) with the latter containing a cameo of Louis Armstrong and Dorothy Dandrige in jazz performance.

For Holiday this decade reflected her most dynamic and varied appearances, equally ascension to widespread popularity as the top singer in jazz polls. *Down Beat* called attention to her 1944 transformation with the photo caption, "the new, stream-lined Billie Holiday" (*Down Beat* 1944). In analysis of individuals seeking the public gaze, "if they are to gain the wide publicity which they desire, they must be constantly different, and this depends to a large extent upon the wearing of different clothing" (Hurlock 1929: 48). Diverse traits that Holiday promoted included printed gowns, skirt suits, platform shoes, fur coats and strong-shouldered dresses. Milbank conveyed the impact Gilbert Adrian, an American designer, made with the latter silhouette in Hollywood. Actresses, such as Joan Crawford, propagated "the broad-shouldered, straight jacket and pencil skirt" accessorized with platform shoes (Milbank 1989: 138). Within the jazz world, the female song stylist, who was a tolerable ornament of the 1930s big band era, took center stage and participated actively in adopting and setting fashion trends.

Three unique styles embraced by Holiday in the 1940s were floral printed gowns, knotted turbans and pompadour bangs. With the first, the *Washington Post* proclaimed an Egyptian tie to the print trend in 1943:

The perennial popularity of prints goes all the way back to Tutankhamin . . . the main reasons for this constant recurrence are (a) patterned fabric is an effective and self-sufficient decorating scheme, (b) it's cheerful, (c) there is great latitude for free expression. This year prints offer brilliant possibilities to designers coping with simplified narrow silhouettes.

(Contini 1943)

Evening and day dresses with flowers and foliage, as with Holiday's gardenia cluster, provided an upbeat quality to the doleful songs about unreciprocated love (Figure 8.1).

More so, the swirling and vibrant designs matched the tendency in allover floral prints for motion picture wardrobes as promoted by Edith Head, costume designer for Paramount Studios. The war years initiated an escapist motive in Hollywood films, where directors focused on plots and settings that featured cheerful sojourns in South America. Movies like *Down Argentine Way* (1940) and *That Night in Rio* (1941) spotlighted the performances of Carmen Miranda in tropical nightclubs accessorized with floral and fruit-laden headpieces. Skillfully, Holiday's union of the gardenias and the floral printed gowns signified a more feminine fashion that challenged the rigid shoulder lines and straight skirt silhouettes; the flowers also camouflaged her choice of heroin use. The *New York Times*, on April 28, 1948, observed a rebounded Holiday wearing the iconic

Figure 8.1 Billie Holiday wears a graphic floral print dress in studio with Jimmy McLin on guitar, 1939. Photo by Charles Peterson. Courtesy of Don Peterson

accessory following her drug punishment: "dressed in scarlet with white flowers in her hair and at her waist and wore elbow-length gauntlets of gold . . . she remains nearly motionless, making every gesture count, singing easily, getting musical effects by control of vocal quality" (*New York Times* 1948a).

During the mid to late 1940s, Holiday was photographed in numerous styles of the turban both solid and printed. The trend of head coverings had made its presence in past decades, for instance the turbans and Tam o'Shanters of the late teens were popularized with lace, tulle and feather trimmings (*New York Times* 1919b). On January 1, 1940, *Vogue* magazine declared "New Triumphs for Turbans" (*Vogue* 1940) that reached widespread consideration through the film, *The Postman Always Rings Twice* (1946). Lana Turner, playing the antagonist, displayed a well-twisted, white turban with midriff baring short set that shed any notion of far eastern locales. The fashion article recited the benefits of the style:

> Turbans are logical. They preserve careful coiffures intact, they're just sense for riding in open cars, trains, airplanes; they're a form of head-dress that looks as smart with dinner-clothes as with slacks. And any mirror can tell you how becoming they are, which is perhaps the best feminine reason of all.
>
> (*Vogue* 1940)

Holiday's method of the turban was akin to *Vogue*'s description of the Javanese variety that "hug the head and wind into a chignon that mimics the gleaming hair-knots of the dancers." This change from the floral clusters permitted the singer to reinvent her public persona, also move beyond the gardenia identity. In images of Holiday with turban, she appeared regal, in control and in possession of international pedigree, often accessorized with tailored jackets and trousers. The exhibition of the turban continued through the 1950s with her displaying a head wrap on her first European tour. Holiday's style adaptations symbolized her determination in the patriarchal recording industry and her earnings in excess of $1000 a week (Nicholson 1995: 148).

The third feature for Holiday was the lacquered bang with braided hairpiece that sat upon her head in similar fashion to the coiffures of the early 1900s, yet with more precision and neatness. In the earlier Gibson girl period, the hair was "pulled up off of the neck and arranged in curls, frizzes, bangs, and bouffant pompadours in front" (Bigelow 1970: 230). The *New York Times*, on October 21, 1943, advanced the trend in these upswept hair-dos that utilized fabricated parts. "Several false hair pieces were used for evening styles, where a more elaborate effect was desired . . . a huge chignon is done entirely with 'boughten' hair, coiled into a figure eight that curves way around to the sides" (Parker 1943). The glossy bang appeared at a pivotal point in Holiday's life, when she was sentenced to one year incarceration for receiving and concealing a narcotic drug. In contrast to the revolting association of heroin user, photographs showed the coif on an elegant and demure Holiday at the District Court of Philadelphia (May 27, 1947) for her sentencing, also worn during her performance at Carnegie Hall (March 27, 1948) following her release from the Federal Reformatory for Women at Alderson, West Virginia. Feasibly, Holiday employed the classic hair-do to mitigate a harmful drug reputation and register a degree of modesty. As described by the *New York Times* in review of similar designs, the "curling bangs gave added allure to their eyes" (Pope 1948). This was evident in the photo from Carnegie Hall, where Holiday appeared reinvigorated, optimistic and graceful as she walked on stage in a textured-bodice gown with cap sleeves and tulle underskirt.

1950s: Beyond the gardenia

In the mid-1950s, African Americans witnessed a battle surge for civil rights. Brown *v.* the Board of Education (1954) and the Montgomery Bus Boycotts (1956) elevated the cause for terminating racial segregation of educational institutions and public buses, continuing into the 1960s with lunch counter sit-ins and marches led by Martin Luther King, Jr. Around this time, jazz began to fragment into different styles, ranging from hard bop to cool jazz and onto free jazz. The chaotic beats and rejections of conventional techniques paralleled the strategies of the Civil Rights Movement. Concurrently, the youthful labels of rhythm and blues, and rock and roll were taking ground, preparing to displace jazz as popular music. Artists such as Bo Diddley, Chuck Berry, Ray Charles and Elvis Presley were bringing a new sound with "songs about fast cars and teenage romance" (Cohodas 2006: 203). Fashion mirrored this instability with modifications of silhouettes and fabrication throughout the decade.

Following the end of the Second World War, Christian Dior altered fashion with the "New Look," a proclamation that cheered the traditional feminine silhouette. Milbank suggested the look had been around in the 1940s but it was now heralded as a day-time look "with its tiny waistline, longer hems, and full skirts" (Milbank 1989: 143). In admiration, Holiday's gowns at the beginning of the 1950s became more structured and decorative with ornate embroideries, lace, jewelling, tulle shells and crinoline supports (Figure 8.2).

Formal gowns were suitable for the theaters, halls and festivals that Holiday was restricted to playing during this period. Having been convicted of a drug penalty, Holiday was denied a cabaret card, which would have allowed her to play in New York nightclubs (Nicholson 1995: 167).

In October 1954, *Vogue* expressed enthusiasm in review of European ball gowns. "The dresses that float, that billow, that drift dreamily into the party: never so pretty in Paris as now, in pure white . . . these endless variations on the

Figure 8.2 Billie Holiday embodies modernity in a streamlined lace gown with satin ribbon at waist, New York, 1951. © Burt Goldblatt Estate Archives/Cynthia Sesso, CTSIMAGES

beautiful, bouffant 'big dress' " (*Vogue* 1954). Photographed in a meditative state at the Hollywood Bowl in 1953, Holiday wears a floor sweeping, strapless ball gown with corseted bodice and tulle layered skirt draped with lace (Figure 8.3).

The photo taken by Herman Leonard signified a trend toward voluminous and elaborate gowns for Holiday that were in contrast to the 1940s where she displayed edgy prints, turbans and impressive gardenias. In 1954, Holiday carried the formal guise to Europe on her first performance tour to the continent. One of the prominent gowns that she was photographed wearing in Amsterdam, London and Paris was a floor-length, off-the-shoulder satin dress with allover floral design. The richness of the embossed fabric and generous cut of the skirt gave Holiday a regal appearance in countries where royals were once fashion arbiters. Holiday injected style accents throughout the tour from an orchid in her

Figure 8.3 Billie Holiday in voluminous ball gown backstage at the Hollywood Bowl, 1953. © Herman Leonard Photography LLC

hair in Paris to a section of tinted hair during her stay in London. Max Jones in *Melody Maker* detailed the latter characteristic:

> Wearing a black dress with a gold thread in it, diamond necklace and earrings, and a patch of silver-sprayed hair a little to one side – where the gardenias used to be pinned . . . and her whole attitude seems spontaneous and very, very hip.
>
> (Jones 1954)

In the 1950s, this hair fad of "touching dark hair in random spots with bleach" received the name "frosting" and was popular along with colored dyes (Bigelow 1970: 271). The *New Musical Express* highlighted Holiday's attention to style on February 12, 1954, "looking as graceful and beautiful as she ever did in a brand new dress bought in London that morning" (*New Musical Express* 1954).

Upon Holiday's return to America, the formal gown was continually referenced through her career in the late 1950s. Notably, a strapless dress that was worn at a 1957 New York jazz festival on Randall's Island featured a bodice embellished with mini-floral appliques, a ruched empire waist and full skirt. The design mirrored a gown displayed by Elizabeth Taylor in the film *A Place in the Sun* (1951). Differing from Holiday's dress, Edith Head, the costume designer, utilized a tulle skirt overlay adorned with floral trimmings that rustled when the actress moved. Both gowns exaggerated the slimness of the waist with bare shoulders and full floral bust. Adding to this visual, Holiday's excesses including alcohol and drugs were evident on her frame with emaciated limbs and a gaunt shoulder profile. The *New York Times* noted the vocal and energy waning on June 17, 1957, "Miss Holiday, making one of her rare New York appearances, was not always in full control of her voice. But once she worked away a tendency toward thickness and lumpiness, she sang with a quiet passion that was deeply moving" (*New York Times* 1957). Jazz artists experienced exacting scrutiny of their performance with comparisons to earlier recordings and successful concerts; as a consequence the function of appearance in pleasing critics and audiences was elevated.

Despite a decline in her vocal range, popularity and earnings, Holiday participated stylistically in the youth uprising of the late 1950s. The most blatant detail was the ponytail that the singer had begun to wear regularly in the mid-1950s, giving Holiday a fresh and sleek exterior. In February 1958, Holiday entered the recording studio for the album *Lady in Satin* that marked her entry into string orchestration. The dominant violins and flowery instrumentation palpable on the recordings from *Satin* were a departure from the raw emotive jazz that Holiday exemplified. "Much of her present potential is stifled in the steady succession of slow, slow ballads and the flaccid accompaniment of Ray Ellis' orchestra," articulated the *New York Times* on July 6, 1958 (Wilson 1958a).

Contrary to the mature, provocative sound achieved on the album, a youthfully dressed Holiday emerged at the recording workspace. Candid snap shots of the session revealed a jazz hipster signified by Holiday's appearance in a dark cardigan sweater set, ankle length tartan slacks, flat casual shoes and mid-length ponytail. Here, she divulged her offstage style that jettisoned, albeit momentarily, the feminine accoutrements of slim midriff gowns, gemstone jewelry and high heels. In the 1950s, the fashion trends of teenagers including scraped-back ponytails, cardigans and strapless dresses that formed their "etiquette of dress" (Milbank 1989: 181) were prominent. Holiday, at the age of 43, was a participant in this fashion reform championed by the youth. During a second trip to Europe in November 1958, she was photographed at the Olympia Theatre sporting the ponytail along with jeweled cat sunglasses, mink coat and African mask earrings that imparted a contemporary image.

An understated garment shape, proclaimed by Cristobal Balenciaga, a Spanish born fashion designer, was seized by Holiday in the months before her death. Fashion shifted away from waist-conscious dresses to semi and loose fitting silhouettes. Balenciaga drew upon the straight hanging frock during the 1950s. As described by Martin and Koda of the Metropolitan Museum of Art, "the fluid effect of the chemise became in Balenciaga's exaggeration the sack dress, forsaking the waist and anticipating the 1960s shift" (Martin and Koda 1995: 34). A few rare images provide a glimpse of the Holiday style that would have likely existed in the next decade. These pictures are so far from the iconic gardenia representation of the singer that they are less employed in popular culture, regretfully limiting the narrative of her complex and ever-changing identity.

In 1959, Holiday traveled to Europe for a brief trip to appear on the *Chelsea at Night* program in London. This event provided the last taped footage of Holiday that trumped her performance on *Lady in Satin* and various live concerts in the latter part of 1958. She wore a knitted mid-sleeve dress accented with a metallic thread with ribbing at the neckline and cuff. The collar was scooped away from the neck at the front and draped in the back, while the body of the garment hung straight in this manner staying true to the chemise trend. A comparable silhouette was demonstrated in a 1958 photograph likely taken during a concert booking in Italy. Holiday is captured walking on the stage adorned in a white sleeveless dress of damask-like fabrication with boat neck and front placket yielding at the waist. The *Washington Post* forecasted the minimalist design that falls straight from the upper bodice. In March 1956, the newspaper detailed the spring silhouette from the Paris based designer, "Balenciaga camouflaged the feminine bosom and waistline with bloused middies and loose tunics" (*Washington Post* 1956). This narrative endured the following year when the *New York Times* asserted that Balenciaga's abstract shapes "were always feminine, soft and rounded, not sharp and angular . . . he was always aware of the woman beneath the dress" (Donovan 1957). In the same manner, Holiday's adoption of the tubular shape paired with a smooth ponytail demonstrated an alluring, reformist style without forsaking her elegance. This modern facade sans the gardenias, elaborate gowns and long gloves, so often attached to Holiday, exemplified her final image. Following a two-month hospital stay and the inability to recover from a liver condition, lung congestion and kidney infection, Holiday died on July 17, 1959 (*New York Times* 1959; Nicholson 1995: 226).

Conclusion

Billie Holiday's representation in popular culture has frequently incorporated photographs and artistic reproductions from the 1940s time period. This is considered her golden period, vocally and visually, thus supporting the focus on this decade. Authors, recording companies, artists, fans and corporations construct and disseminate this data in mass consumption. Allowing for a critique of the singular vision, this chapter has shown a wider view of Holiday's history related to artistic and fashion development. Holiday was propelled to iconic stature following her death, where the legend spawned was a tunnel vision of tragic fame documented with images of sadness and elegant dress. Ultimately, the narrow representation excluded elements that showed the early bombshell expression and post-gardenia narrative.

When asked by Mike Wallace the reason so many jazz greats die at an early age, Holiday replied eloquently, perhaps conveying the verve behind her transformations of dress and appearance. "We try to live one hundred days in one day and we try to please so many people . . . I myself, I want to bend this note and bend that note and sing this way and sing that way and get all the feeling and eat all the good foods and travel all in one day and you can't do it" (Wallace 1956). In assessing the demanding effort, Holiday linked common motives of fashion and jazz, those being admiration, distinction and artistic freedom.

9
AESTHETICS OF THE JAZZ DANDY

Like Gods

When I was a young man in the fifties, the music that was playing in France was jazz. It was due to the fact that many American soldiers, especially black soldiers, would have come to Paris after the war and stayed in Paris in Saint-Germain-des-Prés. Most of them were men—very, very few women. We will see that Dinah Washington never came. Billie Holiday only came twice but for a very short period. It was men.

(Fontanes 2010)

Adding to his narrative, Michel Fontanes, a former executive, author and jazz musician, articulated the French impression of African American male instrumentalists that expatriated to the country. "They were considered in France as Gods. All black musicians not the white musicians." Regarding his trip to Paris in 1949, Miles Davis offered consensus. "It was the freedom of being in France and being treated like a human being, like someone important. Even the band and the music we played sounded better over there" (Davis and Troupe 2011: 126). Dizzy Gillespie affirmed a similar feeling from a 1937 voyage to Europe:

I liked London very much, and we played at the Palladium. I used to jam in a place called the Nest Club . . . interesting how much the Europeans liked our music, even that far back. They took it seriously. They studied it and collected a lot of records. That's how most of the European jazz musicians and, afterwards, the rock musicians first learned how to play our music, by listening to records. They treated you nice over there too and gave you the respect due an artist.

(Gillespie and Fraser 2009: 77–8)

Even earlier in 1919, Sidney Bechet corroborated a similar impression, when he arrived in London with the Southern Syncopated Orchestra. This trip predated his excursion to Paris with Josephine Baker for *La Revue Nègre* (1925) that is considered the stimulus of Europe's fascination with jazz. The orchestra by request gave a Command Performance at Buckingham Palace to the "King and his Servants" (Rye 2010: 5). "Once we got started we had the whole royal family tapping their feet . . . and Will told me later that he'd asked them what it was they'd enjoyed the most, and the King said it was that blues, the Characteristic Blues" (Bechet 2002: 128). Bechet and the ensembles' performance for King George V realized the origins of royal qualities that had been adopted by New Orleans jazz originators through dress, behavior and titles in the late nineteenth century. In relation to Fontanes' designation of supremeness, Louis Armstrong substantiated the divine regard with the account that a Chicago based musician in the 1920s was "treated and respected just like some kind of a God" (Armstrong 1999: 74). The repute of male musicians provides foundation to interpret the appearance and behavior that generated a superior identity of the jazz dandy in America and abroad.

As posited in Chapter 2, male artists wielded discriminating dress with formality, grooming and presence throughout the decades. The individual with an excessive interest in clothing and the tendency toward self-admiration has, in the history of male costume, been classified as the dandy. More so, dandyism has an association with privilege and wealth, which permits the man to exert considerable time towards appearance. In comparison to feminine vanity, Hurlock put forth that "men's clothes throughout the ages have been equally frivolous and absurd, and that the 'dandy' has been a familiar figure in each nation and every age" (Hurlock 1929: 148).

Following a lofty status in the Romantic Period with the likes of Beau Brummel, men's dress discarded the exhibitionist details for "somber, conservative costumes" (Bigelow 1970: 183). This led to the prevalence of the contemporary single-breasted ensemble originating in the late 1800s as the sack and lounge suit featuring sloping shoulders, wide sleeves and high lapels. As consequence of this dress reform, Coolidge asserted that "the standardization of men's clothing has reduced them to a certain uniformity of appearance . . . but it has not done away with the necessity of keeping up with the styles" (Coolidge 1912: 140). Jazzmen since the early progression of brass bands demonstrated conformity to group outfits that over time yielded to individual flair. The attributes of the dandy will be measured in two schools of jazz instrumentation, traditional and modern. In outlining the categories Fontanes validated that the two categories resonated in Europe circa 1950 equal to their standing in America:

There was traditional jazz headed by Sidney Bechet. Bechet was one of the most important musicians of all time. Around Bechet there were hundreds of Dixieland and traditional jazz bands. Albert Nicholas, Bill Coleman—they were current with modern jazz. What I call modern jazz is Charlie Parker and Dizzy Gillespie or people like that.

(Fontanes 2010)

Nicholas and Coleman of the traditional school became permanent expats and contributed greatly to the influence of jazz in Europe.

Traditional dandy: Duke Ellington

In the 1920s and 1930s when jazz orchestras thrived, Duke Ellington and Benny Carter, both being traditional musicians, composers and bandleaders, exemplified the designation of dandy. Their identity was constructed through strategic efforts in dress, lifestyle and behavior that were publicized in media channels. It has been established that the favorable representation of African American jazz performers countered a harmful image sustained by segregation and an ideology of the music's inferiority. On March 10, 1919 prior to the mainstream proliferation of the genre, a *New York Times* critique of two Negro bands testified that "the strange devices known as 'jazz' music were heard last evening" (*New York Times* 1919c). The word choice of "strange" implied a technique that was different, bizarre and varied from accepted norms. Musicians offset this opinion of difference by appearing equal to or better than the exclusive environments in which they played. Regarding his early days in 1930s Chicago, Teddy Wilson recalled the atmosphere at the Gold Coast Club owned by Al Capone. "It was quite an experience hearing these professional gunmen talking so knowledgeably . . . about their favorite stars: the comparative merits of Johnny Hodges and Benny Carter as alto sax players . . . none of them looked like the typical Hollywood-type gangster: to me they looked rather like bank clerks, young professors, or business men!" (Wilson, Ligthart and Van Loo 2001: 17). Jazzmen integrated celebrity promotion and lifestyle ideals that solidified the status of dandy; also, they elevated the black modern man as authoritative with political interest. These qualities in the dandy routine will be identified.

The mark of royalty was placed upon Ellington and Carter with the monikers of "Duke" and "King" respectively. As detailed in *Jazz* magazine, Ellington's title corresponded directly to the quality and presentation of clothing at an early age. "The Duke got his name in high school, because that was the way he liked to dress. Shepherd's plaid was sharp for U Street, if the creases were right and Duke saw to that" (Smith 1942). In examination of elitism, Chapter 4 linked the naming of bands with aristocratic titles that conferred musical innovation, noteworthy dress and genteel behavior. Gioia labeled these practices as "eccentricities of jazz" that fixated on concepts of hierarchy and nobleness (Gioia 1998: 117).

For example Lester Young, known as "Prez," assigned Harry Edison, Billie Holiday and her mother the nicknames, Sweets, Lady Day, and Duchess correspondingly; along with Count Basie they were the royal family in the late 1930s (Holiday and Dufty 2006: 55, Gelly 2007: 55–6). Likely, the unique headings showed respect and endearment among colleagues, as well numbing impediments of Jim Crow. An additional outcome of aristocratic coding was reinforcement of African cultural roots and tribute to this lost history. In his slave narrative of 1814, Olaudah Equiano detailed vast West African kingdoms where chiefs, judges and senators wielded power, wealth and commerce. One of high distinction or grandeur displayed a mark that was achieved "by cutting the skin across the forehead down to the eyebrows" (Gates 1987: 12). In like manner, musicians symbolically trademarked one another with tiered roles within the territory of jazz.

In 1899, Edward Kennedy Ellington was born in Washington, D.C., identified as the "Capital of the Colored Aristocracy" by Gatewood in analysis of the black upper class (Gatewood 1990: 38). It was a locale that afforded social and educational advantages with reduced Jim Crow obstruction, albeit confined to Negro neighborhoods. Langston Hughes illustrated the snobbish tone of Washington's Negro society of 1925:

> For the "better class" Washington colored people, as they called themselves, drew rigid class and color lines within the race against Negroes who worked with their hands, or who were dark in complexion and had no degrees from colleges. These upper class colored people consisted largely of government workers, professors and teachers, doctors, lawyers, and resident politicians . . . They lived in comfortable homes, had fine cars, played bridge, drank Scotch, gave exclusive "formal" parties, and dressed well, but seemed to me altogether lacking in real culture, kindness, or good common sense.
>
> (Hughes 1997: 206–7)

While not immersed in black high society, Ellington grew up in middle class standing with his father employed as a butler and musical training instilled through his parents aptitude of the household piano (Ellington 1973: 10, 17). Ellington, in his autobiography, affirmed his father's socioeconomic philosophy. "J.E. always acted as though he had money, whether he had it or not. He spent and lived like a man who had money, and he raised his family as though he were a millionaire" (Ellington 1973: 10). Hence, the family's principles of conduct including proper speech, good manners and spiritual guidance were parallel to the black elite of Washington.

"It Don't Mean A Thing (If It Ain't Got That Swing)," a 1931 composition by Ellington and lyrics by Irving Mills, intimates the performers approach to music, demeanor and dress. In a key verse, the words advocate that an individual should apply their utmost energy to rhythm of life and image, nodding to Ellington's persona. This smartness was molded in his formative years through impressions of his family, particularly his father and early musical trainers. Ellington's description of a pianist that mentored him in Washington established the dandy quality that transcended the spectrum of dress:

Doc Perry wore glasses and looked very much like the kids try to look today. He was intelligent, had beautiful posture at all times—sitting, walking, in a poolroom, or playing the piano—and talked with a sort of semi-continental finesse. He was extremely dignified, clean, neat, and had impeccably manicured nails and hands.

(Ellington 1973: 26)

Perry enacted social distinctions of a conspicuous manner. According to Barthes in analysis of nineteenth-century dandyism, an intention of the shrewd manner of clothing display among high society was differentiation from the working-class and the bourgeois (Barthes 2006: 23). Ellington's early surroundings, whether at school, cabaret hall or home, reinforced the dandy performance as a social and political imperative.

The obligation of fine dress was evident in Ellington's account of his band the Washingtonians. "We paid quite a lot of attention to our appearance, and if any one of us came in dressed improperly Whetsol would . . . pull down the lower lid of his right eye with his forefinger and stare at the offending party" (Ellington 1973: 70). With assigned social meaning, the gesture portrays a deterrent, that being dismissal among peers for unsuitable style. Hurlock maintained that the follow-the-leader mentality of dress eludes the "pitying glances of their friends and associates" (Hurlock 1929: 41). The members of Ellington's band, as well the social atmosphere of Washington, contributed to an accepted identity of the dandy (Figure 9.1).

According to Banfield on creation of a black music philosophy, these cultural codes are community ideals, "which suggest that certain ways of being, thinking, looking, and styling are normative, preferable, and validated" (Banfield 2010: 9).

Ellington's performance of the jazz dandy was vigorously disseminated in print media from 1930 to 1960 (Figure 9.2).

With positive attitude, periodicals and newspapers, both black and white, formulated a musical genius in terms of dress, language, health and leisure. The importance of dress was accentuated through artifacts that imparted quantifiable consumption. In 1949, *Ebony* itemized Ellington's wardrobe. "He has more than 100 suits. Suede shoes are his current 'kick.' He has dozens of pairs of all colors. Other specialty is white ties" (*Ebony* 1949). Veblen (2007: 340), in analysis of the economic principles of dress, argued that extravagant consumption demonstrates the wearer's ability to purchase without restriction as well "that he or she is not under the necessity of earning a livelihood;" thus social value is heightened. *Look* (1947) and *Band Leaders* (1945) followed this commentary of Ellington's possessions. In turn, the excerpts outlined: "Duke models a grey pin-stripe, part of the 120-suit wardrobe he's famous for" and "he owns about forty-five suits, hundreds of ties, and his shoes, hats and shirts are all custom-made." A requisite of these publications was to exhibit extraordinary news of distinguished African

Figure 9.1 Duke Ellington and his band in wool overcoats and tailored dress signify celebrity status, Los Angeles, 1934. © Bettmann/CORBIS

Figure 9.2 Duke Ellington holding guitar with Cab Calloway at a jam session, New York, 1939. Photo by Charles Peterson. Courtesy of Don Peterson

Americans to a white mainstream readership. The pronouncement of fantastic expenditures by jazz musicians aided the navigation of racial division in media.

Vivid accounts of language and lifestyle legitimized Ellington. Through appraisals and testimonies of eccentric routines, the public facade as narrated in the periodicals was approachable and imitable. "His speech is urbane and colorful—particularly with the ladies—How is the beautiful department?' he will say," wrote *Look* (1947) in an article titled, "The Duke Stays Hot." In the same way as discussed in Chapter 4, Lester Young employed inventive jargon among an exclusive membership that transmitted cultural beliefs and gave prominence to individuality.

Also validating the peculiar quality was Ellington's program to preserve body form. For instance, *Band Leaders* published: "Duke Ellington worries about his health. His consumption of vitamin pills in the winter is enormous . . . the Duke is devoted to massage as a means of keeping his waistline down—a form of synthetic exercise" (*Band Leaders* 1945). The *Saturday Evening Post* matched this tone with the copy, "hypochondriac . . . never in bed before 10am" (Zolotow 1943). As a final reference, *Ebony* (1949) detailed Ellington's food preferences with numerical enhancement. "Crepe suzette is Duke's favorite. He usually skips breakfast, eats heavy brunch. Three half grapefruits will start day. Duke averages three steaks a day, has been known to eat five." These colorful habits contributed to his hygienic, virile and cosmopolitan identity.

Traditional dandy: Benny Carter

As effectual as Ellington, Benny "King" Carter, an instrumentalist, composer-arranger and bandleader, configured a dandy persona that was less flashy yet more international in scope. Carter, identified as the "World's Greatest Exponent of the Alto Saxophone" (*News Press* 1941), was significant in spreading jazz to Europe. From 1935 to 1938, Carter directed and played with international orchestras in France, England and Sweden. The *Melody Maker*, a British weekly, noted on August 14, 1937: "Benny is happy in Holland . . . at present pleasing Dutch swing fans" (*Melody Maker* 1937a). Earlier in the same year, Carter directed an all-British orchestra at the London Hippodrome on January 10. These concerts along with his leadership of an international and interracial band in Holland (Crespo and Hershorn 1999) demonstrated the esteemed status that Carter possessed in Europe, contrasting to the race-mixing restrictions in America.

Carter's appearance was polished with tailored suits and tuxedos, likewise well-groomed coif and upright posture with serious demeanor (Figure 9.3).

Photographic evidence shows that Carter avoided the conk trend that resulted in chemically straightened hair for a traditional short hairstyle. In 1951, *Down*

Figure 9.3 Benny Carter in double-breasted striped suit and his orchestra, New York, 1941. Photo by Charles Peterson. Courtesy of Don Peterson

Beat, an American music journal, categorized Carter as "dapper, debonair, and musically distinguished" (*Down Beat* 1951). Magazines, as with Ellington's romance, augmented the fine gentleman sketch with particulars of leisure activities that had commercial appeal. Concerning this modern masculinity in early twentieth-century publications, Pendergast related that content for men converged on "consumerism, the cult of personality, and the urge toward self-improvement" (Pendergast 2000: 111), such as *Newspic*'s narrative of Carter in 1945 with the following: "he seeks an outlet in sports-horseback riding, bicycle riding, and deep-sea fishing . . . he goes in for seafood-particularly lobsters, clams, crabs and shrimps" (*Newspic* 1945). The African American publication, branded as "The Complete News Picture Magazine," refashioned the jazz dandy into a more athletic, robust individual with a hearty appetite. "By invoking images of success that arose out of physical vitality, talent, 'genius,' or personality . . . these ads and articles offered the first real evidence of a masculinity that was not first and foremost based on race" (Pendergast 2000: 199).

Despite the virtuosity and modern images of Ellington and Carter in periodicals, the reality of racial discrimination was palpable. "An American waiter refused to serve Duke Ellington and members of his orchestra . . . Duke was finally given a seat, but the rest of the boys were placed in the rear away from white diners," disclosed the *Afro-American* in 1941 (*Afro-American* 1941b). Also, in response to black musicians migrating overseas to flee prejudice, Carter avowed, "I prefer to stay and fight" (Hallock 1953). The traditional dandy, always dressed in suit or tuxedo, was embellished in habits of the black male celebrity that confronted racial stereotypes.

Modern dandy: Dizzy Gillespie

Regarding the pioneering sound of bebop that was reconstructing jazz, Ellington made a neutral comment in *Melody Maker*. "It's stimulating and original, which is what I, personally, look for in music" (Feather 1946). Yet, a less complimentary interpretation of bebop performers was outlined in publications. Descriptions around dress, behavior and skill carried negative undertones, for instance *Melody Maker*'s introduction of this genre. "It is an entirely new jazz medium, a style based on augmented chords, elaborate phrases apparently unconnected to each other departing from the traditional use of chord progressions, assimilating fabulous technique and drive, while disregarding conventional jazz accentuation" (Wyse 1946).

Difference, the way in which people or things are dissimilar, was evidenced in descriptions of Dizzy Gillespie and Gerry Mulligan, respectively of bebop and cool jazz. In the late 1940s, articles through colorful text about Gillespie put forth an impression of strange, nonsensical and boorish traits. *Down Beat* targeted Gillespie as the reason for unreasonable style and attitude that was prevailing. "Musicians wear the ridiculous little hats that have been seen around lately because Dizzy wears one" and "stand with a figure 'S' posture, copying Dizzy who appears too apathetic to stand erect" (Schillinger 1946). The spiteful air concerning Gillespie's beret and body position discounted the reverential motive of fashion imitation.

In the same vein, *RCA Victor Record Review*, the magazine of musical fact and comment, printed the follow excerpt in 1949: "Nigeria, South Africa is where Dizzy Gillespie's new leopard skin jacket came from . . . other unusual garments in Gillespie troupe: bop suits worn by musicians (lapelless coats, peg top trousers, berets, floppy ties)" (*RCA Victor Record Review* 1949). The reference to a foreign country linked the "unfamiliar" with "otherness" that being other than American tradition. Stuart Hall's analysis of cultural representation contends that difference is ambivalent through positive and negative readings. Here, the "unusual" quality of Gillespie advanced the musical technique; equally it agitated having origins in African American hands. The sartorial muscle of the dandy changed from the Ellington and Carter tuxedo inculcated image to an individualistic and artful identity embracing race, politics and class. In reflection of his early years in Cheraw, South Carolina, Gillespie pinpointed a sentiment related to formal attire. "Then I saw Duke Ellington in one of those Big Broadcast movies in the early thirties! . . . They were all dressed up in white tails. I had a lot of respect for that" (Gillespie and Fraser 2009: 16). Transitioning from this early influence, Gillespie and others jettisoned the traditional aesthetics and comportment for a more authentic and modern way of being, honed at Minton's Playhouse, the workshop of bebop technique.

Esquire invoked a word that intimated the color and appearance of skin to explain jazz shifts. In 1947, the magazine printed: "So Dizzy and the rest of the Minton coterie have changed the complexion of our music, exerting a force which has influenced countless young soloists" (McKean 1947). The writer seized ownership of music through the possessive pronoun "our." Also, McKean wrote, "it is difficult to judge or compare closely with the swing or jazz you have been listening to" (McKean 1947). The language employed by McKean cautioned that bebop is external to mainstream tastes and beyond the readership's command. Also, subtle difference was assigned to Gillespie's dress and routine:

He wears thick spectacles of the dark-rimmed, straight-templed type so popular with the Museum of Modern Art set, not to mention many of us whose eyes are faulty . . . Dizzy leads a rather quiet life, smoking moderately and drinking little other than copious quantities of milk . . . the Savoy Ballroom clique copy his walk, clothes, glasses, mustache and goatee, his laugh, his bizarre voice which often sounds off-pitch.

(McKean 1947)

The softer account was mitigated with the placement of "bizarre," indicating the quality of being weird or peculiar. Hebdige, in hypothesizing the challenges of subcultures to symbolic order, defined the praise and mockery of style as a double response, which places subgroups outside societal norms (Hebdige 2009: 93).

Heralding the modern style in 1948, *Metronome*, a music-guide magazine, and the *New York Herald Tribune* chose flattering descriptions that matched bebop's rising popularity in Europe. "Dizzy had done plenty of shopping in Scandinavia, his purchases including a Lejea camera, a meerschaum pipe, and a Russian Cossack hat which he wore throughout the tour" (Feather 1948). This quote demonstrated the international and affluent tastes of Gillespie that evolved into embroidered jackets, African textiles, tunic style dashiki shirts and kofia style hats. The headwear, consisting of a pillbox shape with embroidered, crocheted and needlework designs, originated in Kenya and Tanzania. In *Crowning Achievements*, the popularity of African style hats in the late twentieth century indicated "a conscious desire by the wearer to be linked with the African homeland and to celebrate with respect and pride African influences within and outside the continent" (Arnoldi and Kreamer 1995: 96). Gillespie's culturally infused dandyism reconfigured the European manner utilizing African values, dress and artifacts.

Lastly, spiritual context was applied to Gillespie suggesting his ability to perform ritual and charm. The *New York Herald Tribune* printed, "The high priest of Bop is a slender and agile man, with a professional look, horn-rimmed glasses, a moustache and goatee" (McCord 1948). In 1949, *Down Beat* emphasized the performative body: "Gillespie's gyrations and gestures get his band going" (*Down Beat* 1949). Gillespie knowingly merged dance and cadence to create this bewitching effect. A declaration in his memoir established his appropriation of religious expression from South Carolina. "I first learned the meaning of rhythm there (Sanctified church) and all about how music could transport people spiritually" (Gillespie and Fraser 2009: 31). *Jivin' in Be-Bop*, a musical film from 1947, flaunted Gillespie's modernistic style that disrupted the traditional dandy facade. In scenes of Gillespie conducting his orchestra, the routine of "Oop Bop Sh'Bam" and "Salt Peanuts" was enlivened with chants, swinging arms, tapping feet, skipping from side to side and controlled pirouettes. The presentation signaled early forms of African American expressive culture, including ring shouts, call-and-response and spirituals, fused with contemporary dandyism.

Modern dandy: Gerry Mulligan

Gerry Mulligan, a white baritone saxophone player, came into prominence in the 1950s having involvement with Southern California cool jazz and his self-titled quartet. As explored in Chapter 2, the classification had a restrained edge with mollifying arrangements that wandered from the robust nature of bebop. Critic John Wilson noted in the *New York Times* that "Mulligan's men work within tightly constructed arrangements designed for subtle harmonic effects but still played with the pulsing, relaxed beat" (Wilson 1953).

With this fresh sound came a postmodern dandy, who was least identifiable with the tuxedo, abandoning it for "cooler" versions of the suit. Descriptions of cool jazz advocates, like Mulligan and Chet Baker, used wording that designated "difference" from past ideals of white masculinity as promulgated by *Esquire* and *Gentlemen's Quarterly*. A motivation for these publications was "to cast masculinity in terms of its toughness, confidence, and lack of fear of challenge" (Pendergast 2000: 212). In 1953 following the formation of the Mulligan quartet, he was curiously illustrated by *Time*:

A gaunt, hungry looking young fellow named Gerry Mulligan . . . looks more extreme than he sounds. His hair is cut for a Jerry Lewis effect, crew-cropped on top, bangs in front. He has a sleepy face, and on the bandstand he keeps his watery-green eyes closed.

(*Time* 1953)

The language accentuates physiological neglect of appetite, rest and vision. Also, *Down Beat* cited Mulligan's performance at the Storyville in Boston: "the lean, tired-looking baritone sax sensation, assumed a posture of complete fatigue" (Martin 1954b). Like the "cool" promoters, the younger generation's attitude was steeped in moodiness, angst and generational clash as commercialized in films like *The Wild One* (1953), *East of Eden* (1955) and *Rebel Without a Cause* (1955). Descriptions of trumpet-player Chet Baker in *Down Beat* included baby-faced, shy and charming that mirrored the archetype of James Dean, star of the latter two movies (*Down Beat* 1953; Martin 1954a). Like Dean's image in films, Baker was photographed sporting white t-shirts, polo shirts, vests and pompadour hair.

The scrutiny of Mulligan and Baker in music and mainstream publications developed a morose view of youthful masculinity. "It is a common American type, whether looked for in the Ivy League or at a corner drugstore," argued the *Cambridge Review* in discussion of Mulligan's exterior (Coulter 1956). Thus, the "cool" jazz dandy was transformed into a 1950s hipster, negotiating identities within popular culture and black expressive music. Gauging this duality of urban style, Hebdige resolved that "the zoot suits and lightweight 'continentals' of the hipster embodied the traditional aspirations (making out and moving up) of the black street-corner man" (Hebdige 2009: 49).

African American visceral expression was reinterpreted in the late 1950s through a "heavy, dark, impassioned" (Giddins and Deveaux 2009: 355) groove labeled hard bop shadowed by rhythm and blues. Miles Davis, Sonny Rollins and Lee Morgan, among others, ratified new sartorial sensibilities adorning fitted suit jackets, narrow trousers, slim neckties and pointed-toe shoes. This style associated with mods had genesis "from their enthusiasm for modern jazz (Modern Jazz Quartet, Charlie Mingus, Dave Brubeck, etc.) as opposed to the traditional New Orleans jazz then popular in London" (Chenoune 1993: 253). Echoed in the musical virtuosity, dandyism traversed between traditional New Orleans and modern New York aesthetics, and continues to evolve in the present, shedding and reapplying adaptations of the 1800s sack suit.

Decoding jazz aesthetics in Clinton and Obama

Through this binary of traditional and modern, a homology of jazz dandyism is evidenced in the fashioning of the 42nd and 44th Presidents of the United States of America. The former, William "Bill" Clinton, exemplifies the jovial, gregarious and tough quality of the traditional school, wielding his collectedness of reach across the aisle politics. Like Duke Ellington on the pages of *Ebony*, Clinton's masculinity during the 1990s manifested through a stout frame, hearty appetite and instinctual music culture. Clinton's dexterity with the saxophone contributed to his youthful air, equally aided in his diplomacy. Designated as the "saxophone-playing President," Clinton utilized the instrument on the campaign trail and during trips abroad. The *New York Times* reported that Clinton "took up his instrument and jammed with the quartet's pianist" while attending a state dinner in Moscow with President Boris Yeltsin (Apple 1994). Later in the same year, Clinton employed the object during a tour of the Asia-Pacific region. "His day in Manila was filled with pomp and ceremony and he even took up the saxophone at a state luncheon" (Jehl 1994). In addition to conspicuous musicality, the brawniness of Clinton in lightweight, thigh-level running shorts was exhibited in unrestricted jogs along the National Mall. "He prioritized his running as not only a solution to keep pounds off, but also as a way to connect with voters" (Fox 2012). Clinton, as a model of traditional jazz, drew attention to traits of strength, magnetism and showmanship that reinforced his ability to relate to diverse socio-economic backgrounds in a volatile political environment.

In contrast, Barack Obama, the 44th President, signifies the modernist with a measured bearing and remote cosmopolitanism exemplified by the forward-looking architects of bebop and cool jazz. *Men's Vogue* communicated this manner of Obama, when he was a junior senator in 2006. "As a speaker, Obama does not strive for the soulful effect of an African-American evangelical. Nor does he conjure instant empathy with an audience, the way Bill Clinton does. He delivers his message with the understated charisma of a Midwestern news anchor" (Weisberg 2006). Counteracting awkward displays of bowling and hunting, the authenticity of Obama's athleticism, like a hubristic Dizzy Gillespie, had enhanced sartorial expression in a tailored suit hiking the steps of Air Force One and running in oxford lace up shoes with Bo, the Obama's Portuguese Water Dog. An article in *Men's Vogue* in 2008 demonstrated Obama's acceptance of confined athleticism through the senator's comment to an Oregon crowd. "You will not find me on a bull . . . I mean, I have enough trouble bowling" (Martel 2008). Like the qualities of early twentieth-century black publications (*The Colored American Magazine*, *The Crisis* and *Opportunity: A Journal of Negro Life*), Obama's masculinity centers on erudition rather than might. "Such articles urged Negro men to subscribe to the Victorian notion that faithful adherence to certain cardinal virtues created men of character who were bound, as if by laws of nature, to succeed" (Pendergast 2000: 71). In view of this theme on May 19, 2013, Obama using a first-person narrative cited moral expectations for the all-male graduates of Morehouse College, a historically black institution:

> To recognize the burdens you carry with you, but to resist the temptation to use them as excuses. To transform the way we think about manhood, and set higher standards for ourselves and for others. To be successful, but also to

understand that each of us has responsibilities not just to ourselves, but to one another and to future generations.

(Office of the Press Secretary 2013)

The exploration of bebop technique employed a similar fearlessness to transform barriers of race and class, pushing and urging movement beyond limitations of the past. In the same way, Obama's intellect and tenacity, a facsimile of bebop's frenzied riffs and vocal chants, struggled to ameliorate a Congress and nation obstructed by partisan politics. Obama, along the election trail in 2006, stated that the impetus for his work was "to live up to certain values . . . and to figure out how you reconcile those values with a world that is broken apart by class and race and nationality" (Weisberg 2006). In his autobiography's coda, Gillespie matched this philosophy. "So maybe my role in music is just a steppingstone to a higher role. The highest role is the role in the service of humanity, and if I can make that, then I'll be happy" (Gillespie and Fraser 2009: 502). Oscillating between traditional and modern ideals, the aesthetics of the jazz dandy continue to influence expressive culture, society and politics through appearance, behavior and the performative body of elite and marginalized men.

10

PHILADELPHIA NIGHTLIFE, NOSTALGIA AND POPULAR CULTURE

Philadelphia: Jazz city unsung

Although New Orleans, New York and Chicago flourished with neighborhoods of jazz including Storyville, Harlem and the South Side correspondingly, Philadelphia is a setting where innovators and establishments shaped a noteworthy history. The documentation of entertainment outlets was evidenced at the end of the first decade. From 1910 to 1919, society, political and religious groups promoted balls, dances and concerts via the *Philadelphia Tribune*, the African American community paper founded in 1884. Cakewalks and Negro minstrel shows, as discussed in Chapter 2, were prevalent attractions. The all-colored troupes for colored audiences performed variety acts with comedy, dance and songs. For instance, the Professional Club sponsored a Pre-Lenten Ball in 1912 and the Citizen's Republican Club presented the Soap Box Minstrels in 1914. Growth of amusement accelerated in 1914, when John T. Gibson, African American entrepreneur, purchased the Standard Theatre on South Street. Prior to Gibson's entrance, the location of vaudevillian shows and dances included halls, temples and auditoriums. St. Peter Claver's Auditorium, Music Fund Hall and Horticultural Hall were highlighted in the *Philadelphia Tribune* as entertainment settings.

A bounty of African American musical venues flourished particularly from 1920 to 1950. Notifying this renaissance, Ethel Waters cited three saloons that featured Negro performers around 1920. Jack's Rathskeller (Juniper and South Streets), Pop Grey's (South Street) and Barney Gordon's (Kater and 13th Streets) were situated in South Philadelphia just beyond the center city district (Waters and Samuels 1992: 71, 108–9). Of the latter, Waters provided a first-hand account. "We entertained, though, in a big room upstairs where the customers sat at tables. There was only a two-piece band. Toots Moore, the drummer, and a piano player who could play only in two keys" (Waters and Samuels 1992: 108).

Supplying multiple acts, large theaters became the principal outlets for black amusement during the 1920s. This was corroborated by recurring advertisements in the Philadelphia Tribune. By this period, Gibson managed the Standard Theatre (South and 12th Streets) and the Dunbar Theatre (Broad and Lombard Streets), where the fare included dramatic actors, comedians, singers and dancers. References to the imminent growth of jazz music were apparent in the Standard's entertainment promotions in 1919 including the "Merrymakers of Mirth Co. with its Creole Jazz Band" and "Allen & Stokes—A Jazzy Breeze from Dixie—Mirth, Music, Melody." On October 1, 1921 in the *Philadelphia Tribune*, Gibson's Dunbar Theatre publicized the first African American vocalist to be recorded: "The Incomparable Star of the Stage and OKeh Records—Mamie Smith and Her Jazz Hounds." Other musical halls consisted of the Academy of Music (Broad Street), the Palais Royal (South Broad Street) and the Strand Ball Room (Broad and Bainbridge Streets). The social and aesthetic values of these establishments were stressed in a review of the Palais Royal, "The Finest Colored Ballroom in America:"

Going to a dance today is a social occasion—where one meets his friends and makes new acquaintanceships. Beauty and a distinctive atmosphere are of prime importance in supplying the charm which often goes to create fond and lasting memories of such occasions.

(*Philadelphia Tribune* 1926)

On May 14, 1927, the newspaper praised the offering at the Standard: "'Fess' Williams and his Royal Flush Orchestra of New York City took the large crowd of patrons who turned out to welcome him completely off their feet with his peppy fox trots, snappy one steps, dreamy waltzes and low down honest to goodness stomps" (*Philadelphia Tribune* 1927). The article divulged the musical aptitude and diversity of technique necessary for performing at the ballroom. Conceivably due to Prohibition instituted by the 18th Amendment to the U.S. Constitution that banned the manufacture, sale and transportation of alcohol, the black entertainment of the 1920s featured in newsprint emphasized theaters, halls and roller skating rinks, where amusement was increasingly labeled as jazz.

Beyond a decade, prohibition was repealed through the 21st Amendment of 1933. The *Philadelphia Tribune* exhibited a palpable change in the advertisement of entertainment. A multitude of venues in North, South and West Philadelphia began promotion of live music, floorshows, dancing and alcoholic beverages. Here, an excerpt of the Night Life page on May 23, 1935 penned by the "Negro Councilman:"

Mickey Mouse—18th & Federal Sts. (South Philly)
There is only one place in this city that they can really call Harlem and that is South Philadelphia.

Wonder Bar—19th & Montgomery Sts. (North Philly)
When you want to change the spice of sport, then go to the Dixon's Wonder Bar in North Philly.

Joe's Grill—13th & Jefferson Sts. (North Philly)
If your feet are in the mood for dancing then this is the place to go . . . for entertainment and something real I must say that Emerson Sylvester, the world's greatest female impersonator is a wonder.

Bright Spot—601 North 56 St. (West Philly)
Out in West Philadelphia . . . it is really a smart looking little rendezvous.

Hollywood Grille—3616 Market St. (West Philly)
Betty Cobbs, who is called the queen of them all, really swings a beautiful floor show twice nightly and you bear this in mind that they are real floor shows.

Checker Club—Ridge Ave. & Oxford St. (North Philly)
When the show has nearly ended you will then see no other than our own sepia, Gloria Swanson, who is direct from the Grand Terrace in Chicago and then you can tell the world that you have seen a real show.

The influence of Harlem and the legendary Cotton Club with its extravagant floor shows of light-skinned chorus girls are noted in the previous descriptions, as well the naming of the Ridge Cotton Club along the Ridge Avenue entertainment district. In addition, the ubiquitous title of café, such as Art's Café, Pocahontas Café, Hy De Ho Café and The Roseland Café, implied inspiration from Europe and the desire to accentuate superior social mingling. Chenoune detailed that the reading rooms and cafés of early 1800s Paris including Café de Paris, Café Anglais and Tortoni's epitomized the elite settings of high society (Chenoune 1993: 60). The mottos of American venues imparted quality and class, for instance, "All the Glamor of Paris and Broadway" and "The Talk of the Town" employed by The Bright Spot (*Philadelphia Tribune* 1934a). In the 1930s, black nightlife in Philadelphia was highly publicized, competitive and geographically diverse, making necessary the complete hospitality of the patrons with live entertainment, jazz orchestras, celebrities, dancing, food and beverage.

The jazz club renaissance occurred in 1940 when Philadelphia operated over forty musical establishments that were accessible and advertised to African Americans. These places took advantage of unique names to compete in this setting. Durham's Casbah, Post Card, Cotton Bowl, and Bessie's Paradise stood out from others—labeled as bars, grilles or cafés. The propagation of nightlife occurred in tandem with increases in the African American population during and after the Second World War. Philadelphia, among other northern cities, was a beneficiary of the Great Migration, a period when many blacks left the south for economic opportunity, and equally to escape hostile racial segregation and lynchings. From 1930 to 1940, the African American population of the city increased by 14 percent to 250,880 (Levenstein 2009: 8–9).

The neighborhoods of Ridge Avenue and Columbia Avenue in North Philadelphia had significant growth of musical venues. Columbia Avenue, renamed Cecil B. Moore Avenue in 1987, was home to Watt's Zanzibar, Café Society Musical Bar and King Cole Club as listed in the *Philadelphia Tribune* (1946a). Differing from the floorshow prominence of the 1930s, this decade emphasized small jazz ensembles and afternoon jam sessions often, occurring 4.00 p.m. to 8.00 p.m. This change in structure was forecasted in the *Afro-American* on February 29, 1936, when the newspaper proclaimed "nite clubs, hit by repeal depression, want smaller orchestras . . . big bands now too expensive for clubs" (Matthews 1936). Harvey's Café on Ridge Avenue advertised "Come with your friends and enjoy Harvey's Famous Super Jam Sessions" (*Philadelphia Tribune* 1946a). These informal assemblies that kindled exploration of technique and battles of ability were widespread in Philadelphia nightlife. In recollection of his melodic experimentation during the 1940s, Charlie Parker noted: "There was nothing to do but play . . . I did plenty of jam sessions—meant much late hours, plenty good food, nice clean living, you know, but basically speaking, much poverty" (Parker 1954). Miles Davis, providing a local reference of this time, documented that the Charlie Parker Quintet had played in Philadelphia's Downbeat Club (11th and Ludlow Streets) in 1948 (Davis and Troupe 2011: 157).

Another motive for jam sessions was the implementation of the entertainment tax in 1944. Establishments identified as cabarets and rooftop gardens were levied a tax ranging from 20 to 30 percent during the war years (IRS 1944). It is acknowledged that this led to the decline of the big band era with swing dancing. Max Roach noted that patrons started to sit down and listen to ensembles, thus requiring solo skills among musicians. "Because the groups were small, quintets, quartets and trios, in order to have a fuller sound, more was required . . . you had to work hard" (Gillespie and Fraser 2009: 233). Teddy Wilson recalled that the popularity of these displays resulted in a "clamp down" by unions. "Nightclub owners started taking advantage of the fact they could hire a trio or a piano player, and before the night was out there would be ten men on the bandstand" (Wilson, Ligthart and Van Loo 2001: 49).

These assemblies became an intriguing theme in *Jam Session*, a 1944 musical starring Ann Miller. Lighthearted references to jitterbugging and jazz as "hepcat stuff" accented the Columbia Pictures plot. In a segment with the Teddy Powell Orchestra, a zoot-suited white guy with plaid jacket, wide-brimmed hat and lengthy watch chain added theatrics while band members performed a chant with the conductor. This scene demonstrates the appropriation of jazz culture, and also call-and-response technique utilized in early African American songs. Only a month later, Warner Brothers released a short film, *Jammin' the Blues*, which authenticated these gatherings using black musicians like Lester Young, Illinois Jacquet, Joe Jones and others. Virtuosity, song and dance brought to life the true spirit of a session. In the introduction, the master of ceremonies suavely declared: "This is a jam session. Quite often, these great artists gather and play ad-lib hoc music. It could be called a midnight symphony" (Mili 1944). The jamming occurring in Philadelphia and other cities found expression in Hollywood films, likely spawning greater interest in the club trend. Along with advertising fine foods, liquors and nightly music, the notice of jam sessions for an establishment was routine in the period.

The trio, quartet and quintet were ideal for bookings in these small venues; likewise their size was suitable for frequent rotation and performance at jams. Some of the lesser-known musicians that populated the scene in Philadelphia were the Jimmy Golden Quintet, the Stanley Gaines Trio, the King Solomon Trio and the Elmer Snowden Trio. Of the latter, Snowden, an innovative banjoist, was an original member and the business mind of the Washingtonians, a group that Duke Ellington joined and recorded with in the 1920s (Ellington 1973: 70).

Lastly, in this decade, the importance of aesthetic atmosphere was put forth. Bars utilized expressive slogans comprising "smartest," "beautiful," "brightest," and "glamour" to convey quality and attractiveness. For example, The "Last Word" Grille (Haverford and 51st Streets) publicized: "West Philadelphia's Finest Rendezvous, the Showplace Where You'll Meet Your Friends" (*Philadelphia Tribune* 1946b). The Berk's Bar (27th and Berks Streets) appealed directly to women with the following testimonial: "Where Courtesy Fills the Atmosphere, Tables Always Reserved for Ladies" (*Philadelphia Tribune* 1949). Reports of nightclub happenings in the *Philadelphia Tribune* specified styling of dress and music. On March 30, 1946, the newspaper printed: "Sartorially elegant in midnite blue tails, Bobby Lee of TROPICAL GARDENS returned to work this week-end . . . to head a show that is heightened by some newer and groovier features" (Philadelphia Tribune 1946c).

For those unable to witness the surroundings and music of The Hollywood Café (2275 East Williams Street), The Uptown Dreamboat (10th and Montgomery Streets) or The Showboat Musical Bar (Broad and Lombard Streets), venues like the Powelton Café & Music Bar (40th and Filbert Streets) featured a radio broadcast on WHAT-1340. The prevalence of nightlife venues in the *Philadelphia Tribune* was markedly reduced in the 1950s paralleled by modern jazz fragmentation, radio and television ascendency, rhythm and blues growth and popular solo headliners. Of the latter, Billie Holiday, Cab Calloway, Sarah Vaughan, Dinah Washington, Nina Simone and Frank Sinatra drew crowds in Philadelphia. New or reimagined establishments included Club Sada (North Philly), Pink Poodle (South Philly), Lambert Bar (North Philly), Randy's Spot

(Central Philly) and Pep's Bar (South Philly). At these venues, groups such as the Lunatones, Filatones and Bostonians, signified the popularity of vocal harmonizing groups performing Doo-wop (*Philadelphia Tribune* 1956b).

In sum, the African American music landscape signified a workshop of cultural aesthetics that thrived socially outside of white mainstream culture, yet geographically inside. This entertainment imprint through the branding of bars, cafés and theaters demonstrated vicissitudes in the setting, style, structure, depiction and patronage of the music. Indeed, this unique period of ragtime, blues, swing and bebop was, as scripted by Irene's Café, "filled with scores of happy men and women" (*Philadelphia Tribune* 1939b). Live music, fashion, social hierarchy and jazz vernacular pulsated in Philadelphia. The significance of these venues is that they provided a space where people accessed joy and experienced sophistication, equally responding to the racial environment and transforming neighborhood culture. A history of Philadelphia is incomplete without the narrative of these establishments.

Desiring jazz prestige

In 2009, White House|Black Market, a modern women's retailer, echoed the 1930s swing craze with an advertising campaign featuring a polka dot printed dress. The tag line stated "Feel Beautiful" in italicized font, evoking optimism and nostalgia (*Women's Wear Daily* 2009). In the same manner, Billie Holiday wore a comparable dotted halter dress in 1937 at the Apollo Theater. The ensemble heralded Holiday as the innovative jazz singer making initial waves in Harlem (O'Meally 1991: 51). To publicize her return to the Apollo Theatre in 1942, the *Amsterdam News* declared: "Billie Holiday is one of the most unusual and unique of present-day singers . . . she's been on tour chalking up success after success" (*Amsterdam News* 1942). The noteworthy reference to the jazz era is discernible in the clothing brand's marketing.

Continuing this signal, the cover of *Women's Wear Daily* on December 16, 2009 featured the title "Jazz Baby." The issue spotlighted Nikki Yanofsky, a Canadian teen vocalist wearing a bias cut lilac dress with nude back. Yanofsky, who was influenced by Ella Fitzgerald's records, positioned the nostalgic tone of this article: "She introduced me to jazz, and I owe her so much" (Rao 2009). The spirit of jazz was mentioned as important in formulating her distinct style. Yanofsky asserted: "A lot of mainstream music today is very one-dimensional, and I think jazz has made me more intriguing" (Rao 2009). Yanofsky acquired complexity, zeal and depth through the creation of a "jazz-pop-blues" sound. Again in 2012, *Women's Wear Daily* stressed the inspiration of this genre with "Jazz Age Redux," a story about the remake of "The Great Gatsby" and the extensive efforts to recreate the era of men's fashion utilizing the archives and factories of Brooks Brothers. Miles Davis recalled the reputation of this brand in the mid-1940s: "I was wearing my three-piece Brooks Brothers suits that I thought were super hip . . . so couldn't nobody tell me nothing" (Davis and Troupe 2011: 110). Soon after, Davis would jettison this classic-suit silhouette for broad shoulders and wide lapels sported by the uptown Harlem musicians.

As examined in Chapter 4, this admiration for the past was evident with CHANEL. The luxury brand promoted its Chanel No. 5 perfume with a Billie Holiday song, thus retrieving the frankness, melancholy and sexual allure of the classic blues. In 2012, Movado, the luxury watch company, featured Wynton Marsalis, jazz composer and performer, in print promotion. The image of Marsalis playing a trumpet with the subtitle "modern ahead of its time" paired innovation and affluence for the elevated target market. Beyond its reign of popular music, the cachet of jazz has been utilized by numerous brands including Saint Laurent, FedEx, Travelers Insurance, Osteo Bi-Flex and Delta Airlines. Advertisements positioned music, text and photography, in so doing engendering perceptions of quality, luxury, satisfaction and warmth into the product's identity.

In analysis of nostalgia, Wilson argues that the pleasurable feeling experienced comes chiefly from a romanticized perspective of the past, free of the painful aspects (Wilson 2013: 35). The development of jazz in America occurred during extensive periods of strife, brutality and inequality. Embedded in the music is the cultural response of the musicians, singers and audiences, who defied restrictive roles and representations to significantly influence popular culture. The moan of Bessie Smith, the pain of Charlie Parker and the sorrow of Billie Holiday are intricately fused with the good times of the period. Through nostalgic references of jazz that have been blossoming in America, newer generations are informed of the heritage, virtuosity, culture, beauty, passion, struggle and ideology that formed over a hundred-year period.

Last call

Emulating the jazz zeitgeist of the 1920s, a plethora of revival plays, modern productions, orchestral concerts and festivals nourish an insatiable public in the twenty-first century. *Ella: The Musical*, a biographical production of Ella Fitzgerald premiered in 2004, achieving a nine-year run across the United States. Ephemera from the show declared, "you'll fall in love all over again with the magic and soul of Ella Fitzgerald!" (*Ella: The Musical* 2010). Mirroring the jazz era, spectators at Philadelphia's Annenberg Center during 2010 were a gathering of mixed races and ages with men in smart suits and women in chic dresses. Their clothing and demeanor signified a nod to a period when formal fashion was mandatory, structured and ordered among the masses. On December 28, 1939, this authority of style empowered the "Down . . . Fashion Row" column in the *Philadelphia Tribune*:

Fashion decrees that bright corduroys and printed wools shall combine. Especially does the Fashion dictator acclaim the combination for a comfortable ankle-length dinner dress for informal dining at home.

(Dyett 1939)

Jet, *Tan* and *Ebony* magazines, along with African American newspapers, supplied the discourse for proper appearance in the jazz era.

Also in 2010, *Ma Rainey's Black Bottom* by August Wilson, toured Philadelphia, telling the dynamic story of Ma Rainey known as "Mother of the Blues." The show, active for twenty-five years since opening on Broadway in 1984, illustrates the strain of race relations and the complexity of gender in the patriarchal recording industry. Rainey's audaciousness partnered by the blues signaled the role of African American female singers as social revolutionaries with economic clout. In 1926 the *New York Times* substantiated the artistic influence: "Blues, raucous blues! . . . this musical medium of modern life has attained the proportions of a phenomenon worth attention" (Noble 1926). Other revival plays including *Sophisticated Ladies*, a celebration of the life and music of Duke Ellington, *Ain't Misbehavin'*, a tribute to the songs of Thomas "Fats" Waller, and *The Devil's Music: The Life and Blues of Bessie Smith* sustain the enthusiasm for traditional jazz.

In similar fashion, contemporary productions recount the modern period of jazz bringing to life the personalities of Dizzy Gillespie and Billie Holiday. *Last Call at the Downbeat*, a play by Suzanne Cloud, focuses on Gillespie's burgeoning career in Philadelphia during 1941. The production, presented a few blocks from the location of the Downbeat Club where Gillespie honed the roots of bebop, duplicated the nightclub atmosphere with a bartender and small tables flanking the stage. Distinction of Gillespie's dress was achieved through the actor's coverings of a beret, Mackintosh style overcoat, wide lapel double-breasted suit and suspenders. In like manner, *Everyone and I*, written by Elizabeth Scanlon, reflects on the essence of Billie Holiday through musings of Frank O'Hara, an American writer and poet, who penned *The Day Lady Died*, an elegiac poem. The 2013 production at the Kimmel Center for the Performing Arts in Philadelphia was situated near the musical venues where brilliance and misfortune seized Holiday during the 1940s and 1950s. Holiday recalled the details of her 1956 visit in her memoir: "I had worked that week at the Showboat in South Philadelphia. We stayed at a little hotel around the corner in a room with a kitchenette . . . The club was packed. Most of them were customers, but a lot of them looked like fuzz. I closed my first set with 'My Man'" (Holiday 1956: 217–21).

The musical productions about Gillespie and Holiday demonstrate memory and commendation of past artistry. As well, the annual Boscov's Berks Jazz Fest, the 2014 dedication of April as Philadelphia Jazz Appreciation month and the Kimmel Center's Jazz Up Close series of 2011 aim "to keep jazz and the arts moving forward" (Fitzgerald 2012: 30). Jazz aesthetics inclusive of performance, dress, appearance, behavior and language are called upon as cultural legacy advocating future scholarship and art progress in society, equally signaling remembrance of a time when live music, fashion and sophistication were exalted.

CODA

Jazz aesthetics have origins in 18th century America, where the expression of African culture through appearance, song, dance, worship, and jubilee stirred imitation by white mainstream culture. This way of being rooted in a cultural stronghold of spirituality and stamina was compelling in the face of insurmountable odds. By 1840, published sheet music covers documented reproductions of black style in minstrel posture, vernacular and dance. Covers illustrated African American men and women with a distorted attentiveness to their fashion, comportment and relationships. By the century's end, minstrel troupes had disseminated the caricatures to the stage for domestic and international appeal of syncopated music and plantation melodies. These parodies and the manifestation of ragtime fueled the cakewalk vogue that surged in the 1900s.

With numerous brass bands and orchestras that flourished through the teens, New Orleans musicians reclaimed the dignity of syncopated sound. The ensuing years of migration out of the south demonstrated a traversing of jazz success and representation between black and white agents commencing with the Harlem Renaissance's enthusiasm of southern blues and cosmopolitan swing jazz with African orientations, while an economic depression in the 1930s paved the way for the popularity of white orchestras conducted by Benny Goodman, Artie Shaw and Tommy Dorsey. A rebuttal of mundane swing music was posited in the 1940s by architects of bebop sound followed by subsequent explorations of cool, hard bop, avant-garde and fusion. Ultimately with social and political overturn of segregation and separate but equal policy, the musical genres of rhythm and blues and rock and roll coexisted and melded as the end of the century brought folk, disco, funk, pop, rap and hip-hop.

In the twenty-first century, jazz has an authoritative, prestigious and nostalgic permanence in popular culture bound in one hundred years of evolution and contribution to African American equality and American mass appeal. The history linked with remarkable images of fashion and formality resonates in society, where the captivating identities of Duke Ellington, Billie Holiday, Dizzy Gillespie and many others are invoked to engineer value and distinction in literature, theater, cinema, media and advertising. Inseparable from the representations are the artifacts of dress including suits, tuxedos, gowns, furs, gloves, hats, footwear, and jewelry that instituted social, political and economic transformation. Performers of the past advanced their identities through virtuosity, instinctive delivery, high styling and determination generating contemporary urbane reflections. And so, with this association, the phenomenon of jazz that exemplifies freedom of expression, struggles for equality, bonding of community, storytelling of life, and praise of heritage is echoed for newer generations. The congruent practices of fashion and jazz have thrived in self-determination and improvisation, producing a valuable record of artistry, cultural influence and human agency.

APPENDIX I: RECOMMENDED LISTENING

1900s Ragtime
"The Ragtime Dance," Scott Joplin, 1906 Stark
"Down Home Rag," Europe's Society Orchestra, 1913 Victor

1920s Blues
"Crazy Blues," Mamie Smith and Her Jazz Hounds, 1920 OKeh
"West End Blues," Louis Armstrong and His Hot Five, 1928 OKeh
"I'm Wild About That Thing," Bessie Smith, 1929 Columbia

1930s Swing
"It Don't Mean a Thing (If It Aint Got That Swing)," Duke Ellington, 1932 Brunswick
"Jumpin at the Woodside," Count Basie and His Orchestra, 1938 Decca
"Swing, Brother, Swing," Billie Holiday and Her Orchestra, 1939 Vocalion

1940s Bebop
"Salt Peanuts," Dizzy Gillespie and His All Stars, 1945 Guild
"Ornithology," Charlie Parker Septet, 1946 Dial

1950s Cool Jazz, Hard Bop
"Freeway," Gerry Mulligan Quartet, 1952 Pacific Jazz
"Moanin," Art Blakey and The Jazz Messengers, 1958 Blue Note
"The Sermon!," Jimmy Smith, 1958 Blue Note

1960s Free, Fusion
"Free," Ornette Coleman, 1960 Atlantic
"The Sidewinder," Lee Morgan, 1963 Blue Note
"Bitches Brew," Miles Davis, 1970 Columbia

APPENDIX II: RECOMMENDED VIEWING

Hallelujah!, 1929 Metro-Goldwyn-Mayer (morality struggle)
St. Louis Blues, 1929 Paramount (infidelity and melancholy)
Rain, 1932 United Artists (vice versus religion)
Reefer Madness, 1936 Motion Picture Ventures (adolescent drug addiction)
The Blood of Jesus, 1941 Sack Amusement (morality struggle)
Stormy Weather, 1943 20th Century Fox (musical retrospective)
Cabin in the Sky, 1943 Metro-Goldwyn-Mayer (good versus evil)
Jammin' the Blues, 1944 Warner Bros. (authentic jam session)
Young Man with a Horn, 1950 Warner Bros. (celebrity and addiction)
St. Louis Blues, 1958 Paramount (destiny and triumph)
A Man Called Adam, 1966 Embassy (self-destruction)
Lady Sing the Blues, 1972 Paramount (celebrity and addiction)
Bird, 1988 Warner Bros. (celebrity and addiction)

BIBLIOGRAPHY

Abbott, L. and D. Seroff (2007), *Ragged but Right: Black Traveling Shows, "Coon Songs," and the Dark Pathway to Blues and Jazz*, Jackson: University Press of Mississippi.

Afro-American (1937), "7,000 Attend Funeral of Bessie Smith," *Afro-American*, October 9, Institute of Jazz Studies, Newark, Clippings: Bessie Smith.

Afro-American (1938), "Billie Wins Chicago," *Afro-American*, November 5.

Afro-American (1941a), "Calloway May Abandon Famous Hi-De-Ho Style," *Afro-American*, October 25.

Afro-American (1941b), "Duke and Orchestra Face Coast Jim-Crow," *Afro-American*, December 27.

Albertson, C. (2003), *Bessie*, New Haven: Yale University Press.

Amsterdam News (1942), "Billie Holiday, Bennie Carter at Apollo," *New York Amsterdam News*, April 11.

Anderson, L. (1947), *Jivin' in Be-Bop*, Directed by Leonard Anderson and Spencer Williams, USA: Alexander Productions.

Apple Jr., R. (1994), "Clinton in Europe; Clinton, In Russia, Is Firm in Support of Yeltsin's Aims," *New York Times*, January 14, http://search.proquest.com/docview/109315262?accountid=10559 (accessed August 24, 2013).

Armstrong, L. (1999), *Louis Armstrong: in His Own Words*, Ed. by T. Brothers, New York: Oxford University Press.

Arnoldi, M.J. and C.M. Kreamer (1995), *Crowning Achievements: African Arts of Dressing the Head*, Los Angeles: Regents of the University of California.

Ashby-Sterry, J. (1909), "Negro Minstrelsy in England," *Washington Post* (in the *London Graphic*), May 16, http://search.proquest.com/docview/144941173?accountid=10559 (accessed August 5, 2012).

Askwith, R. (1998), "How Aspirin Turned Hero," *Sunday Times*, September 13, http://opioids.com/heroin/heroinhistory.html (accessed January 8, 2012).

Band Leaders (1945), by Weaver, G., "The Duke of Jazzdom," *Band Leaders*, 44–5, Institute of Jazz Studies, Newark, Clippings: Duke Ellington.

Banfield, W. (2010), *Cultural Codes: Makings of a Black Music Philosophy: An Interpretive History from Spirituals to Hip Hop*, Lanham: Scarecrow Press Inc.

Baraka, A. (Leroi Jones) (2002), *Blues People: Negro Music in White America*, New York: Harper Perennial.

Barnard, A. and J. Spencer (eds) (2012), *The Routledge Encyclopedia of Social and Cultural Anthropology*, 2nd edn, New York: Routledge.

Barthes, R. (1973), *Elements of Semiology*, Trans. by A. Lavers and C. Smith, New York: Hill and Wang.

Barthes, R. (1978), *Image, Music, Text*, Trans. by S. Heath, New York: Hill and Wang.

Barthes, R. (2006), *The Language of Fashion*, Ed. by A. Stafford and M. Carter, Trans. by A. Stafford, Oxford and New York: Berg Publishers.

Barton, C. (1944), *Jam Session*, Directed by Charles Barton, USA: Columbia Pictures.

Basie, C. and A. Murray (2002), *Good Morning Blues: The Autobiography of Count Basie*, New York: Da Capo Press.

Bechet, S. (2002), *Treat It Gentle*, New York: Da Capo Press.

Berger, M. (1943), "Zoot Suit Originated in Georgia: Bus Boy Ordered First One in '40," *New York Times*, June 11, http://search.proquest.com/docview/106680550?accountid=10559 (accessed January 8, 2012).

Berkowitz, S. and S. Schlachter (prods.) (2007), *Billie Holiday Remixed and Reimagined*, Compact Disc, © 2007 Sony BMG Music Entertainment.

Berlin, I., M. Favreau and S. Miller (eds) (1998), *Remembering Slavery: African Americans Talk About Their Personal Experiences of Slavery and Freedom*, New York: The New Press.

Bernard, E. (ed.) (2001), *Remember Me to Harlem: The Letters of Langston Hughes and CarlVan Vechten 1925–1964*, New York: Alfred A. Knopf.

Bigelow, M. (1970), *Fashion in History: Apparel in the Western World*, Minneapolis: Burgess.

Black, J. and M. Garland (1975), *A History of Fashion*, New York: William Morrow & Company, Inc.

Blackburn, J. (2005), *With Billie*, New York: Pantheon.

Britton, J. (1964), "The Queen Puts The World Down; Returns to 'Bitter Earth,'" *Jet*, January 2: 50–3.

Brothers, T. (2007), *Louis Armstrong's New Orleans*, New York: W.W. Norton & Company, Inc.

Brown, C. (1931), *Possessed*, directed by Clarence Brown, written by Selwyn, E. and L. Coffee, USA: Metro-Goldwyn-Mayer Studios.

Calefato, P. (2004), *The Clothed Body*, Oxford and New York: Berg Publishers.

California Eagle (1941), "Zute Suit," *The California Eagle*, August 21.

Campbell, M., D. Driskell, D. Lewis, and D. Ryan (1994), *Harlem Renaissance: Art of Black America*, New York: The Studio Museum of Harlem & Abradale Press.

Chamberlain, J. (1928), "When Spring Comes to Harlem: Claude McKay's Novel Gives a Glowing Picture of the Negro Quarter," *New York Times*, March 11, http://search.proquest.com/docview/104613389?accountid=10559 (accessed July 18, 2012).

Chenoune, F. (1993), *A History of Men's Fashion*. Trans. by Dusinberre, D. & R. Martin, Paris: Flammarion.

Chinen, N. (2014), "The Personification of Legends: Plays Promote Personas of Billie Holiday and Louis Armstrong," *New York Times*, April 17, http://www.nytimes.com/2014/04/20/ arts/music/plays-promote-personas-of-billie-holiday-and-louis-armstrong.html (accessed April 20, 2014).

Clarke, D. (2002), *Billie Holiday: Wishing on the Moon*, Cambridge: De Capo Press.

Cohodas, N. (2006), *Queen: The Life and Music of Dinah Washington*, New York: Billboard Books.

Collins, E. and M. Devanna (1992), *The Portable MBA*, New York: John Wiley & Sons, Inc.

Connover, W. (1956), "Interview with Billie Holiday," on *Voice of America Jazz Hour*, February 15, *The Billie Holiday Set*, Track 7, CD, © Baldwin Street Music.

Contini, J. (1943), "In Prints the Trend Is . . .," *Washington Post*, April 4, http://search.proquest. com/docview/151636782?accountid=10559 (accessed August 10, 2012).

Coolidge, M. (1912), *Why Women Are So*, New York: Henry Holt and Company.

Coulter, G. (1956), "Gerry Mulligan," *I.E., Cambridge Review No. 5*, March 20.

Crespo, R. and T. Hershorn (1999), "Virtual Exhibit: Benny Carter, Eight Decades in American Music," http://newarkwww.rutgers.edu/ijs/bc/ (accessed June 26, 2013).

Curtis, W. (1902), "Dress Uniforms Grave Army Topic," *New York Times*, October 19, http://search.proquest.com/docview/96241587?accountid=10559 (accessed June 15, 2013).

Daily Express (1937), "Swing It, Smith!," *Daily Express*, February 25.

Davidson, B. (1966), *African Kingdoms*, New York: Time Inc.

Davies, L. (1943a), "Zoot-Suit Riots are Studied," *New York Times*, June 20, http://search.proquest.com/docview/106627115?accountid=10559 (accessed August 5, 2012).

Davies, L. (1943b), "Zoot Suits Become Issue on Coast," *New York Times*, June 13, http://search.proquest.com/docview/106695646?accountid=10559 (accessed August 5, 2012).

Davis, F. (1994), *Fashion, Culture, and Identity*, Chicago: University of Chicago Press.

Davis, M. and Q. Troupe (2011), *Miles: The Autobiography*, New York: Simon & Schuster.

De Castro, L. (2009), *Patternmaking in Fashion*, Los Angeles: Taschen.

Deutch, H. (1944), *The Psychology of Women: A Pyschoanalytic Interpretation*, New York: Grune & Stratton.

Dewey, J. (1989), *Freedom and Culture*, New York: Prometheus Books.

Dexter Jr., D. (1939), "I'll Never Sing with a Dance Band Again – Holiday," *Down Beat*, November 1.

Donovan, C. (1957), "Fashion Trends Abroad: Paris: Balenciaga Shows 'the Best,'" *New York Times*, August 18, http://search.proquest.com/docview/114171197?accountid=10559 (accessed July 17, 2011).

Down Beat (1944), "Here's an Interesting Shot," *Down Beat*, November 15, Photo by Red Wolfe.

Down Beat (1946), "Parker in Bad Shape," *Down Beat*, August 26.

Down Beat (1949), "Gillespie's Gyrations and Gestures Get His Band Going," *Down Beat*, August 27.

Down Beat (1950), "Capsule Comments: Sarah Vaughan at Café Society, NYC," *Down Beat*, February 10.

Down Beat (1951), "Jazz's Most Underrated Musician? Benny Carter," *Down Beat*, May 18: 16.

Down Beat (1952), "This Washington Mink is on the Up and Up," *Down Beat*, February 20.

Down Beat (1953), "Here's Story of Chet Baker – Horn Star Who'd Rather Sing," *Down Beat*, August 12.

Drug Enforcement Administration (2012a), Controlled Substances Act, http://www.deadiversion.usdoj.gov/21cfr/21usc/index.html. (accessed January 8, 2012).

Drug Enforcement Administration (2012b), Controlled Substances Act, http://www.justice.gov/dea/pubs/abuse/drug_data_sheets/Heroin.pdf. (accessed January 8, 2012).

Du Bois, W. E. B. (2010), *W. E. B. Du Bois: The Souls of Black Folk*, Lexington: ReadaClassic.

Dyett, S. (1939), "Down . . . Fashion Row By Glendora," *Philadelphia Tribune*, December 28: 17.

Ebony (1949), "The Duke and Duchess of the Music World," *Ebony*, October: 20.

Ebony (1959), "The Magic of a 'Paris Original,'" *Ebony*, November: 177–82.

Ebony (1960), "Tops in Fashion," *Ebony*, October: 117–23.

Ella: The Musical (2010), Postcard Advertisement, Philadelphia: Annenberg Center for the Performing Arts.

Ellington, D. (1973), *Music is My Mistress*, New York: Da Capo Press.

Ellison, R. (1995), *Invisible Man*, New York: Vintage Books.

Emge, C. (1955), "Interracial Moulin Rouge Opens in Jim Crow Vegas," *Down Beat*, June 6.

Ewing, E. (1986), *History of Twentieth Century Fashion*, Totowa: Barnes & Noble.

Feather, L. (1946), "Duke Okays 'Be-Bop,'" *Melody Maker*, Institute of Jazz Studies, Newark, Clippings: Duke Ellington.

Feather, L. (1948), "Europe Goes Dizzy," *Metronome*, May, Institute of Jazz Studies, Newark, Clippings: Dizzy Gillespie.

Federal Bureau of Investigation (1949), US Department of Justice, Freedom of Information/Privacy Acts Release, January 25, "Billie Holiday," http://foia.fbi.gov/foiaindex/billieholiday.htm (accessed November 9, 2006).

Fitzgerald, M. (2012), "About Jazz Up Close," *Showcase*, February/March, Philadelphia: Kimmel Center for the Performing Arts.

Flügel, J. C. (1950), *The Psychology of Clothes*, London: Hogarth Press.

Fontanes, M. (2010), Interviewed by Alphonso McClendon, Tape recording, June 25, Fontanes Residence, Bidart, France.

Fox, L. (2012), "Bill Clinton's Running Habit: A Secret Service Nightmare," *US News & World Report*, http://www.usnews.com/news/blogs/washington-whispers/2012/02/29 (accessed August 25, 2013).

Furie, S. (1972), *Lady Sings the Blues*, Directed by Sidney Furie, USA: Paramount Pictures.

Garland, H. (1894), "Our Only Blackman," *Washington Post*, May 1, http://search.proquest.com/docview/139234885?accountid=10559 (accessed August 5, 2012).

Gasnier, L. (1936), *Reefer Madness*, directed by Louis Gasnier, USA: Motion Pictures Ventures.

Gates, H. (ed.) (1987), *The Classic Slave Narratives*, New York: Mentor-Penguin Putnam.

Gatewood, W. (1990), *Aristocrats of Color: The Black Elite 1880–1920*, Bloomington: Indiana University Press.

Gelly, D. (1984), *Lester Young*, New York: Hippocrene Books.

Gelly, D. (2007), *Being Prez: The Life and Music of Lester Young*, Oxford: Oxford University Press.

Ghurye, G. (1995), *Indian Costume*, Bombay: Popular Prakashan Pvt.

Giant Step (2007), "Billie Holiday: Remixed & Reimagined Record Release Party," http://www.giantstep.net/events/797/ (accessed June 21, 2012).

Giddins, G. and S. DeVeaux (2009), *Jazz*, New York: W.W. Norton & Company.

Gillespie, D. and A. Fraser (2009), *To Be, or Not . . . To Bop*, Minneapolis: University of Minnesota Press.

Gilroy, P. (2011), "It Ain't Where You're From, It's Where You're At," in *Cultural Theory: An Anthology*, Szeman, I. and T. Kaposy (eds), West Sussex: Wiley-Blackwell.

Gioia, T. (1998), *The History of Jazz*, New York: Oxford University Press.

Gloag, K. (2012), *Postmodernism in Music*, Cambridge: Cambridge University Press.

Godbolt, J. (1990), *The World of Jazz: In Printed Ephemera and Collectibles*, London: Studio Editions.

Gourse, L. (1994), *Sassy: The Life of Sarah Vaughan*, New York: Da Capo Press.

Greuenberg, C. (1961), "The Duke Calls 'Jazz' The Wrong Word For It," *New York Post*, August 28.

Hall, S. (2011), "Notes on Deconstructing 'the Popular'" (1981), in *Cultural Theory: An Anthology*, I. Szeman and T. Kaposy (eds), West Sussex: Wiley-Blackwell.

Hall, S. (2012), *Representation: Cultural Representations and Signifying Practices*, London, London: Sage Publications.

Hallock, T. (1953), "This US Inquisition Sickens Me," *Melody Maker*, August 8.

Hancock, J. (2009), *Brand Story: Ralph, Vera, Johnny, Billy, And Other Adventures In Fashion Branding*, New York: Fairchild Books.

Handy, W. C. (1969), *Father of the Blues*, Ed. by A. Bontemps, New York: Da Capo Press.

Hebdige, D. (2009), *Subculture: The Meaning of Style*, London and New York: Routledge.

Hentoff, N. (1952), "Lady Day at Storyville," *Down Beat*, January 11.

Holiday, B. (1956), Audio Interview by Willis Connover, Washington, DC, February 15, *The Billie Holiday Set*, CD, Track 13, Ontario: Baldwin Street Music.

Holiday, B. and W. Dufty (2006), *Lady Sings the Blues: the 50th Anniversary Edition*, New York: Harlem Moon.

Hollander, A. (1993), *Seeing Through Clothes*, Berkeley and Los Angeles: University of California Press.

hooks, b. (1990), *Yearning: Race, Gender, and Cultural Politics*, Boston: South End Press.

Houston, D. and J. Bagert (2006), *Jazz, Giants, and Journeys: The Photography of Herman Leonard*, London: Scala Publishers.

Hughes, L. (1997), *The Big Sea: An Autobiography by Langston Hughes*, New York: Hill and Wang.

Hurlock, E. (1929), *The Psychology of Dress: An Analysis of Fashion and Its Motive*, New York: Ronald Press.

IRS (1944), "Annual Report of the Commissioner of the Internal Revenue Service for the Fiscal Year Ended June 30, 1944," www.irs.gov/pub/irs-soi/44dbfuller.pdf (accessed August 25, 2013).

Jehl, D. (1994), "Clinton, on Asia Trip, Faces a Rougher Road," *New York Times*, November 14, http://search.proquest.com/docview/109336870?accountid=10559 (accessed August 24, 2013).

Jet (1951a), "Ten Ways to Get a Mink Coat," *Jet*, November 11: 44–7.

Jet (1951b), "Furor Over Stork Club Bias Grows," *Jet*, November 8: 8–9.

Jet (1951c), "Society," *Jet*, November 8: 41.

Jet (1951d), "Taking a Walk," *Jet*, November 8: 37.

Jet (1955), "Hollywood Gets the Blues; Dinah Lands on Sunset Strip," *Jet*, October 20: 60–1.

Jones, M. (1954), "Max Jones Spends A Holiday with Billie," *Melody Maker*, February 20.

Kaiser, S. B. (1997), *The Social Psychology of Clothing: Symbolic Appearances in Context*, New York: Fairchild Publications.

Keel, R. (2010), "Drug Law Timeline," Schaffer Library of Drug Policy, http://www.druglibrary.org/schaffer/history/drug_law_timeline.htm (accessed July 23, 2010).

Keiser, S. and M. Garner (2008), *Beyond Design: The Synergy of Apparel Product Development*, 2nd edn, New York: Fairchild Publications.

Kliment, B. (1990), *Billie Holiday*, New York: Chelsea House.

Kushner, D. (2009), *Levittown: Two Families, One Tycoon, and the Fight for Civil Rights in America's Legendary Suburb*, New York: Walker & Co.

Levenstein, L. (2009), *A Movement Without Marches: African American Women and the Politics of Poverty in Postwar Philadelphia*, Chapel Hill: The University of North Carolina Press.

Levy, E. (1989), "Ragtime and Race Pride: The Career of James Weldon Johnson," in *American Popular Music: Readings from the Popular Press Volume I: The Nineteenth Century Tin Pan Alley*, T. Scheurer (ed.), Bowling Green: Popular Press.

Look (1947), "The Duke Stays Hot," *Look*, July 22: 69.

Los Angeles Times (1953a), "Jazz Musician Sentenced on Drug Charge," *Los Angeles Times*, September 11.

Los Angeles Times (1953b), "Night Spot Musicians Taken in Dope Roundup," *Los Angeles Times*, April 15.

Lynch, A. (1999), *Dress, Gender and Cultural Change: Asian American and African American Rites of Passage*, Oxford and New York: Berg Publishers.

Lyotard, J. (2011), "Answering the Question: What is Postmodernism?" in *Cultural Theory: An Anthology*, Szeman, I. and T. Kaposy (eds), West Sussex: Wiley-Blackwell.

MacDonald, J. (1989), "'Hot Jazz,' the Jitterbug, and Misunderstandings: The Generation Gap in Swing, 1935–1945," in *American Popular Music: Readings from the Popular Press Volume I: The Nineteenth Century Tin Pan Alley*, T. Scheurer (ed.), Bowling Green: Popular Press.

Marks, C. and D. Edkins (1999), *The Power of Pride: Stylemakers and Rulebreakers of the Harlem Renaissance*, New York: Crown Publishing.

Marley, A. (ed.) (2012), *Henry Ossawa Tanner: Modern Spirit*, Berkeley: University of California Press.

Martel, N. (2008), "Rookie of the Year," *Men's Vogue*, October: 118–23, 147.

Martin, B. (1954a), "Gum Ailment Threatens Baker's Five-Year Plan," *Down Beat*, May 5.

Martin, B. (1954b), "Pipe-and Slipper Jazz is For Me: Gerry Mulligan," *Down Beat*, May 19.

Martin, R. and H. Koda (1995), *Haute Couture*, New York: The Metropolitan Museum of Art.

Matthews, R. (1936), "Are Big Bands Washed Up?" *Afro-American*, February 29: 11.

McCord, B. (1948), "Dining and Dancing," *New York Herald Tribune*, October 27.

McCracken, G. (2008), *Transformations: Identity Construction in Contemporary Culture*, Bloomington: Indiana University Press.

McDowell, C. (1997), *The Man of Fashion: Peacock Males and Perfect Gentleman*, London: Thames and Hudson.

McElya, M. (2007), *Clinging to Mammy: The Faithful Slave in Twentieth-Century America*, Cambridge: Harvard University Press.

McFall, L. (2007), "'Which Half?' Accounting for Ideology in Advertising," in *Critical Marketing: Defining the Field*, M. Saren, P. Maclaran, C. Goulding, R. Elliott, A. Shankar and M. Catterall (eds), Burlington: Elsevier.

McKay, C. (1987), *Home to Harlem*, Boston: Northeastern University Press.

McKean, G. (1947), "The Diz and the Bebop," *Esquire*, October: 90, 212–16.

McPartland, M. (1957), "Mary Lou," *Down Beat*, October 17, Institute of Jazz Studies, Newark, Clippings: Mary Lou Williams.

Melody Maker (1937a), "Holland, Not Hollywood, Has a Soup-and-Fish Cyclist!," *Melody Maker*, August 14.

Melody Maker (1937b), "Swing Music Concert," *Melody Maker*, Benny Carter Orchestra Program, London Hippodrome, January 10.

Melody Maker (1947), "Benny 'Smothered,'" *Melody Maker*, August 20.

Micklin, B. (1973), "A Magic Trumpet Comes Back," *Newsday*, July 23.

Milbank, C. R. (1989), *New York Fashion: The Evolution of American Style*, New York: Abrams.

Milestone, L. (1932), *Rain*, Directed by Lewis Milestone, USA: United Artists.

Mili, G. (1944), *Jammin' the Blues*, Directed by Gjon Mili, USA: Warner Bros.

Milwaukee Journal (1955), "Cool Jewel Anita Gives Something Extra to Notes," *The Milwaukee Journal*, March 15.

Mingus, C. (1991), *Beneath the Underdog: His World as Composed by Mingus*, Ed. by N. King, New York: Vintage Books.

Minnelli, V. (1943), *Cabin in the Sky*, Directed by Vincente Minnelli, USA: Metro-Goldwyn-Mayer.

Moraes, F. (2000), *The Little Book of Heroin*, Berkeley: Ronin Publishing.

Mousouris, M. (1979), "Mary Lou Williams: Musician as Healer," *Voice*, July 23: 81–4.

Nelson, F. (1931), "Broadway Bound," *Pittsburgh Courier*, November 7.

New Musical Express (1954), "Billie Holiday is Here!," *The New Musical Express*, February 12.

New York Post (1961), "Reduce Charge Against Dinah W.," *New York Post*, October 23.

New York Public Library (NYPL) (2000), "Inventory of the William N. and Isabele T. Spiller Papers, 1906–1958," http://www.nypl.org/ead/3988 (accessed June 16, 2012).

New York Times (1859), "Amusements: Ethiopian Minstrelsy," *New York Times*, August 18, http://search.proquest.com/docview/91446639?accountid=10559 (accessed July 6, 2012).

New York Times (1895), "'Black America' at the Garden," *New York Times*, September 17, http://search.proquest. com/docview/95279203?accountid=10559 (accessed June 13, 2012).

New York Times (1896), "Married on the Stage," *New York Times*, September 11, http://search.proquest.com/docview/1016070038?accountid=10559 (accessed June 13, 2012).

New York Times (1901a), "Musicians Condemn Ragtime," *New York Times*, May 15, http://search.proquest.com/docview/96098842?accountid=10559 (accessed June 13, 2012).

New York Times (1901b), "Wide-Open Sunday at Coney Island," *New York Times*, June 17, http://search.proquest.com/docview/96092504?accountid=10559 (accessed June 13, 2012).

New York Times (1903), "A Negro's Music As Sung By A Chorus Of Negroes," *New York Times*, May 3, http://search.proquest.com/docview/96268261?accountid=10559 (accessed June 13, 2012).

New York Times (1904), "At Point Pleasant," *New York Times*, August 28, http://search. proquest.com/docview/ 96385810?accountid=10559 (accessed June 13, 2012).

New York Times (1909), "London Demands Ragtime," *New York Times*, May 9, http://search.proquest.com/docview/96897010?accountid=10559 (accessed June 13, 2012).

New York Times (1912), "Hackett, Carhart Clothing for Men!" Display Ad 10—No Title, *New York Times*, April 19, http://search.proquest.com/docview/97249599?accountid=10559 (accessed July 17, 2011).

New York Times (1914), "Fur is Now All the Rage in the World of Fashion," *New York Times*, January 4, http://search.proquest.com/docview/97580925?accountid=10559 (accessed July 17, 2011).

New York Times (1919a), "Lord & Taylor" Display Ad 64—No Title, *New York Times*, September 28, http://search. proquest.com/docview/100359029?accountid=10559 (accessed July 17, 2011).

New York Times (1919b), "Turbans and Tam O'Shanters," *New York Times*, October 5, http://search.proquest.com/ docview/100366329?accountid=10559 (accessed July 17, 2011).

New York Times (1919c), "Two Negro Bands Play: "Syncopated" at Forty-fourth Street, Clef Club at Selwyn," *New York Times*, March 10, http://search.proquest.com/ docview/100293388?accountid=10559 (accessed July 11, 2011).

New York Times (1921), "Beau Brummels Disappear," *New York Times*, August 17, http://search.proquest.com/ docview/98407955?accountid=10559 (accessed June 26, 2012).

New York Times (1923), "Egypt Dominates Fashion Show Here," *New York Times*, February 25, http://search. proquest.com/docview/103224966?accountid=10559 (accessed July 17, 2011).

New York Times (1926a), "Fashion's Edict Bans 'Jazz' Attire for Men," *New York Times*, September 22, http:// search.proquest.com/docview/103718362?accountid=10559 (accessed July 17, 2011).

New York Times (1926b), "Straton Says Jazz is 'Agency of Devil,'" *New York Times*, May 7, http://search.proquest.com/docview/103889382?accountid=10559 (accessed January 8, 2011).

New York Times (1927), "Period Gowns of Organdy Are Worn," *New York Times*, July 24, http://search.proquest. com/docview/ 104125248?accountid=10559 (accessed July 17, 2011).

New York Times (1934), "President Demands Drive by All Forces of Nation to Solve Crime Problem," *New York Times*, December 11, http://search.proquest.com/ docview/101235483?accountid=10559 (accessed January 8, 2012).

New York Times (1935), "Roosevelt Asks Narcotic War Aid," *New York Times*, March 22, http://search.proquest.com/docview/101570443?accountid=10559 (accessed January 8, 2012).

New York Times (1937), "Diversity Marks Fall Style Show," *New York Times*, September 10, http://search. proquest.com/docview/102173631?accountid=10559 (accessed August 17, 2012).

New York Times (1938), "Extremes Mark Spring Style Show," *New York Times*, March 8, http://search.proquest. com/docview/102706634?accountid=10559 (accessed August 17, 2012).

New York Times (1943), "Two Beaten in Philadelphia," *New York Times*, June 11, http:// search.proquest.com/ docview/106727199?accountid=10559 (accessed January 8, 2012).

New York Times (1944), "Zoot Suit Robbers Hold Up 25 in Shop," *New York Times*, January 1, http://search. proquest.com/docview/106840789?accountid=10559 (accessed January 8, 2012).

New York Times (1945), "Night Club 'Dope' Ring Believed Smashed; Jazz Band Players Among 24 Arrested," *New York Times*, July 10, http://search.proquest.com/ docview/107184760?accountid=10559 (accessed August 5, 2012).

New York Times (1948a), by Harman, C. "Bop: Skee, Re or Be, It's Still Got To Swing," *New York Times*, December 5, http://search.proquest.com/docview/108102612? accountid=10559 (accessed August 5, 2012).

New York Times (1948b), "Holiday's Revue Laden With Stars," *New York Times*, April 28, http://search.proquest. com/docview/108201203?accountid=10559 (accessed August 7, 2012).

New York Times (1949a), "Bebop Doesn't Make Child Musical Moron, Says Expert Here With a School Project," *New York Times*, July 25, http://search.proquest.com/ docview/105790511?accountid=10559 (accessed January 8, 2012).

New York Times (1949b), "FHA Can't Prevent Negro Housing Ban," *New York Times*, March 19, http://search. proquest.com/docview/105707656?accountid=10559 (accessed July 24, 2013).

New York Times (1949c), "Seizures Reach Peak in Cocaine and Heroin," *New York Times*, March 5, http://search. proquest.com/docview/105741284?accountid=10559 (accessed January 8, 2012).

New York Times (1955a), "Red Cross Shoes," *New York Times*, Store Advertisement, March 27, http://search. proquest.com/docview/113459990?accountid=10559 (accessed July 17, 2011).

New York Times (1955b), "Alter-Proof Order for Drugs Sought," *New York Times*, April 26, http://search.proquest. com/docview/113443104?accountid=10559 (accessed January 8, 2012).

New York Times (1957), "'Village' is Scene of Jazz Concert," *New York Times*, June 17, http://search.proquest. com/docview/114210113?accountid=10559 (accessed August 5, 2012).

New York Times (1959), "Three Thousand At Funeral of Billie Holiday," *New York Times*, July 22, http://search. proquest.com/docview/114671901?accountid=10559 (accessed August 5, 2012).

News Press (1941), "Lower Basin Street," *News Press*, December 10.

Newspic (1945), "Benny Carter," *Newspic*, Institute of Jazz Studies, Newark, Clippings: Benny Carter.

Nicholson, S. (1995), *Billie Holiday*, Boston: Northeastern University Press.

Nicholson, S. (2004), *Ella Fitzgerald: The Complete Biography*, New York: Routledge.

Noble, H. (1926), "Sad, Raucous Blues Charm World Anew," *New York Times*, September 26, http:// search.proquest.com/docview/103662484?accountid=10559 (accessed August 5, 2012).

Northup, S. (2010), *Twelve Years a Slave: The Narrative of Solomon Northup*, Ed. by C.S. Badgley, Lexington: Badgley Publishing.

O'Day, A. and G. Eells (1989), *High Times Hard Times*, New York: Limelight Editions.

O'Meally, R. (1991), *The Many Faces of Billie Holiday*, New York: Arcade.

O'Neal, G. (2010), "African-American Aesthetics of Dress as Cultural Genetics," Lecture at Drexel University, Philadelphia, April 21.

Office of the Press Secretary—The White House (2013), "Remarks by the President at Morehouse College Commencement Ceremony," May 19, http://www.whitehouse. gov/the-press-office/2013/05/19/remarks-president-morehouse-college-commencement-ceremony (accessed June 30, 2013).

Our World (1951), "Dinah Washington: Miss Juke-Box," *Our World*, August: 39–41.

Parker, C. (1954), Interviewed by P. Desmond and J. McLellan, WHDH Studio: Boston, January, http://www.plosin.com/MilesAhead/BirdInterviews.html (accessed July 18, 2013).

Parker, M. (1943), "Elaborate Hair-Do Thing of Past; '44 'Head Lines' Are Sleek, Simple," *New York Times*, October 21, http://search.proquest.com/docview/106823678? accountid=10559 (accessed August 5, 2012).

Pendergast, T. (2000), *Creating the Modern Man: American Magazines and Consumer Culture 1900–1950*, Columbia and London: University of Missouri Press.

Peress, M. (2004), *Dvořák to Duke Ellington: A Conductor Explores America's Music and Its African American Roots*, New York: Oxford University Press.

Philadelphia Orchestra Playbill (2012), "Movado – Modern Ahead of Its Time," Movado Advertisement, Movado Group, the *Philadelphia Orchestra Playbill*, November.

Philadelphia Tribune (1912), L. Wollenberger: The One Price Tailor and Clothier Advertisement, December 21.

Philadelphia Tribune (1914), "Tango Dancers," Gibson's New Standard Theatre, Advertisement, May 9.

Philadelphia Tribune (1919), "Exploits in Africa, Mostly Girls," Gibson's New Standard Theatre Advertisement, October 18.

Philadelphia Tribune (1920a), Dunbar Theatre Advertisement, January 24.

Philadelphia Tribune (1920b), S. Rubin & Sons Advertisement, April 24.

Philadelphia Tribune (1921a), Koshland-Clothier and Furnisher Advertisement, September 17.

Philadelphia Tribune (1921b), Dunbar Theatre Advertisement, October 1.

Philadelphia Tribune (1926), "Cotton Pickers and Creole Boys at Palais Royal," *Philadelphia Tribune*, January 15: 3.

Philadelphia Tribune (1927), "'Fess' Williams is Hit at Strand," *Philadelphia Tribune*, May 14: 6.

Philadelphia Tribune (1934a), The Bright Spot Advertisement, November 29.

Philadelphia Tribune (1934b), by Wiggins, E., "Parisians Go Wild Over Eccentric Louie's Music," *Philadelphia Tribune*, November 29.

Philadelphia Tribune (1935), "Night Life and Theatrical Chit Chat," Night Life Page by Negro Councilman, May 23: 13.

Philadelphia Tribune (1939a), "Hundreds Dazzled by Fitzgerald and Jacquet's Virtuosity," *Philadelphia Tribune*, January 20: 12.

Philadelphia Tribune (1939b), "Irene's Cafe," *Philadelphia Tribune*, Dine and Dance Column, December 28.

Philadelphia Tribune (1943), EarlBrook Clothes Advertisement, January 9.

Philadelphia Tribune (1946a), Harvey's Cafe Advertisement and Night Life Page, March 2.

Philadelphia Tribune (1946b), The Last Word Grille Advertisement, May 10.

Philadelphia Tribune (1946c), "Bobby Lee of Tropical Gardens," *Philadelphia Tribune*, March 30: 14.

Philadelphia Tribune (1949), Berk's Bar Advertisement, February 19.

Philadelphia Tribune (1956a), "Lady Cop Exposes Billie Holiday's Dope Cache," *Philadelphia Tribune*, February 25.

Philadelphia Tribune (1956b), Lambert Bar, Club Sada and Pink Poodle Advertisements, January 14.

Pilgrim, D. (2000), "The Coon Caricature," Ferris State University, http://www.ferris.edu/htmls/news/jimcrow/coon/ (accessed June 16, 2012).

Pittsburgh Courier (1929), "Harlem's Cotton Club is Mecca of Beauty and Grace," *Pittsburgh Courier*, April 6.

Pittsburgh Courier (1931), "Henderson, McKinney, Sissle Bunched," *Pittsburgh Courier*, December 5.

PM (1945), "Why Duke Ellington Avoided Music Schools," *PM*, December 9.

Pope, V. (1942), "Fall Styles Spirited Despite WPB Order; Dressmaker Tricks Used in New Gowns," *New York Times*, April 28, http://search.proquest.com/docview/106233706?accountid= 10559 (accessed August 10, 2012).

Pope, V. (1948), "Wide Variety Seen in New Millinery," *New York Times*, July 7, http://search.proquest.com/docview/108093353?accountid=10559 (accessed August 18, 2012).

Quinn, E. (1895), "'Jumped Jim Crow:' Reminisces of Rice, the Father of Negro Minstrelsy. An Original Dandy Darky," *Washington Post*, August 25.

Rao, P. (2009), "Wonder Girl," *Women's Wear Daily*, December 16.

RCA Victor Picture Record Review (1949), "Dizzy Gillespie," October, Institute of Jazz Studies Archive, Newark, Clippings: Dizzy Gillespie.

Redhead, S. (ed.) (2008), *The Jean Baudrillard Reader*, New York: Columbia University Press.

Ridgley, W. (1928a), Personal Communication from J. Calvin Drake, Southern Yacht Club, August 10, Hogan Jazz Archive, Tulane University, New Orleans, Louisiana.

Ridgley, W. (1928b), Personal Communication from Manager, Conn New Orleans Co., August 10, Hogan Jazz Archive, Tulane University, New Orleans, Louisiana.

Ridgley, W. (1928c), Personal Communication, Ridgley's Tuxedo Band Member Contract and Agreement, July 2, Hogan Jazz Archive, Tulane University, New Orleans, Louisiana.

Ridgley, W. "Baba" (1978), Interview Reel I, II, III Summary, Retyped by D. Nadas, February, Hogan Jazz Archive, Tulane University, New Orleans, Louisiana.

Riley, C. (1972), "The Creative Black Man: Artists Struggle to Overcome the Limiting Concepts of Art," *Ebony*, August: 134–9.

Roach, M. and J. Eicher (1973), *The Visible Self: Perspectives on Dress*, Englewood Cliffs: Prentice Hall.

Roach-Higgins, M. and J. Eicher (1992), "Dress and Identity," *Clothing and Textile Research Journal*, 10/4: 1–8.

Rose, G. (2001), *Visual Methodologies: An Introduction to the Interpretation of Visual Materials*, London: Sage Publications.

Rosenbaum, A., M. Rosenbaum and J. Buis (1998), *Shout Because You're Free: The African American Ring Shout Tradition in Coastal Georgia*, Athens: University of Georgia Press.

Rye, H. (2010), "Chronology of the Southern Syncopated Orchestra: 1919–1922," *Black Music Research Journal*, 30/1: 5–17.

Sapir, E. (2007), "Fashion," in *Fashion Theory: A Reader*, M. Barnard (ed.), London: Routledge.

Savage, H. (1905), "Wagner Driving Out Ragtime, Says Henry W. Savage," *New York Times*, May 21, http://search.proquest.com/docview/96530763?accountid=10559 (accessed June 13, 2012).

Sawchuk, K. (2007), "A Tale of Inscription/Fashion Statements," in *Fashion Theory: A Reader*, M. Barnard (ed.), London: Routledge.

Scheurer, T. (ed.) (1989), *American Popular Music: Readings from the Popular Press Volume I: The Nineteenth Century Tin Pan Alley*, Bowling Green: Popular Press.

Schillinger, M. (1946), "Dizzy Gillespie's Style, Its Meaning Analyzed," *Down Beat*, February 11.

Schur, E. (1983), *Labeling Women Deviant: Gender, Stigma, and Social Control*, Philadelphia: Temple University Press.

Smith, C. (1942), "The Duke Steps Out," *Jazz Magazine*, Institute of Jazz Studies, Newark, Clippings: Duke Ellington, Newark.

Smithsonian (2010), "Balm of America: Patent Medicine Collection," Smithsonian National Museum of American History, http://americanhistory.si.edu (accessed July 24, 2010).

Spencer, F. (2002), *Jazz and Death: Medical Profiles of Jazz Greats*, Jackson: University Press of Mississippi.

Spottswood, D. (2002), *The Best of Lucille Bogan* (booklet), L. Cohn (prod.), Compact Disc, © 2004 Sony Music Entertainment, Inc.

Steele, V. and J. Park (2008), *Gothic: Dark Glamour*, New York: Yale University Press and The Fashion Institute of Technology.

Stern, B. (2000), *Jazz on a Summer's Day*, DVD, directed by Bert Stern, New York: Bert Stern Productions/New Yorker Video.

Still, L. (1964), "The Queen is Gone but the Melody Lingers on Forever," *Jet*, January 2: 54–63.

Summers, B. (1998), *Skin Deep: Inside the World of Black Fashion Models*, New York: Amistad.

Suthern II, O. (1989), "Minstrelsy and Popular Culture," in *American Popular Music: Readings from the Popular Press Volume I: The Nineteenth Century Tin Pan Alley*, T. Scheurer (ed.), Bowling Green: Popular Press.

Szeman, I. and T. Kaposy (eds) (2011), *Cultural Theory: An Anthology*, West Sussex: Wiley-Blackwell.

Tanner, P. (1947), "Dizzy at the Down Beat," *Melody Maker*, Institute of Jazz Studies, Newark, Clippings: Dizzy Gillespie.

Terrell, M. (1897), "In Union There is Strength," Presidential Address at National Association of Colored Women, Nashville, September 15, http://www.blackpast.org/?q=1897-mary-church-terrell-union-there-strength (accessed April 2, 2011).

Thurman, W. (1992), *Infants of the Spring*, Boston: Northeastern University Press.

Time (1953), "Music: Counterpoint Jazz," *Time*, February 2.

Tirro, F. (1977), *Jazz: A History*, New York: W.W. Norton & Company, Inc.

Van Vechten, C. (2000), *Nigger Heaven*, Urbana & Chicago: University of Illinois Press.

Variety (1954), "Federal Agents Arrest Anita O'Day," *Variety*, August 25.

Variety (1960), "Fack's II, Frisco," *Variety*, April 21.

Veblen, T. (2007), "Dress as an Expression of Pecuniary Culture," in *Fashion Theory: A Reader*, M. Barnard (ed.), London: Routledge.

Viator, J. (2011), "Sweet and Low," http://www.antiquesroadshowinsider.com/vintage-sheet-music.html (accessed December 4, 2011).

Vidor, K. and R. Mack (dirs.) (1929), *Hallelujah!*, USA: Warner Home Video.

Vivian, G. (1902), "Wafted From the Keys," *New York Times*, November 23, http://search.proquest.com/docview/96179948?accountid=10559 (accessed June 13, 2012).

Vogue (1940), "New Triumphs for Turbans," *Vogue*, January 1, http://search.proquest.com/docview/904290003?accountid=10559 (accessed June 13, 2012).

Vogue (1954), "Fashion: Paris: The New Bouffants," *Vogue*, October 15: 104–5, http://search.proquest. com/docview/904338453?accountid=10559 (accessed June 13, 2012).

Wallace, M. (1956), "Billie Holiday with Mike Wallace," *Night Beat*, Audio Interview, Dumont Television, November 8, *Billie Holiday: The Ultimate Collection*, DVD, 2005, Universal.

Washington Post (1897), "Old-Time Minstrels," *Washington Post*, February 4, http://search.proquest.com/docview/143923183?accountid=10559 (accessed August 5, 2012).

Washington Post (1900), "Ban on Ragtime Music," September 30 (from the *Chicago Chronicle*), http://search.proquest.com/docview/144188239?accountid=10559 (accessed June 13, 2012).

Washington Post (1901), "The Marine Band: Some Views of Its Concerts on Its Western Tour," *Washington Post*, May 7, http://search.proquest.com/docview/144232906?accountid=10559 (accessed June 13, 2013).

Washington Post (1904), "Negro's Part in Music," *Washington Post*, August 14, http://search.proquest.com/docview/144465369?accountid=10559 (accessed August 5, 2012).

Washington Post (1920), "Howard Theater – Mamie Smith," *Washington Post*, December 19, http://search.proquest.com/docview/145771315?accountid=10559 (accessed July 7, 2012).

Washington Post (1927a), "Scanty Dress is Hit by Colored Pastor," *Washington Post*, January 24, http://search.proquest.com/docview/149809038?accountid=10559 (accessed August 5, 2012).

Washington Post (1927b), "New Poetry Comes From Cullen's Pen," *Washington Post*, July 31, http://search.proquest.com/docview/149766419?accountid=10559 (accessed August 5, 2012).

Washington Post (1938), "Billie Holiday, of Blues Fame, On S.S. Potomac," *Washington Post*, September 4, http://search.proquest.com/docview/151047908?accountid=10559 (accessed August 5, 2012).

Washington Post (1949), "Krupa Wars on Marijuana," *Washington Post*, July 28, http://search.proquest.com/docview/152196341?accountid=10559 (accessed August 21, 2013).

Washington Post (1956), "Balenciaga Reveals his Spring 'Camouflage' Costume Collection," *Washington Post and Times Herald*, March 6, http://search.proquest.com/docview/148838064?accountid= 10559 (accessed September 5, 2012).

Waters, E. and C. Samuels (1992), *His Eye is on the Sparrow: An Autobiography by Ethel Waters*, New York: De Capo Press.

Weaver Jr., W. (1951), "Narcotics Clinics Proposed Upstate," *New York Times*, December 1, http://search.proquest.com/docview/112101804?accountid=10559 (accessed January 8, 2012).

Weiner, J. (2012), "Aesthetics," in *The Routledge Encyclopedia of Social and Cultural Anthropology*, 2nd edn, Barnard, A. and J. Spencer (eds), New York: Routledge.

Weisberg, J. (2006), "The Path to Power," *Men's Vogue*, September/October: 118–25, 247.

Welters, L. and P. Cunningham (eds) (2005), *Twentieth-Century American Fashion*, Oxford and New York: Berg Publishers.

West, C. (1999), *The Cornel West Reader*, New York: Basic Civitas Books.

Wilson, E. (2003), *Adorned in Dreams: Fashion and Modernity*, New Brunswick: Rutgers University Press.

Wilson, E. (2013), *Cultural Passions: Fans, Aesthetes and Tarot Readers*, London: I.B. Tauris.

Wilson, J. (1953), "Modern Stylists in Jazz," *New York Times*, September 6, http://search.proquest.com/docview/112556744?accountid=10559 (accessed June 13, 2012).

Wilson, J. (1955), "Revivals in Jazz," *New York Times*, November 13, http://search.proquest.com/docview/113167038?accountid=10559 (accessed June 13, 2012).

Wilson, J. (1958a), "Billie Holiday—Jazz Singer, Pure and Simple," *New York Times*, July 6, http://search.proquest.com/docview/114340805?accountid=10559 (accessed June 13, 2012).

Wilson, J. (1958b), "Billie Holiday Sings With Old Magic In 'All-Star Show' at Town Hall," *New York Times*, September 15, http://search.proquest.com/docview/114539382? accountid=10559 (accessed June 13, 2012).

Wilson, J. (1958c), "Jazz: Revival," *New York Times*, March 30, http://search.proquest. com/docview/114441988?accountid=10559 (accessed June 13, 2012).

Wilson, T., Ligthart, A. and H. Van Loo (2001), *Teddy Wilson Talks Jazz*, New York: Continuum.

Winch, J. (ed.) (2000), *The Elite of Our People: Joseph Willson's Sketches of Black Upper-Class Life in Antebellum Philadelphia*, University Park: Pennsylvania State University Press.

Women's Wear Daily (2009), Advertisement by White House | Black Market, September 15.

Woodham, J. (2004), *A Dictionary of Modern Design*, Oxford Reference Online, http:// www. oxfordreference.com (accessed December 30, 2010).

Wyse, S. (1946), "What is Be-Bop?" *Melody Maker*, August 31.

Yohannan, K. and N. Nolf (1998), *Claire McCardell: Redefining Modernism*, New York: Abrams.

Zolotow, M. (1943), "The Duke of Hot," *Saturday Evening Post*, August 7.

INDEX

In this index photographs are indicated in italics.